Counseling
and Christianity

FIVE APPROACHES

Edited by **Stephen P. Greggo and
Timothy A. Sisemore**

With contributions from
Thomas G. Plante
Mark R. McMinn
Diane Langberg
Gary W. Moon
Stuart W. Scott

Foreword by **Eric L. Johnson**

IVP Academic
An imprint of InterVarsity Press
Downers Grove, Illinois

InterVarsity Press
P.O. Box 1400, Downers Grove, IL 60515-1426
World Wide Web: www.ivpress.com
Email: email@ivpress.com

InterVarsity Press® is the book-publishing division of InterVarsity Christian Fellowship/USA®, a movement of students and faculty active on campus at hundreds of universities, colleges and schools of nursing in the United States of America, and a member movement of the International Fellowship of Evangelical Students. For information about local and regional activities, visit intervarsity.org.

Some names and identifying information in this book have been changed to protect the privacy of the individuals involved.

Cover design: Cindy Kiple
Cover images: Paulo Buchinho/Getty Images
Interior design: Beth Hagenberg

ISBN 978-0-8308-3978-0

Printed in the United States of America ∞

As a member of Green Press Initiative, InterVarsity Press is committed to protecting the environment and to the responsible use of natural resources. To learn more visit greenpressinitiative.org.

Library of Congress Cataloging-in-Publication Data

Greggo, Stephen P., 1956-
  Counseling and Christianity: five approaches / Stephen P. Greggo
and Timothy A. Sisemore ; with contributions from Thomas G. Plante . . .
[et al.].
     p. cm.
  Includes bibliographical references and indexes.
  ISBN 978-0-8308-3978-0 (pbk.: alk. paper)
  1. Counseling—Religious aspects—Christianity. I. Sisemore,
Timothy A. II. Title.
  BR115.C69G74 2012
  253.5—dc23

2012018663

P	22	21	20	19	18	17	16	15	14	13	12	11	10	9
Y	32	31	30	29	28	27	26	25	24	23	22	21	20	

With deep appreciation, the editors dedicate this project to three groups who make this book a step in God's parade of providence for Christians who counsel. We express our heartfelt gratitude

- to the *pioneers* in the foundational volume who gave definition to the core views relating Christian faith, Scripture and social science. David Myers, Gary Collins, Stanton Jones, Robert Roberts, P. J. Watson, David Powlison and Eric Johnson, thanks for your courage, clear thinking and hearts that seek after God.

- to the *clients* who helped forge the wisdom beneath each approach through countless divine appointments. These dialogue partners remain unnamed but their contribution is a gift to acknowledge with respect and honor.

- to the *next generation of people helpers* who will expand and sharpen each approach. Go in grace and truth, and faithfully move the field forward in God-honoring ways.

Thank you, Lord, for all these fellow travelers on the road of faith.

Steve and Tim

Contents

Foreword

Eric L. Johnson

Within the first year after *Psychology and Christianity: Five Views* (2010) was published, I received a number of emails asking whether a similar kind of book on Christian approaches to counseling and psychotherapy could be brought out. Well, here it is! I'm very glad. Though psychology is a much broader discipline, counseling and psychotherapy are clearly what most people think of when the topic of psychology comes up. This is not surprising since these and related areas get the most publicity, and also because the task of improving the psychological well-being of humans is such an important cultural task. Most importantly, the unique challenges and complexity of counseling and psychotherapy warrant their own "five views" book.

This is an extremely important time for followers of Christ to consider deeply what it means to be a Christian in the fields of counseling and psychotherapy. Not too long ago religion was viewed as a topic of disrepute in the fields of psychology, psychotherapy and psychopathology. However, things have changed radically in the past two decades. Perhaps because of the influence of postmodernism, there is an increasing openness to alternative perspectives in the field of psychology. Positive psychology has made the case that "transcendence" is a human virtue or strength (Peterson & Seligman, 2004). Theistic psychology is contesting the dominance of naturalism over the field and arguing that theists (like Christians) ought to consider the relevance of God in the psychological study of human beings (Slife & Reber, 2009). Psychology of religion is enjoying something of a renaissance (Emmons & Paloutzian, 2003; Paloutzian & Park, 2005). Finally, those active in contemporary counseling and psychotherapy have come to recognize that the topics of religion and spirituality have to be addressed in their work, so it is widely acknowledged now that counselors and therapists are ethically obliged to consider the religious and spiritual orientations of those with whom they work. We might consider all of this to constitute something of a revolution in modern psychology. Movement is occurring in some good directions, so Christians have great reason to be encouraged and optimistic about the future. It is very fitting, then, for Christians to think deeply and talk together about their views of counseling and psychotherapy.

At the same time, of all the subdisciplines of psychology, none are so controversial and so fraught with disagreement among Christians. There are a number of reasons for this. First, all of the world's great religions and worldviews concern themselves with the improvement of the psychological well-being of humans. So, modern counseling and psychotherapy have been encroaching upon areas that historically have been considered integral to the Christian religion. And second, since Christianity's founding, "soul improvement" was considered by Christians ultimately to be a gift of God through Christ, and therefore a primary task of the Christian church. Consequently, counseling was being done in local churches, monasteries and convents for centuries before modern psychiatry and psychotherapy arose in the late 1800s, and developed an enormous literature on the Christian healing of the soul. (With many ironies, the root meaning of the relatively recent term *psychotherapy* is literally "soul healing": *psychē* = soul; *therapeuō* = to heal.) Third, and most controversial, is the fact that modern counseling and psychotherapy have been explicitly secular and so have been committed to promoting a kind of "soul healing" that is restricted to human resources and not supernatural. Consider this observation by Singer (1970), a modern psychotherapy theorist: "Man is capable of change and capable of bringing this change about himself, provided he is aided [by other humans] in his search for such change. Were it not for this inherent optimism, this fundamental confidence in man's ultimate capacity to find his way, psychotherapy as a discipline could not exist, salvation could come about only through divine grace" (p. 16). One has to be grateful for such worldview transparency.

Christians as well as naturalists have therefore considered modern counseling and psychotherapy to be, in the most fundamental sense, *com-*

petitors to Christianity with regard to the task of the "healing of the soul" (Adams, 1973; Cushman, 1995; Foucault, 1988; Rieff, 1966; Vitz, 1994). As a result, good Christians are sharply divided regarding how to think about what is called counseling and psychotherapy in our day, how much Christians should borrow from non-Christian counseling and psychotherapy, and to what extent Christians ought to participate in the contemporary mental health field. Even so, such differences among members of the body of Christ usually indicate that the issues involved are complex and that simplistic answers will not be able to address them. All this makes the kind of conversation found in this book extremely important.

No one wants to read a "five views" book that has slightly different versions of basically the same view. Thankfully, this book delivers the goods! The editors wisely gave the contributors a case study to work on (a particularly daunting test case that would make many counselors hasten to refer!), which brought out differences in practice much better than a number of theoretical essays would have. As a result, we are presented with five distinct approaches described by thoughtful and knowledgeable representatives of their respective counseling positions. What stuck out to me were the significant differences in the degree to which Christian content is salient in each approach: reference to the Trinity (and specifically Christ), or merely to God, or to spirituality; beliefs regarding the formative impact of one's personal relationship with Christ; the use of Scripture (in the chapter, in the counseling and as a guide for counseling practice) and prayer as intrinsic to the healing process; the weight given to biblical law and a focus on sin; the therapeutic impact of the counselor's relationship with the counselee; the openness to mainstream psychology and the willingness to participate in the current mental health system; the desire to base counseling practice on empirical research; the attention given to the DSM-IV and clinical diagnosis and the use of diagnostic instruments; the extent to which multiple aspects of the counselee are taken seriously and taken into account; the degree of directiveness that characterizes the counseling; and the humility in presentation (and presumably in counseling style). Where could one get the opportunity to learn from five markedly different Christian counselors how they think about how they counsel? The diversity here offers a remarkable occasion to compare, reflect and learn. The editors are also to be commended for their chapters on the historical and social-institutional context of these presentations. Altogether the book well achieves its end: an in-depth exploration of five significant kinds of Christian counselor in the early twenty-first century.

References

Adams, J. (1973). *The Christian counselor's manual*. Grand Rapids: Zondervan.

Cushman, P. (1995). *Constructing the self, constructing America*. Reading, MA: Addison-Wesley.

Emmons, R. A., & Paloutzian, R. F. (2003). The psychology of religion. In S. T. Fiske, D. L. Schacter & C. Zahn-Waxler (Eds.), *Annual review of psychology, 53* (pp. 377-403). Palo Alto, CA: Annual Reviews.

Foucault, M. (1988). Technologies of the self. In *Technologies of the self: A seminar with Michel Foucault* (pp. 16-29). Amherst, MA: The University of Massachusetts Press.

Johnson, E. L. (Ed.) (2010). *Psychology & Christianity: Five views*. Downers Grove, IL: IVP Academic.

Paloutzian, R. F., & Park, C. L. (Eds.). (2005). *Handbook of the psychology of religion and spirituality*. New York: Guilford.

Peterson, C., & Seligman, M. E. P. (2004). *Character strengths and virtues: A handbook and classification*. New York: Oxford University Press and Washington, DC: American Psychological Association.

Rieff, P. (1966). *The triumph of the therapeutic: Uses of faith after Freud*. New York: Harper & Row.

Singer, E. (1970). *Key concepts in psychotherapy* (2nd ed.). New York: Basic Books.

Slife, B. D., & Reber, J. S. (2009). Is there a pervasive bias against theism in psychology? *Journal of Theoretical and Philosophical Psychology, 29*(2), 69-79.

Vitz, P. C. (1994). *Psychology as religion: The cult of self-worship* (2nd ed.). Grand Rapids: Eerdmans.

1

Setting the Stage for the Five Approaches

LEARNING OBJECTIVES

- *Differentiate pastoral and Christian counseling trends from secular, medically oriented clinical services*
- *Distinguish key features of the five major views for relating the Christian faith to modern psychology*
- *Associate each of the approaches in this volume with the corresponding viewpoint in* Psychology & Christianity: Five Views (Johnson, 2010a)

Walking down the hall in the Student Center, Jake looked like a typical 22-year-old with his holey jeans, mussed hair covering his ears, and a couple of days' growth of beard on his face. Upon closer scrutiny, there was a pained resolve on his face and urgency to his gaze. With a moist palm, he hesitantly opened the door to the Student Support Services office. Somewhat to his surprise, Jake did not back out of his counseling appointment.

Jake was struggling to adjust to life at a Christian college and sought some guidance with his study habits. Yet deep down he knew there was much more to it than that. His short life had overflowed with challenges, joys, sorrows and failures. The Christian faith of his childhood had been battered as he faced the throes of life, and Jake clung to the tattered remnants of that faith as he opened that door. Academic psychology and abstract theology meant little to him at the moment. He needed help—desperately enough to keep this appointment.

Jake, whom we will get to know quite well in the pages that follow, is not unusual. Modern life is challenging, confusing and often daunting. While Christians know their faith is a resource in coping with the trials of life, we struggle to know exactly how this works out in the "real world." For thousands of believers, talking with a counselor is an act of hope that their lives can be better, and their faith stronger. But what should counsel to Christians look like? How do we take the truths of Scripture and apply them to twenty-first-century life? And what do we do with the insights of psychology and its sister mental health disciplines? Do we ignore them and stick to the Bible, embrace them wholeheartedly as gifts from God, or find some via media that incorporates both? Christian counselors must confront these issues if we are to be ready to help the thousands of Jakes who seek our services. It is not enough merely to offer encouragement haphazardly, going with our gut or calling counseling "Christian" simply because we hold to the faith. We must think through how to relate our faith—both beliefs and behaviors—to modern approaches to counseling, but the bottom line is this must translate to practice: what we say and do in session. We intend in the ensuing pages to serve Christian counselors, both those in practice and those still in training, by furthering the connection between theory and practice in relating our faith to the mental health disciplines.

To do so, we will unashamedly build on another's foundation. Eric L. Johnson's (2010a) *Psychology & Christianity: Five Views* offers five major views that represent families of approaches in connecting the discipline of psychology with the Christian faith. These vital theoretical approaches are essential to form a model from which to relate these two fields. Good basic science must always undergird applied science, and likewise biblical wisdom is foundational to biblical advice. Yet for many, a further step is necessary: how do science and biblical wisdom translate into real-life counseling scenarios?

In this introductory chapter, we will document the crucial need for practical application of the theories in Johnson's book before turning to a summary of those views to prepare for the chapters ahead, introducing the clinicians who will guide us as we go.

The Burgeoning of Counseling Services and Providers

How badly do we need to address this issue of how "Christian counseling" should look in the consulting office? We argue that it is vital given the demand for such counsel. Anyone working in mental health who is a Christian can sense the growth of the field over the past few years.

In the world of the twenty-first century, counseling is not just for the seriously mentally ill or wealthy. While it goes by differing names such as psychotherapy, psychoanalysis, therapy, pastoral care, coaching or counseling (depending largely on who is doing it), it is far from uncommon. Why? Seeing a counselor lacks the stigma it once had, which frees many up to seek help who might not have a generation ago. This is especially true for Christians as they accept that being a believer does not immunize one against the struggles of life, nor does seeking help mean one is "mentally ill." The availability of more expert helpers who explicitly state they are Christians or who promote themselves as doing faith-based counseling further enhances the openness to counseling for followers of Christ.

Another reason for the amplified interest in counseling is the increase in mental health problems. While arguments abound as to whether this reflects the stress of (post)modern life or changes in diagnostic criteria, the facts remain. In 2009, the National Institute of Mental Health (NIMH) reported that 26.2% of Americans 18 years of age or older (i.e., roughly one quarter of adult Americans) suffer a diagnosable mental condition each year. That translates to nearly 60 million persons, with 6% of these persons experiencing serious forms of mental illness. Nearly half (45%) of those with one diagnosable condition meet criteria for a second.

One way to look at the significance of this trend is to consider the impact of emotional distress on the economy. Mental illness accounts for 15% of the total impact of disease on the American economy—more than all cancers combined. It is also the leading cause of disability in the United States and Canada. Some 9.5% of the U.S. population meets criteria for depression and 18% for anxiety (NIMH, 2010). Consequently, some 15% of U.S. adults use mental health services each year (U.S. Department of Health and Human Services, 1999). That translates to more than 30 million adults seeking services each year, and while many of those will see a physician for medications, a significant number of them will seek out a talking cure.

Studies focusing on children reveal a similar situation. The NIMH (2010) found 13% of teenagers have a mental disorder. The U.S. De-

partment of Health and Human Services (1999) states that 20% of children
and adolescents experience a mental illness each year, translating to ap-
proximately 10 million young people. Yet some two-thirds of those do not
get the professional services they need. Adding that to the adult totals,
some 70 million Americans suffer from a diagnosable mental illness each
year, and that does not include those who are not diagnosable but who bear
hardships through divorces, job loss and other stressors. Even though
many of these persons do not seek specialized support, a great need for
counseling services obviously exists in the United States and elsewhere.

This demand for services is paralleled by an increase in supply. I (TAS)
can measure it subjectively by tracing the counseling center where I work.
An anomaly in a mid-sized Southern U.S. city when launched in the late
1970s, it has grown to include 15 clinicians plus interns who provide 1100
hours of therapy per month. Even so, several other centers have appeared
in our city in recent years and are also expanding rapidly. Or, track the
growth with book publishing: Christian counseling titles and self-help
books have gained in popularity even as other genres have languished. Or,
consider the burgeoning number of Christian counseling training programs. When I applied to graduate school in 1979, there were only three
programs on the map: Fuller Theological Seminary, Rosemead Graduate
School and Psychological Studies Institute (now Richmont Graduate University). My town alone now has three of its own, exemplifying the ex-
plosive expansion in the number of programs available to believers who
want to counsel in a manner that incorporates faith.

From another vantage point, I (SPG) have been associated with
Christian Counseling Associates (CCA) in the Capital region of upstate
New York. The practice mission is to honor Christ according to his revealed Word, partner with Christian ministries, and assist those hurting
in heart, mind, relationship and health (www.ccahope.com). Birthed by
visionary evangelical leaders over 30 years ago, the intention was to
support pastors and parishioners via advanced therapeutic assistance that
complemented, not crushed, personal faith in Jesus Christ as Lord and
Savior. Increased reliance on third-party funding for medically sanc-
tioned mental health services prompted changes through the years in
both organizational structure and counselor credentials. The heritage of
CCA is typical of Christian practices across the country. For perspective,

in 2010, CCA provided a weekly average of 147.5 billable hours of service. Nearly 80%, or 6,136, of these clinical sessions flowed through a variant of managed mental health care. Despite compliance with oversight requirements and "best practice" expectations, CCA counselors humbly designate our efforts as Christian counseling. In our limited corner of the evangelical world, CCA provides over 7,670 hours a year of professional-level therapy to clients who desire to utilize faith as a critical resource in promoting both overall health and spiritual growth (Greggo, 2007). The demand for service continues to expand.

But maybe national data says it best.

The number of counselors of various ilk is growing to meet the need. As of 2008, there were 152,000 employed clinical, counseling and school psychologists in America (U.S. Bureau of Labor Statistics, 2010), with that number expected to grow by 12% by 2018 to an average of 168,800 among the professions. The number of counselors (including marriage and family therapists) stood at 665,500 in 2009 with a very strong growth rate of 18% expected for the next decade (to 782,200). Mental health counselors are expected to grow even more rapidly at 24%. The 642,000 social workers employed in 2008 should grow to 745,400 (a remarkable 16% increase), with mental health and substance abuse social workers growing even faster at 20%. This adds up to nearly 1.7 million Americans employed in the area by 2018, an extraordinary number even granted that not all of these persons will be counseling.

All of this is not to mention those who counsel as ministers. It is difficult to track how many pastors, chaplains, and pastoral or biblical counselors talk with troubled persons about their burdens. Historically most believers turned to clergy for solace and help, but times are changing. The migration away from pastoral direction and toward secular, medically oriented services continues to trigger strident objection from many conservative Protestants. The core dispute is over the specific parameters for when a ministry or medical setting offers the optimal platform for addressing internal unrest, problems in living or undesirable patterns of behavior (Powlison, 2010a; Adams, 1970).

The profound shift toward evidence-based mental health care is exactly what the current investigation sets out to explore. Within this historical overview, notice that the basic definition of mental health, as offered by the Surgeon General (U.S. Department of Health and Human Services, 1999), contains numerous phrases that plainly tie to value-laden criteria: *productive* activity, *fulfilling* relationships, *adapting* to change, *coping* with adversity, *well-being* and community *contributions*. The implicit understanding of health is embedded in moral and ethical guidelines that shape expectations of typical human behavior. Behavioral norms can be defined by social science using methods of central tendency or by establishing individual baseline functioning. Such norms are utilized to flesh out phrases such as productivity, fulfillment, successful change or coping, health and meaningful contribution to community. Ideal behavioral and ethical practices that transcend "normal" have long been addressed in biblical teaching and Christian tradition through discipleship, pastoral care and spiritual nurture. After all, it was Jesus Christ himself who posed the ultimate reflective question: "What good will it be for a man if he gains the whole world, yet forfeits his soul?" (Matthew 16:26 NIV 1984). Mastery over a mental health concern does not automatically demonstrate spiritual transformation as defined by biblical values. A soul care perspective will be explored shortly.

With the medicalization of mental health, increasing numbers of believers are inclined to consult first with their physicians when feeling a mental health need. If they do specifically seek counseling, they may ask their primary medical provider for a referral to a counselor of one of the varieties just discussed. Insurance coverage of psychotherapy further impacts the direction of service-seekers who may choose providers that are covered on their policies. Christians who practice under the auspices of state licenses have the advantage here, though that begs the question of whether this makes their counsel better than those who counsel within the church or independently as biblical or Christian counselors.

Whether licensed or not, the need for counselors is great, and people are rising to the occasion by entering the field in large numbers. For the growing number of these who are Christians, there is need for great wisdom in determining how to be true to the faith and the teachings of Scripture while in some way responding to the growing data of psychology and its sister mental health disciplines and the current marketplace. Let us briefly trace how believers have responded to "mental health" matters in the past to set the stage for our discussions of the five approaches we will be exploring.

A Brief History of the Christian Care of Souls

Mental health problems are not new; people have long struggled with distress of the soul. Moreover, the debate of who to turn to for such care is also longstanding. The modern Christianity-versus-psychology question is only the latest chapter in the Jerusalem-versus-Athens dilemma that has lasted since before Jesus walked the earth. Johnson (2010b) offers an insightful review with more focus on the study of the nature of persons. We will focus on several themes pertaining to the actual care of souls.

Christian soul care has its earliest roots in the Old Testament. McNeill's (1951) classic work points out that the people of ancient Israel saw God as the Ultimate Guide and the Bible as his wisdom. Yet wise men were guides in discerning this wisdom (a point vital to Coe and Hall's [2010a] transformational model). Central to wisdom was godliness, making the goal of their counsel a clear conscience before God and his Word. This is the background of the rabbi, a term applied to Jesus himself based on his teaching ministry (e.g., Matthew 26:25, 49; Mark 9:5; 10:51; 11:21; and six times in John). Thus, the earliest "counselors" in the Judeo-Christian tradition were men wise in their knowledge of and walk with God, with this wisdom necessarily embodied in a godly life.

However, a competing model arose early, that of the philosophers (McNeill, 1951). Contemplation, religious or not, was a source of wisdom and thus advice. Even so, the "soul" was central, and even Socrates wanted to be considered a "psychiatrist," a "healer of the soul" (much as the word *psychology* means "the study of the soul"—with both terms being ironic given the rejection of the idea of "soul" by most who bear those titles today). Philosophers such as Cicero still found the curing of the soul's irrational arousal to be found in virtue, a morally (though not necessarily religiously) laden idea. Others, such as the Stoics, saw salvation not as moral, but intellectual, with mental control of emotions making the personality whole. Thus, soul care was separated from the religious and no longer clearly tied to godly lives or God himself. The locus switched to human sources for guidance.

The New Testament continues the themes of the Old Testament regarding soul care. As mentioned, Jesus was considered to be a rabbi, though he was much more. While Socrates stressed intellectual clarity as the goal, Jesus' model is quite different. "The transformation of lives he achieves is instituted not in the exposure of error and confusion of thought, but in inducing repentance and commitment to the kingdom" (McNeill, 1951, p. 73). The apostles built on this foundation but included a culture that stressed mutual edification and fraternal correction, communal dimensions of soul care often ignored in our individualistic culture.

In the early church, repentance and consolation (particularly in grief) were themes of the soul care literature (McNeill, 1951). Yet "it was Augustine who formulated both the theology and the psychology that dominated the church for several centuries and, to a large extent, is still the psychology of large areas of the world today" (Kemp, 1947, p. 34). One can only speculate how Augustine's method would be viewed today in the "integration" debate, for he drew from Plato and neo-Platonists in much of his thinking. His contribution, nonetheless, was different. He virtually invented the introspective approach of the *Confessions*, which still is useful in modern counseling (Sisemore, 2001). Whatever one concludes about the influence of philosophy on his thinking, Augustine wrote with great biblical and theological acuity and was quite explicit in the priority of his faith in his thinking.

Space does not permit detailing the progress of soul care through history. It is worth briefly noting, however, one work over seven centuries old by the great Thomas Aquinas, whose wonderful treatise, *Summa Theologica* (1948), offers much guidance to counselors while drawing from Aristotle. These great men of the faith illustrate that soul care drew deep from the Word of God and theology, yet did not ignore the "secular" writers in their thinking. Distinctly writing for "Jerusalem," these greats did not neglect "Athens." As Johnson (2010b) concludes, "In a very real sense, the works of both represent an 'integration' of Christian and non-Christian psychology" (p. 12).

Later scholars of "Jerusalem" were not negligent of the emotional aspects of life and the problems produced. The Puritans are well known for the frequency with which they addressed melancholy, or depression. Noteworthy among the insights of the Puritans was the awareness that melancholy or depression might be physiological. Richard Baxter's *Christian Directory* (1997/1673) might be the first "Christian counseling manual" ever published, addressing issues far beyond depression.

It is not as well known that Christians might have actually "discovered" obsessive-compulsive disorder (OCD). Judith Rappaport (1989) finds the roots of modern OCD in what the Catholic Church originally called "scrupulosity"—the overly rigid attending to morals and proper behavior. Jeremy Taylor (1660) most thoroughly explored it, making it a disorder with a longer history of religious "diagnosis" and "therapy" than secular. These examples illustrate that Christians have long addressed mental health in ways that were progressive for their time. Even as Christian music set the standard for quality in the years around the Reformation, so Christian thought on mental and emotional life was more "cutting edge" than it is now (see, e.g., Noll, 1994).[1]

Let us fastforward to the emergence of the modern discipline called psychology in the late 1800s. In the light of the Enlightenment and emboldened by Darwin's explaining life independent of a Creator, science embraced an empirical approach that allowed only what could be seen and measured, excluding the divine altogether. Whereas the early philosophers generally held to some supernatural beliefs, the new psychologists embraced a methodology that barred the supernatural from the table. Over time, most who practiced psychology abandoned the "soul" of their discipline and embraced a godless worldview to match their methodology. Jones (1994) reported statistics showing academic psychologists to be among the least religious group of scholars, with 50% reporting no religious preference compared to only 10% of the general population. Clinical psychologists were little different, with only 33% claiming religious faith to be the most important influence in their lives in contrast to 72% of the general population. At a time when 90% of the population claimed to hold belief in a personal God, less than one third of counseling and clinical psychologists could endorse a similar claim (Shafranske, 2001). A chasm has developed between the scientific study of persons and faith.

Relating the Christian faith to modern psychology posed new challenges and demanded new thinking and approaches to relating faith to the new, powerful, and popular discipline of psychology. Johnson (2010b) picks up the story at this point, leading us to the need to compare and contrast differing approaches to this task. His focus, appropriate to the focus of *Psychology & Christianity: Five Views* (Johnson, 2010a), is on the

---

[1]The interested reader is referred to Kemp (1947) for a thorough survey of pastoral care in history.

theoretical approaches to relating the disciplines. While there have been efforts to bridge the gap from theory to practice in Christian counseling (McMinn and Campbell's [2007] *Integrative Psychotherapy* being one of the best recent efforts), more Christians who counsel likely have developed their approaches rather haphazardly given the lack of clear models from which to work.

The current volume intends to follow the models presented by Johnson (2010a) to show practical conclusions, comparing and contrasting the five approaches as they are manifest in the counseling room. How much should modern soul care mirror the sages of ancient Israel? What, if anything, can secular thinking and methodology contribute to caring for Christians with mental health challenges? What does all of this mean in a day when a license from a state board, embracing the secular models, is required to counsel in many settings? And most fundamentally, how do we put all of this together to help our friend Jake and others like him?

In preparation for addressing these practical issues, let us review the theoretical underpinnings of the five approaches as laid out in Johnson's (2010a) precursor to this volume.

Theoretical Foundations of the Five Approaches

Approaches to science rarely fit neatly into categories, though such categories enhance communication and enable comparison and contrast among ideas. Thus, the five views in Johnson's (2010a) work are neither orthogonal nor monolithic. They are not orthogonal in that there are points of overlap among them. If one pictures a Venn diagram, the five circles would overlap, though not necessarily with all of the other circles. (This might look strangely akin to the Olympic rings.) For example, while there may be little intersection between biblical counselors and those with a levels-of-explanation approach, there is overlap of biblical counseling with the other three views. These areas of overlap will be even more apparent when we apply these approaches to counseling itself and to Jake in particular.

The five views also are not monolithic. Back to our image of circles, even though there is enough distinction to separate one view from another, there is room for differences within each view within its circle. Thus, if we were covering secular counseling theories and examined psychodynamic theories as a view, Freud would be an appropriate representative. Yet there are, needless to say, considerable differences among Freud, Jung, Adler and the Object Relations theorists who would all fit in this view. Another way to envision this is to think of the taxonomy that organizes living things. Each of the five views might be considered to be more of a genus, containing within it a variety of species. As we move from the authors in Johnson's (2010a) volume to their partners in this one, we will learn that there is similarity enough, but also considerable diversity within each view. Each contributor offers *an* approach from his or her family, but by no means *the* approach. This is important to bear in mind as we proceed.

A levels-of-explanation approach. David Myers, social psychologist and prolific scholar, represents this view in both Johnson's volume (Myers, 2010a) as well as the earlier edition (Myers, 2000). His widely recognized introduction to psychology, now in its ninth edition, may be quite familiar to readers (Myers, 2010b). Despite his stress on science, Myers (2010a) makes clear his Christian commitment from the outset, stressing his work in scientific psychology does not deter him from prayer and Bible reading each day. He carefully defines psychology as "the science of behavior and mental processes" (p. 49) as he accepts the dominant scientific paradigm for the discipline of psychology. Three basic tenets of his view are that (1) science and Christianity both point to a need for humility and awareness of human fallibility, (2) much science provides support for the Bible and theology, and (3) occasionally science will challenge traditional Christian understandings. Myers illustrates point (2) with data from social scientific research and (3) by arguing that homosexuality research should make us rethink biblical teachings on the topic (an interpretation of the data that has been challenged by other Christian scholars, such as Jones and Yarhouse, 2000).

These three tenets flow from Myers's view of the levels of explanation offered by various disciplines, the concept underlying his approach to relating faith and science. Reality, Myers (2010a) contends, is a multilayered unity. So a person can be considered as a group of atoms, a dazzling assortment of chemistry, an object of beauty, a person in a community and a person for whom Christ died. Each layer can be analyzed, or explained, by certain disciplines appropriate to that level. In this particular illustration, the levels might best be examined by a physicist, chemist, artist, social psychologist or theologian, respectively. "Which perspective is pertinent depends on what you want to talk about" (p. 51). Each perspective has its domain, and complements the others. One does not, then, "integrate" the two disciplines of psychology and theology, but honors each in its own domain. Admittedly they will conflict at times, but in general they will cohere, for "In God's world, all truth is one" (p. 52). Persons are to be studied from all levels with humility that becomes scholars of all disciplines.

Myers's position is most common among research and academic psychologists who are Christians. Those who fit in the "genus" of levels of explanation might include Donald Mackay (1991) and Malcolm Jeeves (1997), with an emphasis on neuropsychological research. Everett Worthington (2010) recently has made a compelling case for the importance of science in understanding the person—his theses (p. 13) echo Myers's three major points while his work has focused on more applied and clinical aspects of psychology.

Warren Brown (2004) takes perspectivalism a step further as he wonders if there is any *resonance* among the perspectives of, say, "a nonreductive physicalist account of human nature and a Biblical understanding of persons" (p. 118). His model sees the disciplines as resonating (amplifying and enriching each other as auditory signals in harmony) to yield truth. Brown draws from the Wesleyan Quadrilateral, which holds that knowledge comes from four sources: Scripture, experience, tradition and rationality. He adds science as a fifth source, and argues that information coming from all five sources should "resonate" together in harmony as a symphony orchestra does. When there is dissonance on a subject, the scholar is to arbitrate the differences emanating from each of the sources. This takes Myers's position a step closer to applicability in counseling by addressing the interaction of these fields while not seeing them as being "integrated."

This "resonance" is important when one seeks to draw from science to counsel believing clients as the levels of explanation merge in the counseling office. Science offers descriptions of problematic life issues and has produced techniques that are evidence based as ways to treat them, yet the moral and spiritual dimensions are more often evident in counseling than in the psychological science. In the counseling office, the levels of explanation merge (or resonate loudly) as counselors trained in empiricism serve clients who bring religious and spiritual values and interpretations to the session. These values are now considered as an area of diversity by the major players in the field. The Ethics Code of the American Psychological

Association (APA; 2010) in Principle E requires respect of clients' religion, and in the American Counseling Association's (ACA; 2005) Code, the same is stressed in standard C.5.

Therefore, these major professional organizations have begun publishing material on addressing religion and spirituality in counseling. Burke, Chauvin and Miranti (2003) illustrate the efforts of ACA, while APA's efforts include *Spiritual Practices in Psychotherapy: Thirteen Tools for Enhancing Psychological Health* by Thomas Plante (2009). So, who better to turn to from this perspective to guide us in helping Jake and in understanding how science approaches religion and spirituality in the counseling office? Dr. Plante is Professor of Psychology at Santa Clara University and is also on the adjunct faculty of Stanford University School of Medicine. He has served as president of APA's Division 36 for the Psychology of Religion and Spirituality. He is author of many books, including several addressing the issue of sexual abuse by clergy in the Catholic Church. Plante's familiarity with research and history of addressing spiritual issues in counseling makes him a valuable representative of the levels-of-explanation position.

An integration approach. Johnson (2010b) traces the roots of the second view of relating psychology and Christianity to the 1960s, seeing it arising as a middle ground between biblical counselors and the levels-of-explanation approach by its honoring the former's critique of the latter while still seeing value in scientific psychology. Thus the two disciplines overlap and can be "integrated" in some sense, though what is integrated and how it is done has prompted much discussion.

Stanton Jones (2010) presents the integration view in the Johnson (2010a) volume. He opens by defining the approach as he sees it:

> *Integration of Christianity and psychology (or any area of "secular thought") is our living out—in this particular area—of the lordship of Christ over all of existence by our giving his special revelation—God's true Word—its appropriate place of authority in determining our fundamental beliefs about and practices toward all of reality and toward our academic subject matter in particular.* (p. 102, italics in the original)

Jones concedes that the term *integration* is inadequate to carry the freight of all that is involved in relating faith and secular thought, but asserts that the vital issue is taking a fundamental stance as a Christian in the world of learning and action. He responds to Collins's (2000) concern in the earlier *Four Views* edition of the book about which terms one is to use to define what is being integrated. Jones proposes that it is *science* and *Christianity* that are integrated. *Science* is preferred as psychology owes its legitimacy to its base in scientific knowledge. *Christianity* is chosen over "the Bible" or "Christian theology" as he sees "it is the personal faith convictions and commitments of individual psychologists that can and will shape their scientific and professional work" (Jones, 2010, p. 106), rather than abstract teachings. While greatly valuing Scripture, Jones maintains that much biblical language—even regarding the nature of human persons, the focus of this integration—is imprecise. Science also has its shortcomings, particularly in that it is not as objective as many presume, with facts being influenced by theory, and theory underdetermined by facts. Scientists ultimately cannot avoid addressing metaphysics, something beyond the purview of empiricism.

Jones (2010) does not believe there are "concrete steps" to accomplish this type of integration, but offers some guidelines to the process: the integrationist must keep clear his or her fundamental loyalty to the faith, must be methodologically rigorous, must attend to the tension between the two fields, must conduct science in a way shaped by Christian convictions, and do all in a spirit of tentativeness, patience and humility. Thus, as Myers (2010a) also argues, humility is vital.

Unlike most of the other contributors to Johnson's (2010a) volume, Jones is a clinical psychologist and is well equipped to address the implications of the integration view for therapy (e.g., Jones & Butman, 1991). He remarks that psychotherapy is not completely determined by the (secular) theories of psychotherapy that one might draw from, and a broader understanding of psychotherapy is founded in the therapist's loyalty to Christ and a Christian understanding of the nature of persons. His overall conclusion is that, given the weaknesses inherent in the metaphysical and moral presuppositions of science, "we may need to modify and reshape what we learn from psychology in light of our Christian beliefs" (p. 126). Jones thus differs with Myers in that psychology is reshaped by Christian beliefs rather than challenging them.

Probably the preponderance of writings on relating Christianity and psychology could be termed "integrationism," with most of the authors being psychologists (such as Jones & Butman, 1991; Collins, 2007; Entwistle, 2004). In some instances, the mental health professional teams up with a theologian (e.g., Beck & Demarest, 2005; Shults & Sandage, 2006). (Note that this is also true of the transformational theorists Coe and Hall, 2010a, 2010b.) The major organizations for Christians in the field—the Christian Association for Psychological Studies (www.caps .net) and the American Association of Christian Counselors (www.aacc .net)—are rooted in integration, as are the core journals, *Journal of Psychology and Theology* and *Journal of Psychology and Christianity*. As evidenced in the literature, integration can occur in a variety of ways, but few are as well thought out as the work of Mark McMinn (McMinn & Campbell, 2007; McMinn, 1996, 2008).

Dr. McMinn is Professor of Psychology at George Fox University after helping start the Doctor of Psychology program at Wheaton College. He is also a past president of APA's Division 36, and author of a number of books and articles. Dr. McMinn has demonstrated Christian counseling in a video made by the APA (2006), a rare honor indeed. His recent model of integrative psychotherapy (McMinn & Campbell, 2007; McMinn, 2008) may be the most thoroughly elaborated model of integration to date. This makes him an exceptional choice to represent the integration perspective.

A Christian psychology approach. Johnson (2010b) explains this recent, yet ancient, approach originated with Christian philosopher C. Stephen Evans who, observing the renaissance in philosophy where explicitly Christian models found a hearing, argued that believing psychologists should follow suit. "He challenged Christians in psychology to develop their own theories, research and practice that flow from Christian beliefs about human beings—while continuing to participate actively in the broader field" (p. 36). The call was to reclaim the Christian tradition of thinking about persons (found largely in philosophy and theology) and use it—not modern psychology—as the foundation for our models while not eschewing empirical research. Rather, Christian psychologists engage in research to demonstrate the validity of Christian psychology and to enter dialogue with professionals in the contemporary discipline of psychology.

Central to understanding the Christian psychology approach is breaking free of current use of the term *psychology*. Psychology historically is the "study of the soul," a meaning strangely lost by a modern discipline practiced mostly by those who do not believe in a "soul" to start with. Thus, Christian psychologists are any who study the soul from a Christian worldview, be they biblical authors, theologians, philosophers, novelists, mental health practitioners or empirical psychologists. The term *Christian psychology*, therefore, carries a much broader meaning, as reflected in the name of the journal of the Society for Christian Psychology, *Edification: The Transdisciplinary Journal of the Society for Christian Psychology* (www.christianpsych.org).

Appropriately, then, the two contributors to Johnson's *Psychology & Christianity* (2010a) are a philosopher and research psychologist. Roberts and Watson (2010) begin their case by noting the failure of modern psychology to produce a dominant paradigm or overarching theory, unlike other scientific disciplines. Meanwhile, modern psychology has become more open in admitting that it overlaps with moral functioning, reverting to the older language of the virtues, particularly in the area of positive psychology. This opens the door to Christians working from our own tradition and moral base to propose a model of psychology, a Christian psychology. Roberts and Watson propose two steps in developing this model.

The first step is to retrieve Christian psychology, the biblically rooted understanding of the nature of persons and our psychological functioning and disorder. The fountainhead of this is, of course, the Bible itself, and the Sermon on the Mount, specifically, illustrates this. Roberts and Watson (2010) draw out basics of the psychology of Jesus' teaching in this passage. The Sermon offers a model for personal well-being with the character traits of the Beatitudes and kingdom values, traits that conflict with secular thought at many points. Jesus also points out the "psychopathology" of anger, grudge bearing and anxiety, among others. The psychological explanation for these lies in inwardness explaining actions, such as anger underlying revenge. The "therapeutic interventions" of the Sermon are cultivating the qualities of the Beatitudes and the rest of the moral character of the Sermon, with these again contradicting most secular approaches to therapy. While the authors focus on Scripture, they point also to the rich tradition of Christian thought that develops the basic psychology of the Bible. Roberts and Watson mention Augustine, Aquinas, Pascal and Kierkegaard as examples of "Christian psychologists" from the past, from whom we still stand to learn.

The second step in developing a Christian psychology is to conduct empirical research within the tradition. Roberts and Watson (2010) call out the prejudice of the allegedly "unbiased" theories of modern psychology and argue that "a Christian empirical psychology will begin unapologetically with an explicit normative understanding of human beings" (p. 165) as understood in the Christian tradition. It is thus more intellectually self-aware than other theories. Good research done from this perspective can make a Christian psychology a "worthy intellectual competitor to the secular psychologies" (p. 165). This research can proceed to address explicitly Christian goals and methods, and the authors illustrate this with studies that have already been conducted. Less directly pertinent for clinicians is the task of research to bring the Christian worldview into dialogue with secular models and to expose hidden metaphysical assumptions of establishment psychology, a project reflected in Watson's own research (e.g., Watson, 2011).

A third step might be added to the two Roberts and Watson (2010) propose: an approach to counseling based on the Christian psychology approach advocated above. Johnson (2007) has taken a step in this direction, developing a strong intellectual basis for work in the area, but no clear models of therapy have yet been put forth.

For the present work, we turn to a woman who has been counseling in a manner consistent with Christian psychology (Johnson, 2010b), Dr. Diane Langberg. Author of several books on counseling, she has largely focused on survivors of abuse (Langberg, 2003), including, like Dr. Plante above, those who experienced abuse by clergy (Langberg, 1996). With over 35 years of experience as a therapist, and now serving as director of her own clinic, Dr. Langberg also holds academic appointments at Reformed Episcopal Seminary and Westminster Seminary. She is a leader as well, serving on the boards of the American Association of Christian Counselors and the Society for Christian Psychology. She serves as an experienced guide in bringing Christian psychology into the counseling office.

A transformational approach. Johnson (2010b) notes that this view is new to his volume, not appearing in the earlier *Four Views* (Johnson & Jones, 2000). Since then, a number of integrationists have shifted the focus from intellectual to personal/spiritual matters, arguing "that *how* Christians live out their Christianity in the field of psychology and counseling is at least as important as seeking to understand human beings Christianly" (p. 37; italics in the original). David Benner (1988) was the pivotal pioneer as he looked to historic spirituality for a model of care of souls. He spawned a following, with John Coe and Todd Hall (2010a, 2010b) most fully developing it into a comprehensive approach to reconciling psychology and Christianity.

As Coe and Hall (2010b) present it, the transformational approach might also be called a spiritual formation approach. They de-emphasize relating psychology to faith and argue that psychology, and science itself, is to be transformed into a unity of faith and love. To do this, they propose we are to "get behind the veil" of what tradition tells us is good psychology and do it afresh: "The goal, then, is for each generation in the Spirit to allow *reality* and *faith* to shape this endeavor, to do the work of psychology in faith and then, as a secondary task, reintegrate its findings with those truths and traditions within which it finds itself" (p. 202; italics in the original).

This is therefore a more subjective approach, embedded in the individuals doing such psychology, though certainly objective research has its place as well. The transformational approach is a psychology only for Christians, as it is grounded in Christian realities. The person doing this psychology is fundamental, and the more godly (or healthier) the individual, the better the psychology. "The *good* person is most able to do psychology, for good character transformed by the Spirit and other healthy relationships" (Coe & Hall, 2010b, p. 215) guarantees that the investigator acts out of love and is open to all of reality. Such spiritual maturity is another form of the humility that is a theme in most of the approaches we have surveyed, though here its cultivation is given the most attention as it enables the psychologist to avoid personal biases and distortions.

Coe and Hall (2010b) present a radically relational model, with a strong connection between relation and knowing, in regard to both God and other persons. This is the foundation of the previous point: as we grow in our relationships, we grow in our knowledge. Spiritual disciplines that foster our union with God are a vital part of being a psychologist in the Spirit.

With these basic elements, Coe and Hall (2010b) proceed to lay out the contours of such a transformational psychology. Most basic (Level 1) is the transformation of the psychologist by the spiritual-epistemological disciplines and virtues as we have discussed. Level 2 is the methodology of doing psychology in God. Here the authors look to the Old Testament sage (as is seen, for example, in Proverbs and other Wisdom literature) as their model. Theory and the development of a body of relevant knowledge occur at Level 3. Coe and Hall posit three main dimensions of this: (a) the nature of self as spirit, having a nature and being relational, (b) sin and psychopathology, consequences of original sin, perpetuated by sins of the will and heart, and also result from the demonic and the impact of being sinned against, and (c) psychological health promoted by parental love, Christ's redemptive work, the Holy Spirit, and love to God and neighbor. As one studies their longer explanation in their book, *Psychology in the Spirit* (Coe & Hall, 2010a), it is apparent that much of the model draws from attachment theory in secular psychology. This leads to Level 4 and care of the soul, the place that connects to the consulting office as it takes the model from theory to praxis in counseling and spiritual direction. Level 5 introduces a model of training in transformational psychology, a feature unique to this approach.

This might be a good time to reiterate that each of the approaches is a family, grouping around some central features while having differences with others in the genus. Coe and Hall (2010b) propose a model that incorporates spiritual disciplines, a very intentional relationality and a radical approach to redefining psychology while drawing from attachment theory. Others in this group of approaches might lie closer to Benner (1999), who draws profoundly from the spiritual disciplines while keeping more modern psychology. This forms the core of his edited book on spiritual direction, where he is joined by Gary Moon as coeditor (Moon & Benner, 2004). We will turn to Dr. Moon for help in caring for Jake's soul. Dr. Moon is Director of the Dallas Willard Institute and Chair of Integration at Richmont Graduate University. He is a founding editor of *Conversations*, one of the two publications most germane to this approach (the other is the *Journal of Spiritual Formation and Soul Care*, published by Biola's Institute for Spiritual Formation). Dr. Moon has written widely in journals and authored several books (2004, 2009) on the spiritual life. Trained as a psychologist yet having drunk deeply of the spiritual disciplines and spiritual direction, Dr. Moon is thoroughly qualified to represent the transformational approach.

A biblical counseling approach. Jay Adams (1970) is well known for his strident criticism of modern psychology and Christian adaptations of it. His position is not surprising given the state of affairs at that point in history (Johnson, 2010b). Time has shown this to be a critical turning point, as it played a role in evangelicals' becoming more serious about the integrity of their faith as they worked in psychological fields, and it rallied together those who see the Bible as a basically self-sufficient counseling manual. Founded by Adams in 1968, the Christian Counseling & Educational Foundation has, for many, been the standard bearer of this approach (www.ccef.org). Johnson offers a brief history, and Powlison (2010a) presents a detailed one as biblical counseling, too, has had diversity of opinion. Partly the debate has been on how much dialogue to have with scientific psychology and other approaches. Even since these were published, however, biblical counselors have moved to unite through several meetings in 2010, forming the Biblical Counseling Coalition (www.biblicalcounselingcoalition.org).

David Powlison (2010b) offers a summary of his biblical counseling position in *Psychology & Christianity: Five Views*. Immediately stating his position, he contends, "Christian faith *is* a psychology. . . . Christian ministry *is* a psychotherapy" (p. 245; italics in the original). Conceding that there are many competing psychologies from outside the Christian faith, Powlison would direct us to the only one that is truly rooted in the nature of God and his revelation in the Bible.

Powlison (2010b) begins by stating that merely amassing psychological facts (as in modern science) without keeping God in view is inadequate. In contrast, he maintains three assumptions that underlie his position. First, God is the Maker of all, and to truly know and love this Maker is to be fully human. (Only the Christian faith, then, can show us our ultimate well-being.) Second, the Lord is judge of the living and the dead, knowing and evaluating us completely. We are to be loyal to this God and nothing else. Finally, Christ came to us and for our salvation. This restoration climaxes in a restored relationship with God, which affects all aspects of our psychological functioning.

Building on this, Powlison (2010b) deconstructs current meanings of "psychology" by breaking it into six pieces, progressing from concrete to abstract. Psych-1 is like *a good movie or novel;* it "simply describes how we operate in the world we inhabit" (pp. 249-50). It concerns the person interacting with his or her entire life situation, including behavior, motives, what rules you, and ultimately the living God. Psych-2 is a detailed knowledge of human functioning, like *science*. It includes "close observations and systematic descriptions of human functioning" (p. 253). Here Powlison admits we can learn from secular psychology, but only some "neurotic insights" (p. 255) and nothing systematic given the problems of their version of Psych-3, the interpretive and explanatory level based on Psych-2. For Christians, this must be explicitly a Christian worldview, as it is like *theology*.

This brings us to the focal aspect for our current project. Psych-4 is the practical applications of the above to psychotherapy, and is like *the cure of souls*. For Powlison (2010b), this is a task of Christian wisdom, informing counseling just as it informs preaching or worship. Thus it, too, must be explicitly and wholly Christian as we depend on that (Psych-3) to offer an ideal for human functioning to provide a direction for change. "All counseling does attempt pastoral work, shepherding the souls of wandering, suffering sheep" (p. 258). Other therapies are secular pastoral workers who "heal lightly the woes and wrongs of the human condition" (p. 259).

Psych-5 is a system of professional and institutional arrangements. Powlison (2010b) believes the dominant system in the West is secular and leads to professionals licensed by the state. In contrast, for Christians, Psych-5 is like *church* (and parachurch), where ministry models are integral to the institutions. Finally, Psych-6 is the mass ethos where all of the above takes place—popular culture or *the world*, or spirit of the age. Here Powlison argues Christians should build a counterculture based on biblical wisdom.

In short, only biblical wisdom can form a Psych-3 to understand and interpret the experiences of the person (Psych-1) correctly. Counseling (Psych-4) must follow from that, leaving place only for occasional insights (Psych-2) from secular psychology. Moreover, the context of Christian counseling is more properly outside licensing laws and inside the church or parachurch organizations (Psych-5).

As noted earlier, each approach is more of a family than a singularity. Given the Christian Counseling & Educational Foundation was represented by David Powlison in the *Psychology & Christianity: Five Views* book (Johnson, 2010a), we step outside that organization to get a different perspective from within the Biblical Counseling community. Dr. Stuart Scott is Associate Professor of Biblical Counseling at the Southern Baptist Theological Seminary in Louisville, Kentucky, and Executive Director of the National Center of Biblical Counseling. Prior to this, he garnered over 25 years of counseling and ministry experience, serving most recently as Associate Pastor of Family Ministries and Counseling at Grace Community Church in Los Angeles, where he also taught at the Master's College and Seminary. Author of several books (Scott, 2000, 2009; Peace & Scott, 2010), Dr. Scott has also been active in the formation of the Biblical Counseling Coalition. We look to him as a guide into the use of biblical counseling with Jake.

Charting the Course

Shortly we will let these authors speak and share how these five approaches apply in counseling and, in particular, with Jake. As you read, observe the similarities and dissimilarities to the representative in the earlier volume. These authors focus primarily on case matters and thus will offer only limited commentary to characterize how their own counseling strategies correspond to the overarching view. The practical, applied orientation of this text leaves to the reader the pursuit of the links or distinctions between each theoretical position's spokesperson and practitioner. Such investigation will add depth to an understanding of each view as the flexibility and expertise necessary to move from theory to practice is exemplified. The strategy bound into the chapters ahead is not to expound on the assets or fine points of each unique set of conceptual principles and convictions. Instead, we will witness via demonstration how each unique Christian helping paradigm is manifested in actual application.

There is much to learn for us, and several roads to help for Jake. Let us seek God's guidance as we merge these journeys in the pages that follow.

References

Adams, J. E. (1970). *Competent to counsel*. Phillipsburg, NJ: Presbyterian & Reformed.

American Counseling Association. (2005). *ACA code of ethics*. Retrieved from <www.counseling.org/Resources/CodeOfEthics/TP/Home/CT2.aspx>.

American Psychological Association (Producer). (2006). Christian counseling [Motion picture]. Available from <www.apa.org/pubs/videos/4310744.aspx>.

———. (2010). *Ethical principles of psychologists and code of conduct*. Retrieved from <www.apa.org/ethics/code/index.aspx#>.

Augustine. (1960). *The confessions*. Garden City, NY: Image Books.

Baxter, R. (1997). *A Christian directory*. Morgan, PA: Soli Deo Gloria Publications. (Original work published 1673).

Beck, J. R., & Demarest, B. (2005). *The human person in theology and psychology: A biblical anthropology for the twenty-first century*. Grand Rapids: Kregel.

Benner, D. G. (1988). *Psychotherapy and the spiritual quest*. Grand Rapids: Baker.

———. (1999). *Care of souls: Revisioning Christian nurture and counsel*. Grand Rapids: Baker.

Brown, W. S. (2004). Resonance: A model for relating science, psychology, and faith. *Journal of Psychology and Theology, 23*(2), 110-20.

Burke, M. T., Chauvin, J. C., & Miranti, J. G. (2003). *Religious and spiritual issues in counseling*. New York: Routledge.

Coe, J. H., & Hall, T. W. (2010a). *Psychology in the Spirit: Contours of a transformational psychology*. Downers Grove, IL: IVP Academic.

———. (2010b). A transformational psychology view. In E. L. Johnson (Ed.), *Psychology & Christianity: Five views* (pp. 199-226). Downers Grove, IL: IVP Academic.

Collins, G. (2007). *Christian counseling: A comprehensive guide* (3rd ed.). Nashville: Thomas Nelson.

Collins, G.R. (2000). An integration view. In E. L. Johnson & S. L. Jones (Eds.), *Psychology & Christianity: Four views* (pp. 102-29). Downers Grove, IL: InterVarsity Press.

Entwistle, E. N. (2004). *Integrative approaches to psychology and Christianity: An introduction to worldview issues, philosophical foundations, and models of integration*. Eugene, OR: Wipf and Stock.

Greggo, S. P. (2007). Mending mangled care: The pursuit of Christian service within managed care. *Christian Counseling Today, 15*, 45-47.

Jeeves, M. A. (1997). *Human nature at the millennium: Reflections on the integration of psychology and Christianity*. Grand Rapids: Baker.

Johnson, E. L. (2007). *Foundations for soul care: A Christian psychology proposal*. Downers Grove, IL: IVP Academic.

——— (Ed.). (2010a). *Psychology & Christianity: Five views*. Downers Grove, IL: IVP Academic.

———. (2010b). A brief history of Christians in psychology. In E. L. Johnson (Ed.), *Psychology & Christianity: Five views* (pp. 9-48). Downers Grove, IL: IVP Academic.

Johnson, E. L., & Jones, S. L. (Eds.). (2000). *Psychology & Christianity: Four views*. Downers Grove, IL: InterVarsity Press.

Jones, S. L. (1994). A constructive relationship for religion with the science and profession of psychology: Perhaps the boldest model yet. *American Psychologist, 49*, 184-89.

————. (2010). An integration view. In E. L. Johnson (Ed.), *Psychology & Chris-tianity: Five views* (pp. 101-28). Downers Grove, IL: IVP Academic.

Jones, S. L., & Butman, R. (1991). *Modern psychotherapies: A comprehensive Christian appraisal.* Downers Grove, IL: InterVarsity Press.

Jones, S. L., & Yarhouse, M. (2000). *Homosexuality: The use of scientific research in the church's moral debate.* Downers Grove, IL: InterVarsity Press.

Kemp, C. F. (1947). *Physicians of the soul: A history of pastoral counseling.* New York: The Macmillan Company.

Langberg, D. (1996). Clergy sexual abuse. In C. C. Kroeger & J. R. Beck (Eds.), *Women, Abuse, and the Bible* (pp. 58-69). Grand Rapids: Baker.

Langberg, D. M. (2003). *Counseling survivors of sexual abuse.* Longwood, FL: Xulon Press.

Mackay, D. M. (1991). *Behind the eye.* Oxford: Basil Blackwell.

McMinn, M. R. (1996). *Psychology, theology and spirituality in Christian counseling.* Wheaton, IL: Tyndale House.

————. (2008). *Sin and grace in Christian counseling: An integrative paradigm.* Downers Grove, IL: IVP Academic.

McMinn, M. R., & Campbell, C. D. (2007). *Integrative psychotherapy: Toward a comprehensive Christian approach.* Downers Grove, IL: IVP Academic.

McNeill, J. T. (1951). *A history of the cure of souls.* New York: Harper and Brothers.

Moon, G. W. (2004). *Falling for God: Saying yes to his extravagant proposal.* Colorado Springs: WaterBrook.

————. (2009). *Apprenticeship with Jesus: Learning to live like the Master.* Grand Rapids: Baker.

Moon, G. W., & Benner, D. G. (2004). *Spiritual direction and the care of souls: A guide to Christian approaches and practices.* Downers Grove, IL: InterVarsity Press.

Myers, D. G. (2000). A levels-of-explanation view. In E. L. Johnson & S. L. Jones (Eds.), *Psychology & Christianity: Four views* (pp. 54-83). Downers Grove, IL: InterVarsity Press.

————. (2010a). A levels-of-explanation view. In E. L. Johnson (Ed.), *Psychology & Christianity: Five views* (pp. 49-78). Downers Grove, IL: IVP Academic.

————. (2010b). *Psychology* (9th ed.). New York: Worth Publishers.

National Institute of Mental Health. (2009). *Statistics.* Retrieved from <www.nimh.nih.gov/health/topics/statistics/index.shtml>.

————. (2010). *The numbers count: Mental disorders in America.* Retrieved from <http://wwwapps.nimh.nih.gov/health/publications/the-numbers-count-mental-disorders-in-america.shtml>.

Noll, M. A. (1994). *The scandal of the evangelical mind.* Grand Rapids: Eerdmans.

Peace, M., & Scott, S. (2010). *The faithful parent: A biblical guide to raising a family.* Phillipsburg, NJ: Presbyterian & Reformed.

Plante, T. G. (2009). *Spiritual practices in psychotherapy: Thirteen tools for enhancing psychological health.* Washington, DC: American Psychological Association.

Powlison, D. (2010a). *The biblical counseling movement: History and context.* Greensboro, NC: New Growth Press.

———. (2010b). A biblical counseling view. In E. L. Johnson (Ed.), *Psychology & Christianity: Five views* (pp. 245-73). Downers Grove, IL: IVP Academic.

Roberts, R. C., & Watson, P. J. (2010). A Christian psychology view. In E. L. Johnson (Ed.), *Psychology & Christianity: Five views* (pp. 149-78). Downers Grove, IL: IVP Academic.

Rappaport, J. L. (1989). *The boy who couldn't stop washing: The experience and treatment of obsessive-compulsive disorder.* New York: Signet.

Scott, S. (2000). *The exemplary husband: A biblical perspective.* Bemidji, MN: Focus Publications.

———. (2009). *Biblical manhood: Masculinity, leadership, and decision making.* Bemidji, MN: Focus Publications.

Shafranske, E. (2001). The religious dimension of patient care within rehabilitation medicine: The role of religious attitudes, beliefs, and professional practices. In T. E. Plante & A. C. Sherman (Eds.), *Faith and health: Psychological perspectives* (pp. 311-35). New York: Guilford Press.

Shults, F. L., & Sandage, S. J. (2006). *Transforming spirituality: Integrating theology and psychology.* Grand Rapids: Baker.

Sisemore, T. A. (2001). Saint Augustine's Confessions and the use of introspection in counseling. *Journal of Psychology and Christianity, 21,* 324-31.

Taylor, J. (1660). *Ductor dubitantium, or, the rule of conscience in all her general measures; serving as a great instrument for the determination of cases of conscience.* Retrieved from <books.google.com/>.

Thomas Aquinas. (1948). *Summa theologica.* Notre Dame, IN: Ave Maria Press.

U.S. Bureau of Labor Statistics. (2010). *Occupational outlook handbook* (2010-2011 ed.). Retrieved from <www.bls.gov/oco/>.

U.S. Department of Health and Human Services. (1999). *Mental health: A report of the Surgeon General—Executive summary.* Rockville, MD: U.S. Department of Health and Human Services, Substance Abuse and Mental Health Services Administration, Center for Mental Health Services, National Institutes of Health, National Institute of Mental Health. Retrieved from <www.surgeon general.gov/library/mentalhealth/summary.html>.

Watson, P. J. (2011). Whose psychology? Which rationality? Christian psychology within an ideological surround after postmodernism. *Journal of Psychology and Christianity, 30,* 307-316.

Worthington, E. L., Jr. (2010). *Coming to peace with psychology.* Downers Grove, IL: IVP Academic.

2

Moving Models into Practice

LEARNING OBJECTIVES

- *Identify the motivation, core values and personal passions from your spiritual journey that sustain your interest in becoming a counselor who engages others in strategic conversation to address change.*
- *Define the consultant role and pinpoint how expert consultation can strengthen counseling services.*
- *Examine your initial reactions and emotional response to the prospect of becoming Jake's counselor.*

We met Jake briefly in chapter 1, and we intend now to get to know him well. Before hearing Jake's full story, it is important to consider a few preliminary matters. Our panel of experts will each assume the role of consultant to display how clinical priorities and Christian worldview translate into client care. When exposed to the models that depict the relationship between psychology and Christianity, both novice and skilled clinicians inevitably question: *What would that view look like in real-life counseling?* (Johnson, 2010). Through the procedure of case consultation, the opportunity is ripe to move beyond defining each position and demonstrate how each greets the gritty, fast-paced and demanding world of client care. How does each approach enlighten the change-oriented communication known as counseling in ways that consistently conform to a Christian faith perspective?

Helpers who seriously consider how their relationship with Jesus Christ can shape a counseling encounter undertake a monumental feat. Initially, the venture requires prayer, meditation, study and diligent reasoning to recognize the value of each conceptual model in managing the intersection of faith, culture and modern science. This step involves contemplating theology, worldview, scientific philosophy, dimensions of personal faith and the priority ascribed to Scripture. Once these key parameters are put into place, another daunting task immediately ensues. It is one matter to diligently assess how the disciplines of Christian theology and scientific psychology sort out matters of epistemology—how we know what we know. It is quite another venture to implement a paradigm establishing the lines of interdisciplinary authority as an instructive grid to inform interpersonal, helping conversations. Clinicians and pastors who adopt a version of these five views must tame abstract philosophical debate and domesticate a sensible approach that flourishes in the rough-and-tumble reality of helping relationships.

Counseling is an applied discipline that utilizes information and methods from various sources. It can be succinctly defined as person-to-person dialogue to guide and support change (Collins, 2007). An alternative but related generic description might be a candid, pastoral style of speaking the truth in love to further change through the application of biblical teaching (Powlison, 2010). Either way, this type of conversation may involve facilitating personal transformation, comfort for one adjusting to a loss or gain, or a turbulent combination of both. Placing the emphasis in counseling on coping with the dynamics of change may be basic, but it is anything but simplistic. Complexities in counseling arise on three levels, and interaction effects among them abound. First, change can be unwelcomed, overwhelming, fear provoking, alien and/or demanding. Thus, the initial level considers the impact of the current situation on the client. Second, each counselee has a unique set of past experiences, distinctive personality features, a customary approach to interpersonal relationships and preferences for how best to address novel situations. Characteristic patterns create an urgency to maintain or return to the equilibrium bound within the status quo. Thus, the second level involves the motivation of the client to adapt, modify or abandon conventional ways of facing others, the world and the spiritual reality of being a created person. Third, the relationship between counselor and counselee must be skillfully navigated to successfully negotiate the intricate motives radiating through the change process. The counseling literature informs helpers how to establish roles, engage participants and respect the host of influential forces that impact strategic discourse (Egan, 2010; Kellemen, 2004). Counseling aims to maximize creative interpersonal conversation to pursue problem management or resolution, enhance coping and relational abilities, and advance personal healing and maturation.

This chapter considers the relationship between adopting a conceptual model and maintaining vitality in one's role as a counselor. In subsequent chapters, our notable panel of experts will each make transparent how their selected model becomes useful for the counselor who comes alongside Jake to journey toward change. Each view of the relationship between Christian faith and counseling praxis uniquely shapes expectations for client service. Each renowned author will press toward the goal of extrapolating best practice procedures for merging Christian faith into clinical and ministry-oriented counseling. The consultants show how each approach proceeds in actual conversations with a client such as Jake.

Our proposal is that one's Christian worldview will be exhibited in a commitment to an interface model regulating faith and clinical practice. This establishes a range of crucial and significant expectations. Consider the following application questions across the five models to relate counseling to Christianity.

1. What does a "psychologically" healthy person look like, and how is such health or wholeness defined?

2. What is psychopathology, or what are the types of problems addressed in counseling?

3. How does Scripture inform, regulate and bring life to the helping encounter?

4. What is the connection between physical well-being and the soul, medically/behaviorally oriented treatment and soul care, individual autonomy and participation in Christian community?

5. What are the goals of counseling?

6. How are goals established and interventions selected?

7. What are the steps or processes that lead to this goal?

8. What accounts for change in the counseling process? What is the source of healing and growth?

9. How does the counselor determine when the conditions are in place to end counseling?

10. How informed or involved are ministry leaders in the particular helping process or with follow-up and aftercare?[1]

So, to state it simply, counseling involves deliberate conversations that focus on change. Let's consider a few crucial variables that inspire the passions of persons who voluntarily step into the role of change agent (Kottler, 2010; Orlinsky & Ronnestad, 2005). Perhaps you may catch glimpses of yourself in the formational experiences of helpers such as Andy, Sonia, Ray and Anita.

From Comforted to Comforter

Andy recently began a new career as a helping professional. For years he performed admirably as a stellar student while constantly rebuking inner doubts surrounding worth and competence. Fortunately, as his academic credits accumulated during his undergraduate years, his spiritual life soared, thanks to an amiable denominational chaplain and an active campus fellowship. Andy set his occupational trajectory toward the field of social work. This vocational choice was acknowledged as the outward symbol of his emergence from a lifetime within a family system infused with alcoholism. Andy was committed to giving fresh opportunities to persons in families with similar embedded dysfunction. Those marginalized by chronic illness, addiction, poverty or injustice deserve the opportunity to break out of the destructive cycles that enslave. As he himself was set free, his career objective is invigorated by an excitement that others might enjoy a similar energizing release to the spiritual renewal that made it possible for him to thrive.

When Sonia walks the aisle in her academic cap and gown to receive her master's hood, the honor her family will experience may well exceed any private sense of accomplishment. Medical missionaries supplied the remarkable procedure that kept her father alive following his accident. A supportive church opened the path for her parents to immigrate following his conversion. She could flawlessly recite this family testimonial. Obtaining

---

[1]This question set may be useful for individual reflection and group discussion following review of each consultant's approach.

an advanced degree for one with her pedigree symbolized a bright new beginning and was a worthy cause for an entire community to celebrate. Following Bible college, her education continued with courses in Christian education and counseling. Currently, her practicum is with an agency that supports victims of domestic violence. Sonia is shocked at how extraordinarily difficult it is for women to sever bonds with malicious men who too often inflict harm. In her family, the potency of Scripture and church fellowship was the secret to a clean start. Her inner prayer is for a future position where the Bible will inform her healing efforts. Sonia would like her clients to have the full advantage of the identical resources that brought her family to a whole new world. Chains can be broken.

Ray reached a major career objective by becoming a proficient accounting manager of a mid-sized company in a service industry. In subsequent years he endured more than his fair share of battle scars from the wearisome war of never-ending number crunching and office politics. He surprised even himself by enrolling in a counseling degree program for "recreation." Remarkably, that revitalizing educational sideline diminished the cruel impact of one of those milestone birthdays, the big 50. Ray's pastor urged him on, along with every grateful participant in his long-running men's Bible study. His exemplary faith journey and welcoming charisma mark Ray as an invaluable lay soul-care leader. Listening to this supportive choir, he made the bold transition from his stable position in a healthy business into a new livelihood as a professional counselor. Fortunately, Ray does not intend to leave his faith behind as he enters this fresh field and novel vocation. From Ray's perspective, direct investment in people helping feels far more thrilling than tracking the movement of funds that belong to others.

Anita is the mother of a pair of teenagers who will soon be exploring colleges. She is adjusting to the routine of reentry into the work force in her new employment as a psychologist. She easily recalls the spiritual progression that brought her to this juncture. The ruin from the privacy of her past was ultimately resolved by a profound spiritual conversion. Her heart holds a vibrant memory that once, while basking in the delight of a ministry conference, she cast her life without reservation upon her beautiful Lord. Her imagination was instantly flooded with astounding images of future missionary service. The inner press to fulfill that promise was satisfied for a decade by volunteering as a pregnancy and birthing coach at a church-based center. Given her private life decisions, it was indeed a blessing to be there for mothers-to-be facing personal and financial obstacles. Anita expresses heartfelt gratitude for the day her eyes perused the acceptance letter conveying an invitation to enter a doctoral program in mental health with an emphasis on Christian faith. The disquieting voice of reason had screamed out the realities and improbabilities. Fortunately, from the center of her being she was empowered to pray, "Lord, as my life priorities must soon be redirected, how might I keep my steps on your path as I pursue my earnest commitment to serve and honor you?" Her educational quest is now history, complete with miraculous accounts of how the Lord supplied her needs. Anita offers similar prayers to the Lord daily as she engages empathically with the life stories of her clients.

The backgrounds for helpers such as Andy, Sonia, Ray and Anita may be distinct, but examine each thoroughly and a common thread will become evident. It is the cord that unites these with thousands of similar counselor stories. Christians who are motivated to make interpersonal connections via counseling routinely have an intense passion to serve their neighbors, following the Lord's instruction in the parable of the Good Samaritan (Luke 10:29-37). Jesus originally spoke that parable in response to a highly religious attorney who probed our Lord about securing eternal life. The lawyer-inquirer knew without hesitation that the requirement of the great commandment was to unreservedly love God and neighbor. The intention of the Old Testament decree that Jesus referenced was not ambiguous in terms of *what* to do. The subject for hairsplitting was discerning *who* actually qualified to receive such precious compassion, esteem and affection. So the question posed was, "Who is my neighbor?" Jesus touched the heart of all his hearers by sharing about an unfortunate traveler who was victimized by thieves, severely beaten and left by the roadside for dead (Luke 10:29-37). Religious leaders passed by the wounded sufferer but were unresponsive. What purpose would there be in defiling oneself by touching a dying person when the cause was hopeless? The unlikely rescuer who stepped up was identified as a member of an ostracized and despised ethnic group. Only a kindhearted Samaritan offered comprehensive assistance. For his unselfish act of neighborly grace, the Samaritan was granted the place of highest honor in our Lord's story. Thereafter, from a biblical perspective, a "neighbor" is one who is near and manifests a need.

Living in love with the Father, Son and Holy Spirit manifests itself in an overflow of compassion to others as an act of worship. Helping in tangible ways expresses the desire of Christ followers to offer a bowl of hot soup, cup of cool water or warm clothes to the Lord Jesus himself (Matthew 25:31-46). Providing assistance displays heavenly devotion. The energy from this transcendent force excites Christian people helpers as they aid and equip clients. Many who enter the field of counseling recognize silently that beneath all the overt circumstances, surface scenarios and diverse characteristics, those being served are entirely like us. The role of counselor and counselee could easily be reversed. For this reason, the person in this parable from our Lord with whom counselors may most identify is not the Good Samaritan. Rather, it is the one robbed, beaten, abandoned and left for dead at the side of the road. A Samaritan once made a detour on our behalf. An aspect of a counselor's calling may be to return the favor and follow the example.

Broken souls are soiled by sin, yet human persons perpetually bear a resemblance to their Creator. The Scripture states that human beings represent their divine origin to the world (Ephesians 1:3-14). We were designed to participate in heavenly blessings and were thus made in the imago Dei, in the image of the Triune God (Genesis 1:26-28). Nonetheless, a combination of relational struggles, situational pain and internal burdens can make too many of life's moments a living hell. It is such seasons of adversity that ignite a helper's inner zeal to be beneficial to others. God himself supplies the basic necessities for relief. The God of the Scriptures *is* the Lord of all comfort. This transcendent God of the universe routinely performs custom-made miracles of grace in the ordinary ordeals of our humanity. Recognition of such divine grace and action inspires loyal servants to become ministers of consolation, mercy and goodness to those similarly afflicted (2 Corinthians 1:3-11). The instruction from the Word is forthright and unambiguous. Endurance through affliction is sustained by the Lord God, who delivers marvelous comfort. This renewing spiritual experience is the qualifying process for having a ministry of comfort to others (Robertson, 1997).

In his earthly life, the Master's numerous miracles of divine intervention inspire hope and model compassion. His teaching stories include those unforgettable parables that communicate ways to bring spiritual blessings down to earthly life. And prior to his departure to heaven, Jesus prompted his closest followers to persistently feed and love his sheep (John 21:15-19). Hearts afire to serve God are the ongoing evidence of conformity to the great commandment. "'Love the Lord your God with all your heart and with all your soul and with all your mind.' This is the first and greatest commandment. And the second is like it: 'Love your neighbor as yourself'" (Matthew 22:37-39 NIV). Christians strengthened by the soothing of the Holy Spirit in turn participate in health restoring and social justice ministries. This has been the pattern of a Christ-inspired love since the outpouring at Pentecost (Acts 2:1). What is unique in counseling is that the movement of the Spirit rustles like the wind through the deceptively empty space between self and other. The therapeutic relationship, the bonds formed to cross the divide between counselor and client, are anointed and become sacred (Olthuis, 2001). The Spirit's trail can be traced via the supplies of refreshment that are presented to others in a world fraught with physical sickness, fractured families, poverty and human stagnation.

If you are a supervisor, skills trainer or counselor educator, listen to the background stories of people helpers who serve in Christian settings or who enter training programs that have an explicit faith mission. Discern what brought each person to the demanding fields of counseling, pastoral care, psychotherapy and spiritual formation. Based upon our experience with scores of students in Christian seminaries and universities, we predict that a core theme will emerge. The occupational decision to enter these sectors of service is often associated with a period of exceptional spiritual awakening. This correlation spotlights a critical priority for those who train Christ followers to assume positions in the wide range of mental health professions and pastoral care opportunities that are available today.

Worldview and Personal Spirituality

Those who train Christians to counsel, such as educators, clinical supervisors or mentoring pastors, move into a relationship that has dual roles. One role is that of gatekeeper to a professional guild. Or, if the setting is ministry, the senior shepherd has a role similar to that of gatekeeper in the decision to bestow an anointing, blessing or ordination. This is in line with Paul's instruction to Timothy not to be hasty in the laying on of hands (1 Timothy 5:22). The ethical responsibility to protect future clients or a congregational community will be impacted by the work of the apprentice professional or ministerial counselor. The second role is equally important. It is that of influential spiritual mentor. To both separate and align these roles well enough so that the net effect is complimentary, not fraught with conflict, requires intentionality (Greggo & Becker, 2010; Hathaway, 2009).

Educators and leaders in an explicitly Christian milieu do have the responsibility to listen and cooperate with the ongoing movement of the Holy Spirit in the lives of those being trained. Our charge is to foster delight for compassionate service while simultaneously shaping the skills, competencies and mindset to meet the opportunities and constraints within the contemporary context. The former feeds their devotion. The latter not only steers counselors toward effectiveness, but it also protects mental health professionals and pastoral caregivers alike from the common malady of compassion fatigue. A fate darker than burnout is the dampening of God's good gift of faith. The risk of such an occurrence is multiplied when counselors harbor unrealistic expectations regarding how, when and in what ways the Holy Spirit will produce favorable, recognizable results in and through everyday helping relationships.

Forging a purposeful, hope-empowered and credible outlook for counseling begins in the furnace where the forces of the therapeutic and redemptive are fused. An understanding of the helping encounter eventually emerges and matures into a conviction regarding the process. One's perspective on what enhances or inhibits personal change is ultimately connected to worldview, commonly described as an internally embedded comprehensive perspective on how, what and why the universe operates. Worldview informs the establishment of a counselor's theoretical orientation. This in turn fashions one's role and function as agents to empower change. A Christian worldview is concisely defined as grasping our place in Scripture and history (Vanhoozer, 2010), implying the recognition that a benevolent Creator still oversees the universe, down to the level of each uniquely formed person. The Lord of the universe has intentionally revealed himself in Word through the Scriptures and in the person of Jesus

Christ. The Trinity has moved throughout history working out God's eternal plan of redemption. The requirement that follows such understanding is this: Christian helpers are on a journey to grow in grace and in depth of understanding about their place in salvation history. Counselors are not finished products, but like all God's children, are by grace working out their own salvation in fear and trembling. God is at work to accomplish his purpose (Philippians 2:12-13).

As the movement of this walk of faith proceeds, counselors are required to commit to a preferred viewpoint on the interface of core Christian beliefs with the premises found in the social science literature that govern their chosen vocation. This is an important decision. Fortunately a significant literature base will assist in this merger of worldview with conceptual model, most explicitly in the next phase. Once a conceptual model is selected, practitioners strive to become proficient in making the core assumptions from that view operational in actual practice. Since these views are variations on evangelical faith traditions that take personal commitment to spirituality extremely seriously, self-assessment is a distinct phase in the application of worldview to basic helping procedures.

Increasingly, therapist awareness of cultural assumptions and spirituality is a crucial element in clinician education and supervision (Frame, 2003; Hagedorn & Moorhead, 2011; Hagedorn & Gutierrez, 2009; Hagedorn, 2005; Wiggins, 2009). Ultimately, one's effectiveness and adherence to professional guidelines when making direct client contact regarding faith perspectives will hinge on the productive results of an earnest therapist's self-reflection. Reciting one's spiritual journey or authoring a spiritual autobiography is regularly prescribed as a method to further contemplation. This will heighten the ease of recognition of central individual spiritual themes, identify key influencers, highlight crucial developmental moments and solidify memorable lessons (Wiggins, 2009). Helpers will persistently strive to increase awareness of private subjective experience and influences. This sharpens one's alertness to the wealth and liabilities that spiritual resources contain. This type of deliberation facilitates personal growth, honing the self as helping agent into a potential curative force (Dreher & Plante, 2007; Wiggins, 2009). Spiritual self-examination is an exceptionally crucial preparatory exercise for those who perceive the intersection of faith and healing to be a place they intend to visit consistently. This domain raises profound tensions while remarkably opening amazing resources. Identity development and growth in spiritual maturity grinds the lenses that interpret the correlates of the secular and the sacred. The objective is to prime the counselor so that the self, with its compilation of religious, transcendent and spiritual experiences, can be brought into the presence of a client in a manner that is predominantly effective and incontrovertibly ethical.

Partnering for Consultation and Collaboration

Consultation in mental health settings is traditionally conceived as a partnership formed between a specialist with an acquired exceptional expertise and either an individual colleague or an entire treatment team (Dougherty, 2009). The purpose of consultation is to make the most of the extensive knowledge base of the consultant as a supplement to the existing skills of the clinician or team. In essence, the care of the client remains the responsibility of the assigned clinician, while particular aspects of the treatment approach or outcomes are placed under the direction of the consultant. A consultant might be secured to provide assistance on a single case with features that are presently beyond the competency of the counselor to address (e.g., a specific client with severe health concerns due to anorexia). Or the consultant may be available to provide assistance on a category of cases (e.g., any case where eating issues are identified). If a counselor is assigned to provide care for a client but lacks the competency necessary to provide appropriate treatment, both sensibility and professional ethics mandate that one of two options be implemented: (1) the client could be referred to a suitable clinician who has the proficiency necessary to assume care, or (2) the counselor could secure consultation support to benefit and protect the client while expanding the counselor's own set of qualifying competencies. Consultation is an in vivo (live and real) training experience designed to benefit clients while fostering the growth of participating clinicians (Tack & Morrow, 2009).

Routinely in academic, clinical and ministry settings that provide supervision to emerging counselors, a direct supervisor is in the prime position to both ensure quality client care and foster the development of the apprentice counselor. In addition, there may well be other mentors who make available precise training in a specific technique, treatment of a specific disorder or in a therapeutic model. For example, a mentor counselor may be available to train a counselor in leading an anger management group or in coming alongside clients with food, substance or behavioral addictions. As a counselor considers ways to make a Christian worldview explicit in the counseling process, a consultant may be a useful resource to serve clients and nurture the counselor. Academic training programs with mission statements that hold dear Christian ministry values will often incorporate specific consultation services or educational seminars to fieldwork experience for the purpose of furthering understanding and for making applications in this domain. The overarching commitment to accomplish this educational objective is so critical that highly specialized training consultants are secured to mentor in this particular arena.

Collaboration is another variation of mental health service that retains many features of consultation with the notable distinction that the direct care of the client is fulfilled jointly by clinician and specialist. In other words, consultation is a hands-off course of action with the expert assisting the counselor behind the scenes, whereas collaboration is hands-on with both clinicians sharing in a defined manner in the responsibility of client care (Dougherty, 2009). A unique feature of biblical counseling has been the extensive use of collaboration as the prevailing training modality (Powlison, 2010). The session itself is conducted by a skilled biblical counselor, while one or perhaps more counselors-in-training participate or observe. This is an excellent example of collaboration applied in a ministry context. In summary, a mental health consultant engages only the professional peer, while a collaborative treatment arrangement implies that the expert has a presence with the counselee.

In elaborating on the following case scenario, our experts have been charged principally to assume the role of consultant. The opportunity to collaborate remains entirely open and is at the discretion of the consultant. The rationale for this arrangement is that the charge before these specialists is to coach clinicians in the principles and procedures representative of their view of the relationship between counseling and Christianity. Therefore, it is not the expectation or duty of the consultant to extrapolate all the details of the care plan necessary to service this multifaceted client. For this investigation we assume that the counselor in the lead position has the requisite informational base and mastery of a therapeutic skill set at the level equivalent to the average professional in the field, but the counselor *lacks* and *desires to learn* the methods and techniques to offer treatment that is distinctively Christian according to the assumptions of a particular overarching view.

The examinations of the case study ahead offer an informed response to the ten application questions posed earlier in this chapter. Each model will likely establish and prioritize these questions somewhat differently. Experts will display how these or similar queries guide the helping relationship and process. The goal is to grow in understanding the contribution and relationship between the Christian theology and counseling ventures. Here are Christian approaches that clinicians such as Andy, Sonia, Ray and Anita can plainly evaluate for adoption into their own helping activities. As counselors such as these four make the link between interface model and explicit practice, occasions will arise when assistance from an accomplished consultant will be most welcomed. Since a direct consultant partnership is not always available, this written account has been formulated to fill a gap in this important component of training.

One conspicuous omission in the case scenario that follows will be immediately evident. No details are articulated in regard to the mental health or pastoral counselor with whom Jake will actually be conversing. Counseling services at college centers are frequently problem focused and intentionally time limited. Given Jake's forthright request to get his academic life off to a good start, his initial session was with Cheryl, an available mental health clinician who would shortly shift her employment role. As Jake's story unfolds, Cheryl offers immediate support, gathers information and forms an agreement to match him with a suitable counselor. The juncture arrives for the transfer of Jake's care. The references to Andy (social worker), Sonia (biblical counselor), Ray (licensed professional counselor) and Anita (psychologist) are indeed representative of the array of counselors with Christian faith convictions who could easily be pictured sitting across from Jake and entering respectfully into his story. However, no specific counselor profile will be sketched or outlined. Consider this rationale and then evaluate the challenge. As editors, we would propose that each reader actively *imagine and assume the role of primary therapist.* From this point forward, Jake is *your* client. The direction selected will be influenced by *your* assessment. The care he receives is under *your* responsibility. Fortunately, as Jake's counselor, you are not alone in devising a strategy that addresses his concerns, meets his needs and honors the Lord. When you as reader step into the participatory role as helper to Jake, the best consultants with Christian convictions and professional credentials will be advocates by your side for this therapeutic journey. Let's open the case record, meet your new client, and ponder the clinical and faith-enhancing encounters that are about to unfold.

The Case of Jake

Jake, a 22-year-old Caucasian male, reluctantly made an appointment at the counseling center at the Christian college where he recently matriculated.[2] Following his medical discharge from the Army, Jake spent nearly a year recovering and setting a direction. He is starting college for the first time. As he met with the counselor for an initial consultation, Jake admitted that his personal saga was "pretty messed up." Though he had only been on campus for two weeks, he stated emphatically that there was no way he would ever fit in.

Despite all this, Jake entered counseling ostensibly only to seek assistance in getting class assignments completed. "I never applied myself much in school. Now I am ready to work for that piece of paper that leads to a real job that pays big bucks." When asked what he would like to do after graduation, Jake said that he had absolutely no idea. Jake made decent scores on standardized tests, enabling him to get into college despite a less than stellar academic history. Being a veteran certainly didn't hurt. His Army chaplain had written a polite letter of recommendation noting that Jake was "hungry to grow in his faith." In contrast, Jake himself said that most days he is not even sure that he belongs at a Christian college. The whole "Jesus thing" felt fake, phony and dull. Now that he was actually living on a college campus, he reported that he can't get into sitting still to study even though he knows that's what he needs to do.

Fifteen minutes into the session, Cheryl, his counselor, surmised that Jake was presenting with a simple case of adjustment-to-college-life "blues" combined with strong reverberations from syllabus shock and accompanied by a

---

[2]This case scenario is a fictional composite composed specifically for training purposes in the counseling classroom. The details and issues were drawn from the actual experience of several clinicians across multiple clients and settings. Jake's history and presenting concerns are indeed multifaceted and complex. Mental health professionals who engage regularly with clients who have characteristics similar to Jake's indicate that this account, though fictitious does convey features that are typical, realistic and clinically relevant.

rather severe case of academic anxiety. There should be no trouble finishing a round of short-term care during the remaining month that she had available before her transition to a new position. The full tale that was eventually disclosed across the next several sessions, however, revealed a more troubling series of concerns.

"If I can't make it here, I really have no place to go. I might as well get blown into oblivion." This set off an alarm in the counselor's head. She could sense rapidly that Jake harbored considerable anxiety regarding his academic prowess. Yet this apprehension could point to a deeper theme of discouragement that could be churning internally due to multiple causes. There were signs of impulsive tendencies and decisions nearly everywhere behind his candid self-destructive statement. The conversations that ensued elicited the following details.

Jake confessed that while he had learned a few names and faces during the orientation, he could not connect with the "kids" in the dorm. There was no tightly knit squad of comrades at this school like he had experienced in the Army. The situation wasn't helped by the fact that he paid for a single room, so he did not have a roommate. Jake reported sitting alone most nights, playing around on his computer. He said that short naps during the day or whenever he gets too tired are all he really needs to keep him going. Jake explained that he has "nasty" dreams, so he doesn't like to sleep. He has two medications prescribed by a psychiatrist from the Army, but he doesn't remember what they are and only takes those when he's having a bad day. "Those clowns in the military stuffed me with so many pills that it still makes me wanna puke." Jake reported that nothing he has tried has done much to aid him in getting to sleep or to help him settle down since he was discharged from the service. While Jake is aware that he should not get high for medical reasons, he admitted smoking marijuana "on occasion" to chill out, relax and get to sleep. Jake argued that if God really is such a great God, he should fix his problems immediately and give him all of his life back. Until God pulls this off as a sure sign of blessing, it is perfectly acceptable, according to Jake, to do a little dope to feel more like a normal person.

Jake reported flashbacks from his days in the military. He spent nearly a full session telling numerous horrific war stories that he had heard from other vets whom he met when in the hospital. Though he had never been in an actual combat zone himself, the stories he had heard seemed so real to him that he re-experiences them in nightmares on a regular basis. He also has flashbacks from his direct personal experience of an accident on a night training mission. A helicopter loaded with guys from his unit crashed for absolutely no reason. "It blew up and fell out of the sky." Jake witnessed the accident scene firsthand, arriving while the wreckage was fresh and still burning hot. He professed that now he wakes up at night in a cold sweat and can "smell human flesh cooking." Jake explained that he was supposed to ride in that chopper later in the training exercise. He repeated over and over as he shook his head, "That shoulda been me." He claimed that he can see the face of one of his bunkmates at the very second that the helicopter hit the ground. Jake did acknowledge that he never literally saw his friend's physical body at the accident site, nor did he take in the sight of any of the other casualties with his own eyes. Still, he carries a vivid visual picture in his head. This dramatic vision seems to stem from the strange bond he felt toward this training buddy. This friend had once told Jake that he was going to college right after discharge, and that inspired Jake to do the same.

Following that tragic event of the fatal training mission, Jake claimed, he started getting high whenever he could. Up until that point, he would only sip a few "brews" when off duty. "I went back to my old ways and started druggin' with whatever stuff I could get, whenever I could get it." "Mostly, I smoke dope." Once in a while, he admitted, he would do crack. He claimed that previously his favorites were club drugs like coke and ecstasy.

Eight weeks after the accident, Jake was in a bar with friends and became totally "wasted." A brawl broke out, and he was at the center of it. He was hit hard in the head by a table leg. His head trauma was so severe that it was questionable whether or not he would live. Jake's mother was told that his injuries might leave him in a permanent vegetative state in a nursing home. While Jake claimed to remember nothing, he knew that he was airlifted to a special hospital where severe brain injuries were treated. Jake was in intensive care for nearly two months and in rehab for several more. Following this incident and extended recovery, he received a medical discharge from the Army. He was told that his brain could not be subjected to any further injury. Jake had a considerable amount of testing done while he was in rehab, but he couldn't recall any detailed description of the results. He did recall being told that he may not be able to remember things the way that he used to before the injury. However, the medical staff said that since he was young, he had a good chance of doing fine. Now that he is in school, Jake worries if he will be able to remember well enough to do okay on exams and to write papers. He wonders aloud if there is any special help available to compensate for his learning needs.

During rehab, Jake had been required to attend an Alcoholics Anonymous (AA) group. This seemed foolish to him since he did not believe he ever had an alcohol problem. He did like the chaplain who helped run the group, so he went as he was told. This relationship played a key role in his return to the Christian faith conveyed to him by his mother. But Jake's longing to hook up with his old girlfriend again is what focused his energy on getting out of the hospital. He began writing her, but by Jake's report, she did not respond to phone calls, letters or e-mails. Still, his recovery progressed to where the medical staff indicated that it was remarkable and perhaps even miraculous. Jake had decided that God had a purpose behind letting him get this whack up the side of his head: to get home and be a father to the child, likely his child, that his former girlfriend was raising with the help of her parents.

Jake's description of his family background was sparse. He had a younger sister who was about to start in a four-year Christian college after two successful years at a community college. She was hoping to become a teacher like their mother. Jake's mother is and has always been a "God-fearing woman" who tends to get a little "wacky" about religion. His mother has been an elementary school teacher in a low-income neighborhood that is known to be gang territory and is notoriously violent. This is her mission field, and she gives much to her students. Jake's sister seems to share both her mother's faith and passion for "God's little ones." His mother attends a "Holy Roller" church and really gets into marathon prayer meetings. Jake attended a few such gatherings with his mother after he left the rehab hospital. He was under the impression that he had been completely healed after having preachers at these meetings lay hands on him on several occasions. His current trouble sleeping and concentrating on his studies aside, he did not believe that he has any continuing physical or mental problems. God did a miracle.

Jake's father died when Jake was 10. His dad was a truck driver who drank whenever he was not on the road. Jake's only memories of his father are seeing him sleeping on the couch or fighting with his mother. Jake recalled coming home from school one day and being the one to find his father dead in the bathroom with blood coming out of his nose and mouth. He was never really told how his dad died. His mother said that the Lord took him because of his constant drinking. While she claims to miss him terribly, his death was an answer to her prayer. Jake told the story of getting into a big fight once with a kid at school who said his father had died from doing drugs. He had never heard that from anyone within his own family. There were no close relatives, and his mother was the only authority figure in his life, though Cheryl realized that term *authority* must be applied with caution. Mostly, his mother left him alone and let him do whatever he wanted. She said that he looked and acted too much like his father. Eventually, supported by the presence of her pastor, she told Jake that he better go away to school or get back into the service because he could not live at home if he wasn't working and free to "do who knows what staying out all night long." This pushed Jake off to college to pursue the dream that his deceased buddy passed along to him.

Jake had done well in elementary school but hit a wall in middle school. He did fine on tests without much effort to study, and rarely did he do any homework. Fights with peers were common. Jake did not like to read long books. He had ways of getting his mother to help write papers, and her pleading with teachers enabled him to get by in school. Jake began to party hard in high school. He went out with a good girl with a church background during his junior and senior years. Missy wasn't a partier, so he "hid" his rowdy activities from her. Jake believed she really knew all about his wild side but pretended not to notice. She never made it an issue between them. Missy was a grade behind him, so after high school he took a pizza delivery job for nearly a year, waiting for her to graduate. They were not sexually active until he signed up to go into the Army. As the date came closer for him to leave, he successfully pressured her to have sex with him. Jake was angry when Missy told him she was pregnant, and they fought when he tried to convince her to have an abortion. Her parents always hated Jake, but when Missy became pregnant, they did everything they could to have her break off all contact, and even moved to another town. It was not until he was in rehab that he started relentlessly attempting to reestablish contact with her. Despite all his pleas to make amends, Missy would not speak to him. Jake did hear through old contacts that she is now dating other people. He has never seen the child, sent Missy any child support or made any attempt to establish a legal relationship with the child. Missy has never asked him for anything. He is fairly sure that the baby is his based on their long relationship and the timing of the birth. He did recall that her father called him a loser, like his own dad had, and said a "drug-dealing, pizza delivery boy" was not worthy of his daughter. The reality that God has not given him back his girlfriend irritates, annoys and at times outrages Jake.

After five sessions with Jake, Cheryl is perplexed and concerned. Every treatment approach that starts in one direction runs smack into another issue that takes center stage. Jake has not followed through on practical ideas about getting his academic work done. The goal to get him involved with tutoring has not yet been met. Jake misses his tutoring appointments and "forgets" to follow through. After speaking with a professor, Jake voiced to Cheryl the desire to figure out how his screwy family and absent father might still be messing up his life. But when the counselor would invite Jake to explore his previous family experience, he would change the subject or claim that he could not remember details. Jake has not been cooperative with obtaining any medical or psychiatric records. Jake saw a psychiatrist while in rehab and several times afterward. Once he moved back home with his mother, he did not see that doctor anymore because he was several states away. Jake said that he may need a referral to see a shrink, as there are forms to fill out to keep his medical disability funds flowing. Jake cannot explain his actual medical condition and has not provided documentation about it either.

The resident advisor on Jake's floor is suspicious that someone has been smoking or even getting high in the dorm. Thus far, there has been no confirmation or formal complaint, but the evidence is starting to point toward Jake.

During one session Jake asked the counselor to contact his girlfriend's family and tell them that they need to forgive, forget and start to get along. "Isn't that the Christian thing to do?" Jake queried. When the counselor hesitated before answering, Jake became angry and sullen, making comments that hinted at self-harm. These were loose and without threatening details, such as driving a car into a wall at high speed. He muttered that he has a recurring desire to no longer live the life he is living.

Before the counselor could establish a clear direction, Jake reported that a crisis had occurred the weekend before their fifth appointment. His RA told Jake that a young woman he had spent time with had reported to her RA that they had been drinking off-campus. She reportedly told her RA with tears flowing that Jake coaxed her to get high with him but she refused. She also said when they got back to his room, he had been physically rough and sexually inappropriate with her. She is not pressing charges, denies being raped and is embarrassed because she believes her own behavior was not honoring to God. The RA confronted Jake. He wants Jake to come clean, take responsibility, and get evaluated for a drinking and drug problem. Jake told his counselor that he did have a few beers with this girl. It was all in fun and nothing happened. This is all really no big deal.

Due to a shift in responsibilities, Cheryl will no longer be able to continue offering Jake counseling sessions. The anticipated brief, academically focused treatment is not going to fit the matters that are so important to Jake and to the college community. The case will therefore be transferred, and treatment will be ongoing. In addition, consultation assistance will be made available to his counselor to ensure that Jake's Christian faith is incorporated in the treatment. Jake and his counselor come to an amiable agreement. He is determined to cooperate fully with Cheryl's recommendations and says he will make every effort to make progress with the counselor selected for him. Jake realizes that his future at this college is tenuous and that his plan to move ahead in his life is currently in jeopardy.

What's Next for Jake?

Jake has a counseling appointment on your schedule. Establishing expectations, setting goals and guiding Jake through these numerous individual, community, academic and family upsets is your mission. Furthermore, you have in this case the exceptional opportunity to learn how prominent views on the relationship between psychology and Christianity could form a distinctive approach that is strategically implemented moment by moment and session to session. Five consultants with extensive expertise in a particular Christian approach to counseling are available to partner with you in your ongoing care for Jake.

References

Collins, G. R. (2007). *Christian counseling: A comprehensive guide* (3rd ed.). Nashville: Thomas Nelson.

Dreher, D. R., & Plante, T. G. (2007). The calling protocol: Promoting greater health, joy, and purpose in life. In T. G. Plante & C. E. Thoresen (Eds.), *Spirit, science, and health: How the spiritual mind fuels physical wellness* (pp. 129-42). Westport, CT: Praeger.

Dougherty, A. M. (Ed.). (2009). *Casebook of psychological consultation and collaboration in school and community settings*. Belmont, CA: Brooks/Cole Cengage Learning.

Egan, G. (2010). *The skilled helper: A problem management and opportunity development approach to helping* (9th ed.). Belmont, CA: Brooks/Cole Cengage Learning.

Frame, M. W. (2003). *Integrating spirituality and religion into counseling: A comprehensive approach.* Pacific Grove, CA: Brooks/Cole.

Greggo, S. P., & Becker, S. P. (2010). The attachment paradigm: A secure base for counselor education? *Journal of Psychology and Christianity, 29,* 16-36.

Hagedorn, W. B., (2005). Counselor self-awareness and self-exploration of spiritual and religious beliefs: Know thyself. In C. S. Cashwell & J. S. Young (Eds.), *Integrating spirituality and religion into counseling* (pp. 63-84). Alexandria, VA: American Counseling Association.

Hagedorn, W. B., & Gutierrez, D. (2009). Integration versus segregation: Applications of the spiritual competencies in counselor education programs. *Counseling and Values, 54,* 32-47.

Hagedorn, W. B., & Moorhead, H. J. H. (2010). Counselor self awareness: exploring attitudes, beliefs and values. In C. S. Cashwell & J. S. Young (Eds.), *Integrating spirituality and religion into counseling* (pp. 71-85). Alexandria, VA: American Counseling Association.

Hathaway, W. L. (2009). Clinical use of explicit religious approaches: Christian role integration issues. *Journal of Psychology and Christianity, 28,* 105-12.

Johnson, E. L. (Ed.). (2010). *Psychology & Christianity: Five views.* Downers Grove, IL: IVP Academic.

Johnson, E. L., & Jones, S. L. (2000). *Psychology & Christianity: Four views.* Downers Grove, IL: InterVarsity Press.

Kellemen, R. W. (2004). *Soul physicians: A theology of soul care and spiritual direction.* Taneytown, MD: RPM Books.

Kottler, J. A. (2010). *On being a therapist* (4th ed.). San Francisco: John Wiley/Jossey-Bass.

Olthuis, J. H. (2001). *The beautiful risk: A new psychology of loving and being loved.* Grand Rapids: Zondervan.

Orlinsky, D. E., & Ronnestad, M. H. (2005). *How psychotherapists develop: A study of therapeutic work and professional growth.* Washington, DC: American Psychological Association.

Powlison, D. (2010). *The biblical counseling movement: History and context.* Greensboro, NC: New Growth Press.

Robertson, A. T. (1997). *Word pictures in the New Testament* [Logos Research Systems version]. Available at <www.logos.com/product/815/word-pictures-in-the-new-testament>.

Tack, R. E., & Morrow, D. F. (2009). Mental health case consultation. In A. M. Dougherty (Ed.), *Casebook of psychological consultation and collaboration in school and community settings* (pp. 35-47). Belmont, CA: Brooks/Cole Cengage Learning.

Vanhoozer, K. J. (2010). Forming the performers: How Christians can use canon sense to bring us to our (theodramatic) senses. *Edification: The Transdisciplinary Journal of Christian Psychology, 4*, 5-16.

Wiggins, M. I. (2009). Therapist self-awareness of spirituality. In J. D. Aten & M. M. Leach (Eds.), *Spirituality and the therapeutic process: A comprehensive resource from intake to termination* (pp. 53-74). Washington, DC: American Psychological Association.

3

A Levels-of-Explanation Approach

USING A BIOPSYCHOSOCIALSPIRITUAL
AND EVIDENCE-BASED MODEL

Thomas G. Plante

LEARNING OBJECTIVES

- *Explain the key features of a scientifically informed, biopsychosocialspiritual approach to assessment and case conceptualization.*
- *Evaluate how the empirical basis of the levels-of-explanation approach exemplifies the ethical principles endorsed by professional codes of ethics.*
- *Select a significant feature of this consultation that you find particularly valuable and describe its worth for your own counseling practice.*

Introduction, Priorities and Initial Impressions

To say that Jake has a lot of problems is an understatement. These likely include polysubstance abuse; impulsivity and perhaps attention deficit hyperactivity disorder; anger management problems and a probable impulse control disorder in general; posttraumatic stress; depression; suicide risk; learning problems and possible learning disabilities, among other difficult challenges. His social and occupational functioning appear to be poor, as does his prognosis. His Global Assessment of Functioning (GAF) score using the American Psychiatric Association's *Diagnostic and Statistical*

Manual (DSM-IV-TR) would be rather low for sure. Where does a counselor (or a consultant working with the counselor) even begin addressing all of these complex areas of concern?

Any counselor working with Jake likely will feel overwhelmed rather quickly with the breadth and depth of his multiple troubles. Additionally, in contemporary professional practice there are usually many limitations to the services that can be provided to clients due to managed care and general insurance limitations. Furthermore, in order to make progress the client has to be willing to work hard toward behavior change and trust that the counselor can help them to do so. This can't be assumed with Jake or with many other clients either. When someone has multiple troubles, counselors typically want to utilize a wide variety of services that may or may not be available in the community or even allowed by insurance coverage. Moreover, services offered may not be supported by the client or the client's family. So, in working with Jake, the counselor must first take a very deep breath, say a prayer and think through ways to best help him—perhaps by triage or prioritizing assessment and intervention strategies, and keeping options, possibilities and limitations in mind.

Although Jake has an overwhelming array of concerns, the counselor can indeed be hopeful. Many potentially effective tools and strategies are available to help Jake make progress and have a more satisfying, productive and health-promoting life. While the bad news is that Jake has enormous and concerning problems, the good news is that psychology and related fields have much to offer him to address these troubles. In the levels-of-explanation approach discussed by David Myers (2010), the best available information in science and practice can be brought forth to help our understanding of human behavior and thus maximize our intervention strategies to improve human functioning. The sciences, not only in psychology but in medical and other fields as well, can all be put to good use to help Jake.

These levels of explanation include a biopsychosocialspiritual approach that is evidence-based (i.e., informed by the best research data available and consistent with guidelines for clinical practice supplied by the American Psychological Association, 2006). We need to better understand Jake from a biological, psychological, social and spiritual perspective in order to plan our intervention, being attentive to multiple aspects of Jake and his functioning as well as the research to support each assessment and intervention approach.

For example, many of Jake's issues may have a biological origin or biological implications that should be considered and addressed. His ongoing substance abuse as well as his significant head injury may have altered his brain and brain functioning, which can manifest itself in his difficulties with impulse control, reasoning and judgment. His brain may well be compromised, which could be assessed and treated as part of this intervention.

On another level of explanation, many of Jake's difficulties also may have a psychological origin. His challenges from his family of origin and stress including the loss of his father at a young age through severe alcohol abuse, combined with Jake's military experiences and trauma, his rejection by his former girlfriend and her family, and other stressful life experiences may have taken their toll on Jake's psychological functioning, contributing to feelings of depression, anxiety, anger, isolation and low self-esteem.

Social factors may also play an important role in Jake's many issues. For example, being a college student yet feeling very different from his peers due to being older, perhaps being less well prepared for academic life, and having traumatic military experiences may all lead to loneliness, withdrawal and not fitting in with others. As Jake compares his skills, talents and place in life to that of his classmates, he most likely feels that he comes up short. Feeling that he doesn't belong, is inferior in some ways and doesn't measure up may lead to further isolation, withdrawal, frustration, substance abuse and self-esteem challenges.

Spiritual factors likely play an important role as well in Jake's concerns. He chose to attend a Christian college, and his mother is reported to be very religious and highly engaged in her spirited church community. Although he expressed reservations about his own Christian commitment and engagement, a spiritual void likely fuels his difficulties and, at the very least, prevents him from engaging in the many benefits of religious coping.

Thus, there are multiple levels of explanation to understand and ultimately treat Jake's many challenges. Of course, one can't treat all of his troubles all at once. We must triage (i.e., prioritize what should be accomplished first based on the most serious and immediate problems) as well as take into consideration Jake's desire for change and relief from the issues that matter to him most.

It is important to determine what needs to be addressed first. Typically, the issues that cause serious and immediate harm to self and others are the very first on the list. Since Jake has made statements about harming himself, evaluating and potentially treating his suicidality becomes the highest priority. However, Jake has a recent history of violence toward others as well, and so examining his potential for homicidality also becomes extremely important right away. The combination of impulse control challenges, alcohol and substance abuse difficulties, access to (and skills with) firearms, his breakup of a significant intimate relationship, and a history of violence toward others is highly concerning and may place Jake at substantial risk for impulsive acting-out behaviors such as violence.

Jake may also be at risk for dropping out of treatment—his failure to attend recent appointments by "forgetting" or not showing up is highly troubling. Thus, addressing the therapeutic alliance and finding ways to engage Jake so that he can come to value and appreciate the counseling endeavor is critical to make any therapeutic gains. After all, you can't help someone if they either don't want to be helped or if they fail to show up for scheduled appointments. As they say, "you can lead a horse to water but you can't make it drink."

Finally, some of the practical limitations of professional counseling services (such as fees, managed care policies, scheduling conflicts, transportation) must be immediately addressed as well so that thoughtful assessment and treatment can proceed given the often limited resources and options available. Typically university counseling centers allow students a limited number of sessions on the order of 12 or less. Since Jake came to the university counseling center, it may likely mean that only a handful of sessions will be authorized. His numerous issues are unlikely to be adequately addressed with such limitations in the number of sessions allowed or available. Therefore, knowing the number of available sessions ahead of time (assuming limitations are expected) can help the counselor to prepare a realistic assessment and treatment plan.

In summary, Jake has a lot of difficulties that need attention. His many serious troubles might be overwhelming not only to him but to the treating counselor as well. There is a lot of work to do, and yet there may be limited resources to make adequate and lasting progress. The clinician needs to take a deep breath, roll up his or her sleeves, and get to it. Jake needs to do the same. The levels-of-explanation approach suggests that we take the very best that science and practice has to offer and apply that knowledge to this particular individual and the unique challenges that he faces. Quality science, not only in psychology but also in related fields as well, can help us provide a state-of-the-art and biopsychosocialspiritual, multifaceted approach to hopefully help Jake better manage his many issues and live a healthier, productive and satisfying life. The good news is that he can be helped. The bad news is that it will take much work not only by the counselor but by Jake himself, and it is unclear if he is up to the challenge.

Assessment

Before counselors begin an intervention or treatment plan, they must know exactly what they are treating. A helpful and effective tool available in psychology involves thoughtful psychodiagnostic assessment. The assessment process can utilize a levels-of-explanation approach, assessing the biological, psychological, social and spiritual dimensions of Jake's problems, which can give both the counselor and Jake a better sense of what might contribute to his many difficulties. The counselor could inquire about the availability of psychological testing reports and notes from previous treatment with Jake and, with his permission, secure these reports by contacting the institutions and professionals who have worked with Jake in the past.

Jake's history of head injury and polysubstance abuse may suggest brain impairment, which may also be at the root of his impulsive and disorganized behavior as well as his poor judgment and school performance. A comprehensive neuropsychological evaluation is likely needed, assuming that it hasn't already been conducted recently. Furthermore, an evaluation by a physician (perhaps by an internal medicine physician first and then, if the physician deems it appropriate, by a neurologist) would likely be helpful in the assessment process as well. These evaluations can be time consuming and expensive, and so being mindful of insurance limitations is important. Since Jake is a veteran, a local Veteran's Administration (VA) hospital may be able to provide these services at no charge to Jake. A comprehensive and state-of-the-art physical, neuropsychological and neurological evaluation could help assess the biological influences on Jake's troubles. The counselor might wish to determine if Jake would be willing to participate in this type of evaluation.

Again, it is possible that a complete neuropsychological and neurological evaluation has already been conducted with Jake during his extensive treatment for his head injury. There is no sense in reinventing the wheel; if complete assessments have already been recently conducted on Jake, then the counselor could well benefit from getting those reports.

In addition to attending to the biological influences on Jake's many problems, the counselor must assess the psychological influences too. Psychological tests examining personality, affective and general psychological functioning would be helpful to better understand Jake. One of the most popular and commonly used general psychological tests available is the Minnesota Multiphasic Personality Inventory, second edition (MMPI-2; Tellegen & Kraemmer, 1989). It provides scores relative to national norms on numerous psychological, affective and personality dimensions. In addition, tests such as the Millon Multiaxial Clinical Inventory, third edition (MCMI-III; Millon, Millon, Davis & Grossman, 2008) highlight personality dysfunction in particular and can act as a supplement to the MMPI-2 assessment. These tests are objective psychological tests, generally inexpensive to administer and score. While they may take Jake several hours to complete, they need little time from the clinician to administer and score. Depending on the particular questions that need to be addressed in the psychological testing process, additional tests might be selected for use with Jake as well. These could include projective instruments such as the Rorschach (Exner, 2003), the Thematic Apperception Test (Murray, 1943), a sentence completion test and projective drawings, among others. These tests are more costly than the objective psychological tests such as the MMPI-2 and MCMI-III since they are individually administered by a clinician and can take a fair amount of time to both administer and score. Additionally, these tests must be completed by a psychologist and thus might not be available to many other counselors to use. Furthermore, controversy about the validity of projective techniques continues to exist among professionals. Since copyright has now expired with the Rorschach in particular, detailed information about this instrument is readily available on the Internet.

Social functioning can be assessed through a variety of means. With Jake's permission and cooperation, it could prove useful to examine his social functioning by talking with relevant others who have had the opportunity to observe him in various settings. These include his instructors, relatives, roommates and so forth. However, confidentiality is a concern, and obviously no communication can occur between the counselor and others in Jake's life without written permission and full and informed consent from Jake. Social observation can also occur by watching Jake in social settings such as college classes, social events and the like. Again, any direct observations outside of the counseling setting would need to be considered carefully with informed consent and permission granted by Jake.

Spiritual assessment might occur through the use of clinical interview as well as a variety of questionnaires that assess spiritual matters. For example, counselors may wish to use the Brief Multidimensional Measure of Religiousness/Spirituality (Fetzer-NIA; Fetzer Institute, 1999), the Santa Clara Strength of Religious Faith Questionnaire (SCSORF; Plante & Boccaccini, 1997; Plante, Vallaeys, Sherman & Wallston, 2002), the Duke Religious Index (DUREL; Koenig, Meador & Parkerson, 1997), the Religious Commitment Inventory-10 (RCI-10; Worthington et al., 2003) or the Religious Coping Scale (RCOPE; Pargament, Koenig & Perez, 2000). Each questionnaire is easy to use and complete, and has certain advantages and disadvantages measuring various aspects of spirituality, religious coping and so forth. Additionally, unlike the MMPI-2, MCMI-III, Rorschach and others mentioned above, these instruments can be used by any counselor and do not need to be utilized only by a psychologist. Further details about these and other spiritual assessment devices can be found elsewhere (e.g., Plante, 2009).

All of these assessment tasks take time, effort and varying amounts of money. The counselor must be mindful of the resource limitations as well as Jake's willingness to participate in the assessment process. Evaluating Jake from multiple levels assessing his biological, psychological, social and spiritual functioning can help best diagnose his troubles in a way that will hopefully lead to more thoughtful and effective treatment interventions. The counselor would be well advised to consider the costs and benefits of assessment carefully with Jake.

Conceptualization

An appropriate assessment process is foundational to developing a thoughtful conceptualization of any clinical case, including Jake's. For example, if a neuropsychological examination reveals that Jake has a significant brain tumor or lesion greatly impacting his executive functioning such as his judgment and impulse control, the clinician would conceptualize Jake's case very differently than if no brain compromises exist. Or if cognitive testing reveals that Jake has limited intellectual functioning or a significant learning disability, one might conceptualize his case differently than if testing reveals that he has outstanding intellectual and cognitive functioning. The point is, conceptualizing a case is difficult until some assessment process has been conducted and completed to understand the various factors that contributed to Jake's presenting difficulties.

However, the levels-of-explanation approach using a biopsychosocial-spiritual perspective does guide us in conceptualization even when a full and complete assessment has not been conducted. Attending to the biological, psychological, social and spiritual influences on behavior has become fundamental in counseling and psychology defining the biopsychosocialspiritual framework. While biological, psychological, social and spiritual factors are all viewed as relevant in this perspective, they may not each be equal in their contribution to every problem or disorder. Thus, in the case of a primarily biological disorder such as cancer, for example, psychological, social and spiritual factors provide important contributions to the course and treatment of the disease but are not given equal etiological or treatment consideration. Similarly, while a grief reaction following the loss of a loved one may at first glance appear purely psychological, social factors such as family and community support, spiritual factors such as beliefs about the afterlife and about God, and biological factors such as disrupted sleeping and eating patterns can all complicate or alleviate the severity of symptoms. Thus, an intelligent blending and weighing of these factors constitutes the challenge of biopsychosocial-spiritual integration. Melchert (2007) well states the need for biopsychosocialspiritual integration and conceptualization when he says, "replacing the traditional reliance on an array of theoretical orientations with a science-based biopsychosocial framework would resolve many of the contradictions and conflicts that characterized (earlier) era(s) in (professional psychology)" (p. 34).

The biopsychosocialspiritual approach is contextual such that the interaction of biological, psychological, social and spiritual influences on behavior must be addressed in order to improve the complex lives and functioning of people who seek professional health and mental health services. This framework applies a systems theory perspective to emotional, psychological, physical and behavioral functioning (McDaniel, 1995; Schwartz, 1982, 1984). For example, the "approach assumes that all human problems are . . . systems problems; each biological problem has psychosocial consequences, and each psychosocial problem has biological correlates" (McDaniel, 1995, p. 117). Miller (1978), for example, discusses seven levels of systems, each interdependent on the others. These include functioning at the cellular, organ, organism, group, organization, society and supernatural levels. Furthermore, Miller outlines 19 additional sublevels present at each of the major seven levels of functioning. Dysfunction at any level of functioning leads to dysregulation, which in turn results in dysfunction at other levels. Thus, changes in one area of functioning (such as the biological area) will likely impact functioning in other areas (such as the psychological area). Chemical imbalances might occur at the cellular level in the brain, leading to mood dysfunction in the form of depression. The depressive feelings may then lead to interpersonal difficulties that further impact job performance and self-esteem. Stress associated with these problems at work, school and home may then lead to further brain chemical imbalances and further depression. The biopsychosocialspiritual perspective is holistic in that it considers the whole person, and specifically the holistic interaction of biological, psychological, social and spiritual influences.

Conceptualization must be evidence based. As psychology has evolved over the years, more and more quality research has become available to guide assessment, conceptualization and treatment. No longer can professionals do as they wish based on their own view of human behavior and behavior change strategies. In fact, the American Psychological Association (e.g., 2002, 2006) has issued a variety of position papers based on the work of several task forces in recent years that support an evidence-based approach to professional practice. Thus, our conceptualization of Jake must be considered through the lens of empirically supported research, practices and strategies. For example, many of the problems that Jake appears to experience (e.g., depression, impulsivity, substance abuse, posttraumatic stress) have a great deal of research to support our understanding, conceptualization and intervention for these issues. A thoughtful counselor must be responsive to these research-supported approaches to these problems.

For example, gradual exposure and response-prevention interventions for posttraumatic stress symptoms have been supported by quality research (e.g., Cooper & Clum, 1989). Medication and both cognitive-behavioral and interpersonal psychotherapy have been found to be helpful for those who experience depression (Cornes & Frank, 1994; Cuipers, van Straten & Warmerdam, 2007; Elkin et al., 1989; National Institute for Health and Clinical Excellence, 2007). Although counselors must be mindful of the empirical support for any clinical intervention conducted with Jake as well as with any other clients, this does not mean that counselors treat their clients using a cookbook, or that they treat the diagnosis rather than the person. Everyone has a unique story and an individual set of circumstances that contributed to why they experience the symptoms and troubles that they have and why they seek the professional services of a counselor. Research thus *informs* (and does not *dictate*) professional practice.

If you had a physical problem that needed the attention of a physician to evaluate and treat, you would hope that this doctor is caught up on the most up-to-date research and practice to provide you with state-of-the-art care. You should expect the same from a psychologist or a counselor. In an era of evidence-based practice, all mental health professionals must be up-to-date on the science behind clinical interventions. Thus, the counselor treating Jake must be attentive to the research literature that speaks to the types of symptoms and concerns that he experiences. This includes depression, impulsivity, substance abuse, posttraumatic stress and other matters. All of this data comes together in conceptualization in order to figure out how best to help Jake cope with his many challenges.

Given what we know thus far about Jake (and without the ability to access additional information other than what is presented in his case description), I would offer the following conceptualization about his case for the counselor's consideration. Of course, after a more formalized assessment procedure has been conducted, a more thoughtful and nuanced conceptualization of the case would likely occur.

Jake likely has a variety of biological, psychological, social and spiritual contributions to his many troubles. Sadly, he has experienced a brain injury and a highly significant one at that. In addition to his brain injury due to his bar fight, he also has a reported history of significant substance abuse, which also impacts brain functioning. Depression, impulse control problems, attentional troubles and poor judgment, among other symptoms and challenges, can all be expected for many with these types of brain injuries. Jake clearly has psychosocial issues as well. His growing-up years were stressful as were his military service and relationship challenges. He feels traumatized by many of his experiences and is quickly having troubles in school and in his general functioning. These psychosocial troubles may result in additional brain injury through continued substance abuse and other poor decisions (e.g., engaging in bar fights), making matters much worse for him. Jake also has spiritual problems as well. Although he finds himself at a Christian college, he clearly is ambivalent and challenged by his religious tradition and seems to be feeling distant from his faith tradition, beliefs and relationship to God. These spiritual troubles may lead to additional poor decisions that, again, make matters worse for him. Thus, Jake has a variety of biopsychosocialspiritual challenges that interact with each other and result in dysregulation on multiple levels.

Treatment Plan and Techniques

Once assessment and conceptualization occurs, the burning question is what to do about it in treatment planning and intervention. In consulting with the treating counselor, the following might be offered for consideration.

First, the counselor needs to build rapport and have "buy in" from Jake. You can't help someone if they refuse to be helped. You can't work through a treatment plan if they don't show up for scheduled appointments. This may be an ongoing issue that likely will need to be revisited regularly.

Second, it is important to understand the resources that are available for treatment and to use these resources wisely. As we've discussed, Jake's insurance plan or the university's counseling center may likely have limits to the number of sessions and extent of treatment available. A rather small number of sessions are likely allowable. It is important to know what these limitations might be in order to develop a reasonable treatment plan. The counselor could also work with Jake about supplementary services too. For example, since he is a military veteran, he is likely entitled to many veteran benefits. Contacting the local VA hospital could be productive to determine what additional services Jake is entitled to. VA hospitals usually have extensive mental health services available including assessment, treatment, and self-help or peer-led programs such as Alcoholic Anonymous and other 12-step groups. Church communities also often offer social services that may be helpful to Jake. Knowing what resources are available to Jake outside of the counselor's services can be very useful in order to develop a total treatment and intervention package.

Third, we need to prioritize our intervention to address the most serious and immediate issues. Jake has so many difficulties that it is challenging to know how to address each one. Some may need immediate attention while others can wait. Usually, symptoms that are life threatening (e.g., suicide, homicide, drunk driving, domestic violence) need immediate attention. In Jake's case, suicidal and homicidal concerns are relevant and need to be assessed and attended to. Ongoing assessment and possible intervention regarding danger to self and others may be needed in Jake's situation. All jurisdictions call for breaking confidentiality when there is reasonable suspicion of immediate danger to self and others in order to keep clients and others safe. Inpatient hospitalization and involuntary commitment may be necessary if he appears to be in imminent danger of harm.

Jake may weigh in on what concerns he wants to address. Particular issues such as his estrangement from his child and former girlfriend or his problems fitting in and doing well in school may be on the forefront of his mind, desiring immediate attention. In order to keep Jake engaged and supportive of the treatment plan, the counselor needs to address the issues that are most concerning for Jake. Some of Jake's troubles may get appropriately and adequately managed elsewhere (e.g., working with a physician regarding his brain injury or attending a specialized substance abuse program for his addiction problems), and thus the counselor may only need to periodically check in with Jake and perhaps the other professionals working with him on these matters.

Fourth, the counselor may wish to help Jake understand that the science and practice of psychology using a biopsychosocialspiritual and evidence-based levels approach can be very helpful to him. Principles from both science and practice can be used to better understand his troubles and to develop coping strategies for him.

Dysregulation and systems theory, as discussed earlier, is relevant for Jake's problems, for example. If Jake stays up late each night playing on his computer, his lack of sleep won't be helpful to him to do well in his classes the next morning. That will result in poor academic performance leading to depression and frustration, perhaps leading to additional substance abuse and sleep troubles. Jake must come to understand that dysregulation and systems theory can help him better plan his days to better ensure that he takes adequate care of himself and his needs in a health-promoting (rather than health-damaging) manner.

While we can't know for sure how Jake will respond to a treatment plan or suggestions, for the purpose of this chapter I'll outline the key treatment issues that should be addressed in a biopsychosocialspiritual framework the counselor might wish to keep in mind while working with Jake. Since this book focuses on Christianity and counseling, the spiritual elements of the treatment plan will be highlighted in more detail than the other factors.

Biological. Jake's head injury and substance abuse is concerning. He may have permanent cognitive impairment that must be addressed. He may need to develop (with assistance) strategies to cope with his impairment. His goal of completing college may or may not be realistic, and selecting an educational and vocational plan needs to take into consideration his cognitive strengths and weaknesses.

Jake may also need medication management to address his biologically related challenges. Medication for impulse control, attention deficit, depression and substance abuse may need to be addressed by an appropriate physician, such as a psychiatrist or neurologist.

Psychological. Jake's psychological needs are numerous. He likely feels rejected by many, including his parents, his former girlfriend and her family, among others. He clearly feels isolated from other students, not fitting in on campus. These issues may also surface as he develops a professional relationship with the counselor, and thus attending to transference issues and projections becomes important. For example, he might expect the counselor to reject him or judge him negatively as he believes others do. He may have trouble being honest and open or admitting distress to his counselor.

Jake may also feel burdened by his belief that he needs to fulfill the educational goals of his military friend who died. College may not be his calling, yet he feels compelled to complete the goals of his fallen soldier friend. It would be important to work with Jake to determine what life plan and goals make sense for him, separate from the goals of his now deceased fellow soldier.

Often those who have similar troubles as Jake set themselves up for failure by sabotaging their efforts. For example, Jake's habit of staying up all night or abusing alcohol and substances may provide him with an excuse for not doing well in school. He may conclude that his failures are due to these habits rather than something that might feel more uncomfortable and threatening, such as not being smart enough for college work. He may believe that his lack of satisfying relationships is due to the fact that he is an older student who has experienced military service rather than due to his difficult personality, acting-out behaviors and poor social skills.

The counselor may wish to carefully address these issues with Jake, trying to minimize a defensive reaction from him. There are many techniques and strategies to accomplish this goal. First, a rapport and a trusting relationship with the counselor is very important. Then, for example, it could prove productive for Jake to create some distance from his own conflict by talking about a hypothetical third person who experiences the very same challenges and behavioral responses that Jake does. The counselor could ask Jake to advise this third party on how to handle his difficulties. In this way, the counselor puts Jake in the therapist or trusted advisor role where he may have more distance from his own emotional reactions to his problems.

Social. Jake's college milieu may very well create a social comparison that isn't helpful to him. He may not have much in common with the typical students in his classes and living quarters. While he may be older and more hardened from his life experiences and military service, they may be better prepared for college work and social life. These issues should be discussed with Jake, and perhaps strategies could be implemented for him to feel more socially connected (if not on campus then perhaps through off-campus activities). Working to improve his social functioning is also part of the treatment package.

Spiritual. Addressing Jake's spiritual needs and perhaps feelings of alienation are important too. Jake may feel distant from his faith tradition and from God for a variety of reasons, including his losses and stresses in life and his conflictual relationships with his parents, or perhaps from feeling like God has not blessed him in ways that he expected. It would be helpful to discuss these matters with Jake and develop strategies for spiritual renewal. Research clearly demonstrates a variety of physical and mental health benefits to religious and spiritual engagement as well as the use of religious coping and contemplative practices (Plante, 2009, 2010; Plante & Thoresen, 2007). For example, examining Jake's prayer life and satisfaction with a faith community, and discerning his calling may prove very useful for him. In my careful review of the spiritual and religious traditions, there appear to be many spiritual and religious tools that could be well integrated into counseling for Jake and others (see Plante, 2009). I'll briefly review 13 tools here and then focus on a few of them that might be especially useful for Jake.

Meditation. Research has demonstrated that there are many mental and physical health benefits from regular meditative contemplative practices (Kabat-Zinn, 2003; Plante, 2010; Shapiro & Walsh, 2007). These benefits include stress reduction, acceptance of self and others, as well as improved coping and enhanced interpersonal relationships. Many physical benefits such as lower blood pressure and tempered stress reactivity are also probable for those who meditate in an ongoing manner. Jake may wish to explore meditative techniques to help him manage his stress and discontent. These could include specifically Christian approaches (such as centering prayer) or meditative approaches from Eastern traditions such as mindfulness meditation or yoga.

Prayer. Research from a variety of quality studies suggests that there are both mental and physical health benefits of engaging in regular prayer activities, including enhanced psychological functioning, well-being and meaning, and stress reduction (Masters, 2007). Jake may wish to examine his prayer life, perhaps seek spiritual direction from a clergy member or prayer mentor/director, and work toward a more satisfying prayer life.

Vocation, meaning, purpose and calling in life. Spirituality and religious engagement provide direction and opportunities to develop and nurture an enhanced sense of meaning, purpose, calling and vocation in one's life. Jake's life appears rudderless, and he could likely benefit from efforts to find more purpose and meaning.

As mentioned, Jake may somehow feel compelled to complete the goal of education in response to his fellow soldier buddy who died. This may have been the deceased soldier's calling but not Jake's. One technique that might help Jake is the use of the "calling protocol" (Dreher & Plante, 2007). It uses the principles from the Spiritual Exercises of St. Ignatius (founder of the Jesuits) to help people develop a better sense of vocation, calling and purpose in their lives, and also to help discern one's own calling (and not that of someone else).

The calling protocol highlights the four *Ds*: *discovery, detachment, discernment and direction*. *Discovery* refers to the development of a better understanding of personal strengths or gifts. The positive psychology literature refers to these as "signature strengths" (e.g., Snyder & Lopez, 2007). Gaining a solid appreciation of one's gifts can then be used to determine how these gifts can best be enlisted to improve one's sense of meaning and purpose. For example, social skills, the ability to counsel others, musical talents and organization skills are possible gifts or strengths that can be employed to improve quality of life and help find one's calling and vocation. It is important to have a realistic understanding of our gifts to maximize the odds that they can be used effectively. Jake may not feel that he has too many gifts, and so exploration with him may help him identify them. For example, some of the skills that he learned in the military (e.g., the ability to triage, be organized, follow a protocol) might be highlighted so that they could be used in his recovery now.

In the calling protocol, *detachment* refers to working to move away from problematic and sometimes debilitating behaviors, thoughts and attitudes that prevent someone from understanding and nurturing their gifts. These behaviors and tendencies might include consumerism, greed, workaholism, alcoholism, dysfunctional relationships, low self-esteem, fear, anxiety, and a variety of other damaging addictions and behavior patterns that distract us from our vocation and calling as well as prevent us from nurturing our gifts. These behaviors, attitudes, thoughts and life circumstances are thus roadblocks to nurturing and using the gifts defined during the discovery phase. Jake has plenty of these obstacles. If he can see that they prevent him from using his gifts and from becoming the person he is called to be, he may develop more energy and motivation to tackle his maladaptive and health-damaging behaviors.

Discernment refers to thinking through how we can best live our lives and use our gifts that might lead us to experiences of consolation rather than desolation. Consolation leads to peace, solace and joy, while desolation leads to depression, anxiety and other damaging feelings, thoughts and behavior. Thinking about and working through the process of discernment is needed to secure more meaning, purpose and vocation in life.

Discernment helps us to better appreciate how our gifts can be used productively and realistically in a way that gives us comfort and peace. Jake may feel that his gifts are not tied in with college life, for example.

Direction refers to developing a vocational path to live a more meaningful and purposeful life. Direction is the action plan that emerges when the discernment process is complete. Spiritual direction within many religious traditions has used variations on these four steps to help their clients develop more calling, purpose and meaning in life. These strategies can also be used with people in general to develop a better life path.

Certainly the four *D*s defined above are not unique. Perhaps what is unique is the integration of a spiritually based mindset to help people such as Jake find a way to better achieve a sense of calling, vocation, meaning and purpose in their lives.

Acceptance of self and others (even with faults). Religious and spiritual traditions provide wise counsel regarding the benefits of accepting ourselves and others even with faults and imperfections. The traditions offer various strategies for redemption, forgiveness, reconciliation and acceptance from others and also from the divine. The often quoted and well-known "serenity prayer" beautifully articulates what so much of psychotherapy tries to accomplish. It states: *"God, grant me the serenity to accept the things I cannot change; courage to change the things I can; and wisdom to know the difference."* The serenity prayer is also an important part of 12-step programs, which may benefit Jake as well.

Ethical values and behaviors. The religious and spiritual traditions have spent hundreds and even thousands of years fine-tuning many time-tested guidelines and principles for ethical living. Living more ethically has psychological, relational, community and other benefits (Plante, 2004). Additionally, the primary ethical principles endorsed for psychologists and articulated in the ethics code (American Psychological Association, 2002) overlap with many of the same ethical guidelines offered and supported by the various religious and spiritual traditions. These include guiding principles and values such as respect, responsibility, integrity, competence and concern for others ("RRICC"; Plante, 2004). For example, both the professional ethics codes and religious and spiritual traditions encourage people to be concerned about and help improve the welfare of others (and especially those in greatest need), to be honest and maintain integrity in all that we do and say, and to be respectful to everyone and to life. Jake may well benefit from examining his behavior and finding ways to develop ethical principles that mean much to him. This may also assist in his efforts to improve his psychological and behavioral functioning.

Being part of something larger and greater than oneself. The religious and spiritual traditions contribute to being part of something larger than ourselves. Religion and spirituality offer a path to help place life and our many challenges in a better and bigger perspective. If Jake can feel part of something bigger and perhaps more important than himself, he may cope better with the many stressful challenges and transitions in his life.

Forgiveness, gratitude, love, kindness and compassion. The religious and spiritual traditions encourage people to be forgiving, grateful, loving, kind and compassionate. Many research studies have demonstrated the positive mental, physical and community health benefits of forgiveness (Koenig, McCullough & Larson, 2001). Forgiveness is a foil to anger, hostility and bitterness. Jake could certainly benefit from working on his anger and bitterness.

Gratitude highlights the ability to be thankful for what one has or what has been given, as well as the ability to appreciate and savor daily events and experiences. It involves "counting your blessings" and is encouraged within all of the major religious traditions. Research has indicated that those who experience more gratitude tend to sleep better, are more optimistic and more energetic, and maintain better interpersonal relationships too (e.g., Emmons & McCullough, 2003). Jake could work to be more grateful for his blessings. Unlike many of his peers, he survived his military experience and has the good fortune to be able to live life.

Additionally, Jake could learn to be more loving, kind and compassionate, which is also supported by his and other religious traditions (Armstrong, 2006). This way of being also has many mental, physical, community and relational benefits (Snyder & Lopez, 2007). Treating others as you wish to be treated, popularly referred to as the golden rule, is a way of life and could be used to help Jake in his treatment.

Jake clearly needs to learn to be more gracious toward himself and others. This is a spiritual issue as well. The religious traditions encourage loving kindness to others along with compassionate behaviors, which can not only make the world a better place but have many physical and mental health benefits as well (Plante, 2009; Plante & Thoresen, 2007). For example, in one of our recent studies (Plante, Lackey & Hwang, 2009), we found that students who participated in an alternative school break focusing on "faith that does justice," which involved helping others in solidarity, returned from their experience more compassionate than when they left and coped better with school and other stressors to boot. Jake could consider volunteer activities, perhaps helping other veterans or other groups (e.g., homeless persons, children). This may be therapeutic for Jake and help him become less self-focused.

Volunteerism and charity. Religious traditions universally encourage and support charitable works and volunteerism that attempts to help those in great need and tries to make the world a better place for everyone. Remarkably, research suggests that two hours per week or more of volunteer activities is associated with mental and physical health benefits and actually reduces mortality risks over time as much as 40% (Oman & Thoresen, 2003).

The religious traditions generally offer an effective organizational structure to nurture productive community engagement, which most often emphasizes helping those in greatest need such as the poor and marginalized of society. Furthermore, ongoing volunteerism usually provides the volunteer with an enhanced sense of meaning, purpose and calling that can often help keep their own troubles and stressors in better perspective. Jake could certainly help his own case by engaging with others in need.

Ritual and community support. Research over many years and in many ways has consistently found that mental and physical health benefits can be secured from social support. Religious and spiritual practices, services, rituals and other activities provide ongoing community social networking opportunities shared with others who maintain similar values, beliefs, perspectives and traditions. Regular religious service attendance, Bible or other scripture studies, and many holiday celebrations within family and faith communities all provide organized and ongoing opportunities for social connection, networking and support. Jake may wish to incorporate ritual and community support into his treatment plan.

Social justice. The religious and spiritual wisdom traditions all support social justice ideas and activities to make the world a more humane and just place. Furthermore, social justice activities and engagement help people to be less focused on themselves. It is often hard to feel overly stressed and caught up by our own daily hassles and challenges when confronted with the serious and often fatal challenges of poverty, oppression, violence and disease experienced by the majority of the world's population. Again, Jake may become less self-centered if he can attend to the issues and concerns of others.

Spiritual models. Religious and spiritual models provide followers with excellent exemplars to imitate (Oman & Thoresen, 2003, 2007). The recent highly popular question "What would Jesus do?" (WWJD) is a perfect example.

Ancient religious models such as Jesus, Buddha and Mohammad, as well as many of the more contemporary religious and spiritual models such as Gandhi, Mother Teresa, the Dalai Lama, Martin Luther King Jr., and even one's family and friends can act as a template or model for how to live and act in a better way. Research has indicated that observational learning is a very powerful method to acquire new skills and behaviors (Bandura, 1986). Observing spiritual and religious role models can be a highly productive way to help motivate and inspire others to "go and do likewise" (Luke 10:37). Jake may wish to examine who can be good models for his life and could perhaps nurture a mentoring relationship with him.

Bibliotherapy. Psychologists and other health care professionals have used bibliotherapy to help others for decades. They have encouraged their clients to read various self-help and other books to augment their treatment and enhance their lives. Many of these materials are also used for psychoeducational purposes such as learning more about a particular diagnosis and the treatment options. These books are also frequently used to increase client motivation or provide inspiration. The religious and spiritual traditions also usually encourage their members to read sacred Scripture such as the Bible, as well as other sacred readings and commentaries on sacred texts to improve their faith, spirituality and lives in general. There are plenty of excellent books that Jake might consider reading to help him better cope with his troubles.

Sacredness of life. The religious and spiritual traditions all nurture and support the notion that life is sacred and that the divine lives within all of us. This concept—that we are all very important, sacred and perhaps a "child of God"—has many implications and ramifications for how we perceive ourselves and interact with others. The religious faith communities and traditions instruct and underscore that if we are in fact sacred, then everyone must be treated with a great deal of respect, kindness, love and compassion. Psychologists and other professionals can then use this perspective of sacredness in their psychotherapeutic work. The counselor can encourage Jake to enhance his self-worth as well as his interpersonal relationships by getting a better sense of the divine within himself and others.

Attending to the biopsychosocialspiritual needs of Jake in a comprehensive and evidence-based manner hopefully will result in behavior change for him and a more satisfying and healthy life and lifestyle. Additional services and resources can be enlisted to help as well. These might include those offered by veteran groups, the college where Jake attends and local church communities.

Evaluation and Follow-Up Care

As treatment progresses, ongoing evaluation and outcome assessment is needed to determine if adequate progress is being made. Treatment can get derailed for many different reasons. Some of the assessment instruments discussed earlier (such as the MMPI-2) might be readministered to determine if objective decreases in symptoms and pathology can be found. Additionally, other client satisfaction and treatment outcome measures and checklists can be used to evaluate progress and determine if treatment has stalled or is in trouble. These results can also be used clinically with Jake to help adjust treatment goals and change the course of treatment if and as needed. Often this data is necessary to justify continued services (especially services funded by insurance) as well.

Typically, following treatment termination, periodical follow-up or booster sessions are needed to check in. Termination ideally would occur when treatment goals are met and when Jake is managing his life and troubles in a healthy, productive and sustainable manner. Relapse prevention strategies are needed as well (especially for those like Jake who experience addictions). Jake may likely need some kind of ongoing follow-up care indefinitely. This might involve professional services, but it could also potentially involve self-help, paraprofessional or community services such as those offered by veteran hospitals and church communities. For example, he may attend AA meetings indefinitely not only to help him manage his addictions but also obtain the kind of spiritual fellowship he likely needs.

Conclusion and Recommendations

Although Jake has numerous and serious problems that involve biological, psychological, social and spiritual factors and dysfunction, the science and practice of psychology has much to offer him if he is willing to engage in the process of counseling. Counselors must do their part, and Jake must do his part as well. Together they can work as a team to help Jake improve his functioning and life. Consultation will likely be needed from other professionals, as well as supplemental services provided outside of the counseling sessions. Hopefully, Jake can look forward to a better future if all of the elements work together for his well-being.

References

American Psychological Association. (2002). Ethical principles of psychologists and code of conduct. *American Psychologist, 57,* 1060-73.

American Psychological Association Presidential Task Force on Evidence-Based Practice. (2006). Evidence-based practice in psychology. *American Psychologist, 61,* 271-85.

Armstrong, K. (2006). *The great transformation: The beginning of our religious traditions.* New York: Anchor Books.

Bandura, A. (1986). *Social foundations of thought and action.* Englewood Cliffs, NJ: Prentice Hall.

Cooper, N. A., & Clum, G. A. (1989). Imaginal flooding as a supplementary treatment for PTSD in combat veterans: A controlled study. *Behavior Therapy, 20,* 381-92.

Cornes, C. L., & Frank, E. (1994). Interpersonal psychotherapy for depression. *Clinical Psychologist, 47,* 9-10.

Cuipers, P., van Straten, A., & Warmerdam, L. (2007). Behavioral activation treatments of depression: A meta-analysis. *Clinical Psychology Review, 27,* 318-26.

Dreher, D. E., & Plante, T. G. (2007). Rediscovering the sense of calling: Promoting greater health, joy, and purpose in life. In T. G. Plante & C. E. Thoresen (Eds.), *Spirit, science and health: How the spiritual mind fuels physical wellness* (pp. 129-42). Westport, CT: Praeger/ Greenwood.

Elkin, I., Shea, M. T., Watkins, J. T., Imber, S. D., Sotsky, S. M., Collins, J. F., . . . Docherty, J.P. (1989). National Institute of Mental Health treatment of depression collaborative research program: General effectiveness of treatments. *Archives of General Psychiatry, 46,* 971-82.

Emmons, R. A., & McCullough, M. E. (2003). Counting blessings versus burdens: Experimental studies of gratitude and subjective well-being. *Journal of Personality and Social Psychology, 84,* 377-89.

Exner, J. E. (2003). *The Rorschach: A comprehensive system: Vol. 1. Basic foundations* (4th ed.). New York: Wiley.

Fetzer Institute/National Institute of Aging Working Group. (1999*). Multidimensional measurement of religiousness/spirituality for use in health research: A report of the Fetzer Institute/National Institute on Aging Working Group.* Kalamazoo, MI: John E. Fetzer Institute.

Kabat-Zinn, J. (2003). Mindfulness-based interventions in context: Past, present, and future. *Clinical Psychology: Research and Practice, 10,* 144-56.

Koenig, H. G., McCullough, M. E., & Larson, D. B. (2001). *Handbook of religion and health.* New York: Oxford University Press.

Koenig, H. G., Meador, K., & Parkerson, G. (1997). Religion Index for Psychiatric Research: A 5-item measure for use in health outcome studies [Letter to the editor]. *American Journal of Psychiatry, 154,* 885-86.

Masters, K. S. (2007). Prayer and health. In T. G. Plante & C. E. Thoresen (Eds.), *Spirit, science and health: How the spiritual mind fuels the body* (pp. 11-24). Westport, CT: Praeger/ Greenwood.

McDaniel, S. H. (1995). Collaboration between psychologists and family physicians: Implementing the biopsychosocial model. *Professional Psychology: Research and Practice, 26,* 117-22.

Melchert, T. P. (2007). Strengthening the scientific foundations of professional psychology: Time for the next steps. *Professional Psychology: Research and Practice, 38,* 34-43.

Miller, J. G. (1978). *Living systems.* New York: McGraw-Hill.

Millon, T., Millon, C., Davis, R., & Grossman, S. (2008). *Manual for the Millon Clinical Inventory-III.* Minneapolis: Pearson.

Murray, H. A. (1943). *Thematic apperception test.* Cambridge, MA: Harvard University Press.

Myers, D. G. (2010). A levels-of-explanation view. In E. L. Johnson (Ed.), *Psychology & Christianity: Five views* (pp. 49-78). Downers Grove, IL: IVP Academic.

National Institute for Health and Clinical Excellence. (2007). *Depression: Management of depression in primary and secondary care* (Quick reference guide, amended). London: Author.

Oman, D., & Thoresen, C. E. (2003). Spiritual modeling: A key to spiritual and religious growth? *The International Journal for the Psychology of Religion, 13,* 149-65.

———. (2007). How does one learn to be spiritual? The neglected role of spiritual modeling in health. In T. G. Plante & C. E. Thoresen (Eds.), *Spirit, science and health: How the spiritual mind fuels physical wellness* (pp. 39-56). Westport, CT: Praeger/Greenwood.

Pargament, K. I., Koenig, H. G., & Perez, L. (2000). The many methods of religious coping: Initial development and validation of the RCOPE. *Journal of Clinical Psychology, 56,* 519-43.

Plante, T. G. (2004). *Do the right thing: Living ethically in an unethical world.* Oakland, CA: New Harbinger.

———. (2009). *Spiritual practices in psychotherapy: Thirteen tools for enhancing psychological health.* Washington, DC: American Psychological Association.

——— (Ed). (2010). *Contemplative practices in action: Spirituality, meditation, and health.* Santa Barbara, CA: Praeger/Greenwood.

Plante, T. G., & Boccaccini, B. F. (1997). The Santa Clara Strength of Religious Faith Questionnaire. *Pastoral Psychology, 45,* 375-87.

Plante, T. G., Lackey, K., & Hwang, J. (2009). The impact of immersion trips on development of compassion among college students. *Journal of Experiential Education, 32,* 28-43.

Plante, T. G., & Thoresen, C. E. (Eds.). (2007). *Spirit, science and health: How the spiritual mind fuels physical wellness.* Westport, CT: Praeger/Greenwood.

Plante, T. G., Vallaeys, C. L., Sherman, A. C., & Wallston, K. A. (2002). The development of a brief version of the Santa Clara Strength of Religious Faith Questionnaire. *Pastoral Psychology, 48,* 11-21.

Schwartz, G. E. (1982). Testing the biopsychosocial model: The ultimate challenge facing behavioral medicine? *Journal of Consulting and Clinical Psychology, 50,* 1040-53.

———. (1984). Psychobiology of health: A new synthesis. In B. L. Hammonds & C. J. Scheirer (Eds.), *Psychology and health: The master lecture series* (Vol. 3, pp. 149-93). Washington, DC: American Psychological Association.

Shapiro, S. L., & Walsh, R. (2007). Meditation: Exploring the farther reaches. In T. G. Plante & C. E. Thoresen (Eds.), *Spirit, science and health: How the spiritual mind fuels the body* (pp. 57-71). Westport, CT: Praeger/ Greenwood.

Snyder, C. R., & Lopez, S. J. (2007). *Positive psychology: The scientific and practical explorations of human strengths.* Thousand Oaks, CA: Sage.

Tellegen, A., & Kraemmer, B. (1989*). Minnesota Multiphasic Personality Inventory (MMPI-2): Manual for administration and scoring.* Minneapolis: University of Minnesota Press.

Worthington, E. L., Jr., Wade, N. G., Hight, T. L., Ripley, J. S., McCullough, M. E., Berry, J. W., . . . O'Connor, L. (2003). The Religious Commitment Inventory-10: Development, refinement, and validation of a brief scale for research and counseling. *Journal of Counseling Psychology, 50,* 84-96.

4

An Integration Approach

Mark R. McMinn

LEARNING OBJECTIVES

- *Explain how the integration view balances psychology, theology and spirituality.*
- *Locate how the theological assertion that humans are created in God's image is applied in attending to the functional, structural and relational aspects of Jake's presenting concerns.*
- *From the session dialogue samples, describe the benefits of Recursive Schema Activation (RSA) to reveal behavioral patterns connected to core cognitive beliefs.*

I puzzle over the adage "to have your cake and eat it too." If one has cake, why wouldn't they eat it?[1] To have your cake and *not* eat it just seems silly. In the same way, if Christian counselors have the rich theoretical and scientific tradition of psychology to draw upon, why wouldn't they do so? And if the counselor has access to biblical revelation and the theological wisdom of the centuries, of course the counselor should rely on these resources also.

A substantial risk is that counselors might easily resort to haphazard means of relating psychology, theology and spirituality, drawing on Christian and

---

[1]The correct interpretation of this adage is that the cake is gone after one eats it. In this sense, we cannot have our cake and eat it too. But the saying is typically used to suggest we cannot have two things we want regardless of how consumable they may be, and that is what puzzles me. When it comes to integration, I want to hold psychology, theology and spirituality together at the same time.

psychological resources whenever one or the other seems most convenient, popular or pragmatic. Stanton Jones's chapter on the integration view in *Psychology & Christianity: Five Views* (Jones, 2010) is an excellent corrective to those who may practice these haphazard forms of integration. As is true of his earlier work (e.g., Jones & Butman, 1991), Jones defines and describes a thoughtful sort of integration that maintains the rightful authority of Christ and Scripture. During my 13 years at Wheaton College, Stan was first a colleague and then a supervisor (when he became provost), and always a friend and role model of Christian maturity. Like Stan, I believe integration needs to begin with a Christian understanding of the human condition, that we need a measure of humility in recognizing that we do not interpret Scripture without human error, that science is a value-laden enterprise and that psychological science can prove helpful in the work counselors do.

I appreciate how Jones (2010) considers Christianity to be bigger than Christian theology. Likewise, in my previous work I have argued that spiritual formation ought to be considered alongside theology in the context of counseling (McMinn, 2011). Like three legs of a tripod, psychology, theology and spirituality are all important to consider in formulating and providing clinical services. Most of the approaches in this book will consider these three, but one will explicitly trump the other two when providing treatment to Jake. In this chapter, I attempt to play Three No Trump.[2] That is, my approach with Jake will be influenced by all three—psychology, theology and spirituality—with all of them highly valued.

This is not to say that psychology, theology and spirituality are equally authoritative or that they are all used at every moment in counseling. Integrative counseling calls for adaptability, fluidity and sensitivity to the current moment, and for an ability to see different realms of authority in relation to the particular situation being faced. For example, I take biblical and theological wisdom to be more authoritative than psychology in understanding the deep cries of human existence. When a client is weeping in my office, confronted with the deepest pains of loss and struggle, I may occasionally ponder the psychological theories I learned in graduate school, but much more often I am thinking about a Christian view of persons. In situations such as this I sit stunned anew by the depth of brokenness that pervades the human condition. I am inwardly groaning

---

[2]This is a term from the card game bridge. Three No Trump is a common bid, with none of the suits trumping the others.

in harmony with my client's outward groans, yearning for all creation to be re-deemed (Romans 8:22-23). Conversely, psychology is more helpful than the-ology when treating symptoms of panic disorder. Advances in cognitive and behavioral interventions have proven highly effective in treating symptoms of panic, and I would be quite irresponsible if I failed to provide those treatment options to clients who need help. The third leg of this tripod—spiritual for-mation—is a primary goal of faith communities, and can be a worthy consider-ation for counseling as well. The deeply personal and experiential nature of spiritual formation defies taxonomies, but I find that when I am open to hearing about my clients' spiritual journeys, they are eager to tell me.

In working with Jake, I would pray for discernment and wisdom in bal-ancing psychology, theology and spirituality. All three are important, but the effective counselor must be discerning and wise about how these three com-ponents are emphasized at any given moment in the treatment process.

Preliminary Considerations

I once heard Dr. Larry Crabb introduce a talk by telling of a time when he was sitting with a difficult client shortly after Crabb had received his Ph.D. in psychology. As Dr. Crabb listened to the complexity of the cli-ent's life, he thought to himself, "Oh my, this person needs a profes-sional!" I had a similar reaction when reading the case study about Jake, wondering what I had gotten myself into by agreeing to write this chapter. This is a complex case.

 Who is the client? One of the early considerations from an ethical perspective is identifying the client. Is Jake being referred to another counselor in the Christian college's counseling center, or is this a counselor in the community? If the former, then it is important to clarify whether the counselor's primary com-mitment is to the university (as an employee) or to Jake (as a counselor). Who is the counselor's primary client, the university or Jake? This may come to bear later if Jake continues to violate behavioral standards at the college. For ex-ample, if Jake admits to using or selling drugs, or to sexual aggression, will the counselor be obligated to report this to the college? The ground rules for re-porting behavioral infractions need to be specified in advance, and in writing, to minimize the chances of misunderstandings and violations of confidentiality later. If the counselor is expected to protect the college from students like Jake, then Jake needs to know this in advance, before deciding how much to disclose.

From a therapeutic perspective, the ideal situation would be a counselor who has no reporting requirement to the Christian college. This provides Jake with a greater degree of confidentiality and a sense of safety. Counselors have primary ethical and legal obligations to their clients, and if a counselor anticipates a potential conflict of interests between an employer and a client, then the counselor needs to work this out in advance by informing the client and/or renegotiating the employer's expectations. Jake will not make much progress in counseling if he does not experience it as a safe place to be open and honest.

Treatment goals. Psychotherapists speak of client autonomy, and theologians speak of human agency; both point in the same direction when it comes to Jake. That is, Jake needs to determine what he wants to work on in the context of counseling. If it were up to me, I could come up with quite a list of behavioral changes for Jake to consider, but I don't have the sense that Jake wants to make changes in his behavior. Not yet, at least. He seems to be saying, "I want to feel better" rather than, "I want to change the destructive things I am doing."

Does this mean that a counselor should simply accept Jake's goals for treatment? Yes and no. At first, Jake's goals ought to be the primary focus of treatment. If a counselor asserts an overly directive voice at this point, Jake will simply head for the door. It is important for Jake to set his own direction for therapy, both because client autonomy is an ethical commitment for licensed counselors, and because it is how God treats us. From the earliest pages of the Bible we see God allowing human freedom, even if that freedom is ultimately self-destructive. The price of human agency is enormous, yet God chose it over predetermining how people would behave. Still, I hope that Jake's goals for treatment may deepen and grow over time. At first he may simply want to feel better and study more effectively, but as he recovers from trauma, learns more about himself, and begins to trust the process of counseling, he may also realize the need to change behaviors and take more responsibility for what lies ahead. Change takes time.

This raises a question that Christian counselors often face: is sanctification the goal of Christian counseling? This question defies simple answers. On one hand, if we answer yes, that sanctification *is* the goal of Christian counseling, then we put many licensed counselors and psychologists in an unavoidable conflict because they are accountable to state licensing bodies and insurance providers. Most counselors are trained in assessment, diagnosis, treatment planning and psychotherapy, and are responsible to provide these services to clients. These mental health goals are not the same as the Christian notion of sanctification. On the other hand, if we answer no, that sanctification *is not* the goal of Christian counseling, then we remove virtually all spiritual formation from the counseling process, and we are left with little more than mainstream counseling practice with a few spiritual metaphors or Bible verses attached. My conclusion is that every Christian relationship has the potential of promoting sanctification because close relationships help us see things more clearly. With effective counseling, the counselor does the professional work he or she is trained to do, remaining open to discussions of faith in the process, and as this occurs the client develops a deepening awareness of self in relation to God and others. This quite naturally has a sanctifying effect. Growing in sanctification is not the goal of counseling, but it is, at least to some extent, the inevitable outcome of an effective counseling relationship between Christians.

Initial impressions. In considering Jake's situation, I have many initial impressions that will be important to consider in counseling. I will limit myself to a top-ten list.

First, he has a background of trauma that ought to be explored and understood. The immediate trauma occurred in a combat training exercise and other related military experiences, but he also experienced a childhood trauma with his father's death. Some clinicians believe substance abuse problems should be treated before any other issues are addressed in counseling. In contrast, I think the substance abuse may be a coping response to the trauma, so I would like to see the trauma addressed first, or at least simultaneously with substance abuse.

Second, he has a recent brain injury. Traumatic Brain Injury (TBI) can cause profound changes in mood, personality and cognitive abilities. This needs to be assessed, and previous medical records obtained.

Third, his views of God concern me. Jake claims some level of Christian commitment, but the nature of this is not clear. Was his conversion meaningful and sincere, or more a way to please a military chaplain or to try to win back his former girlfriend? Jake seems to hold to what Smith and Denton (2005) call Moralistic Therapeutic Deism—an increasingly common set of beliefs suggesting that God is a "Divine Butler and Cosmic Therapist" (p. 165) who should provide for his needs without making many demands on how he lives.

Fourth, I am concerned about depression and potential suicide risk. He might even be dangerous to others. What does Jake mean when he says, "I might as well get blown into oblivion"?

Fifth, I wonder about his academic ability in the context of his college experience. With his modest high school performance and his recent brain injury, does Jake have the academic ability he needs to succeed in college? His standardized test scores suggest that he does, but test scores are far from perfect predictors of college achievement. Does the college have a learning resource center where he can be assessed for a possible learning disorder and receive help if he needs it?

Sixth, it seems clear that there are substance abuse issues that ought to be considered. Jake has used and abused various substances, and he seems to deny the seriousness of this even after mandatory time in an Alcoholics Anonymous (AA) group during his medical rehabilitation. Could his substance use be an effort to cope with the trauma and depression he faces?

Seventh, there are diversity issues to consider here.[3] What sort of socioeconomic background does Jake have, and how does his background affect his experience at a Christian college, which presumably comprises middle- and upper-middle-class young adults? How does Jake perceive women? What is it like for Jake to be several years older than other new students at the college he attends? What, if anything, should be made of Jake's "strange bond" to his military bunkmate? Is Jake offering a cloaked allusion to an experience of same-sex attraction?

Eighth, I want to explore the nature of his relationships with others. He seems somewhat socially anxious, at least in the Christian college context, and he may respond by isolating himself at times. Social isolation coupled with a brain injury may compromise his social judgment when he is around others.

Ninth, I am concerned about the possibility of an emerging personality disorder. With this, I am referring to a category of disorder in the *Diagnostic and Statistical Manual*, currently in its fourth edition (DSM-IV-TR; American Psychiatric Association, 2000) and soon to be released in its fifth edition. Not all authors in this volume are comfortable using the

---

[3] I appreciate the input of my colleague Dr. Winston Seegobin regarding the diversity issues presented in this case example.

DSM to categorize psychological disorders, and while I concur that any taxonomy system can be misused, I find it quite a useful tool to conceptualize clients, guide treatment and communicate with other professionals. Still, I don't find the *DSM* particularly useful in describing the human condition. It is a tool—a useful one, in my opinion—but should not be mistaken for an authoritative guide to human struggle or flourishing. For these purposes, an integration approach goes to Scripture and the riches of our Christian tradition.

Jake may have met *DSM* criteria for conduct disorder during his teenage years, which heightens his risk of antisocial personality disorder during adulthood. Those with antisocial personality disorder seem to lack remorse for their deeds, and they seek their own pleasure at the expense of others. Jake's dismissive attitude toward the college woman who complained about his being sexually aggressive fits this possibility, though many other explanations are possible as well. A personality disorder is a serious diagnosis that may carry implications for a client's future, and I would not make it without compelling evidence.

Tenth, I am interested in Jake's experience of hope. The Christian faith calls us to hope amidst struggle (e.g., Romans 5:3-5). Though psychologists study hopelessness more than hope, in Jake's case I find hope much more interesting. At times he seems to have unrealistic hopes, such as seeing college as an automatic ticket to the middle class, but at other times he seems to lack hope: "If I can't make it here, I really have no place to go. I might as well get blown into oblivion." What is the source of Jake's hope? He tends to view God as owing him a way to escape his problems, rather than seeing a deep sense of hope in God's loving and redeeming character. This cannot be confronted directly in therapy because hope cannot be mustered by willpower. As Jake grows in self-awareness, he might also progress in the Christian journey toward trusting God's goodness in the midst of life struggles, and this will produce hope: "Not only so, but we also glory in our sufferings, because we know that suffering produces perseverance; perseverance, character; and character, hope. And hope does not put us to shame, because God's love has been poured out into our hearts through the Holy Spirit, who has been given to us" (Romans 5:3-5 NIV).

Assessment

In *Psychology, Theology, and Spirituality in Christian Counseling* (McMinn, 2011), I suggest three dimensions related to Christian mental health care. The first is a healthy sense of self. Do I know myself well? Am I aware of my thoughts, feelings, motives, inner conflicts, struggles, desires and hopes? Second is an awareness of our human brokenness. Christianity teaches us that all creation is fallen, all of us tainted by the pervasive influence of sin. With regard to health, am I humble enough to see myself as fallible, vulnerable, capable of making mistakes and hurting others? Do I accept responsibility and apologize when I hurt others? Do I try to grow and become more and more the person God wants me to be? The third dimension of health pertains to relationships. Do I fill my life with rewarding and close relationships? In all three of these dimensions, it seems that Jake has some level of health, but also has work to do.

Sense of self. We see evidence that Jake has some sense of himself. He has enough confidence and self-awareness to be quite clear and honest about his faith-related questions. He also is able to talk about his difficult military experiences—something that not every veteran is willing to do. Also, he seems forthcoming, willing to talk about matters quite directly and openly.

Even with these positives, I am concerned about Jake's self-awareness. He seems somewhat defensive and self-protective, and at times quite self-absorbed. Rather than seeing his own behavior as the obstacle to getting back together with his former girlfriend, he projects the blame on his ex-girlfriend's family, suggesting that they are not doing the Christian "thing" of forgiving and forgetting. He seems to minimize his substance abuse problems. Jake's views of God also seem quite self-serving.

Awareness of brokenness. Jake has made modest progress in the second dimension of health—awareness of his brokenness. His nominal return to faith signals some personal insight about his need for someone greater than himself. Also, he reached out and came to the counseling center for help, which suggests a measure of humility in recognizing that he has needs he cannot meet on his own.

That said, there is also ample evidence that Jake does not fully understand his complicity in his life problems. His faith seems somewhat superficial. He is not so interested in humbling himself before a majestic God as he is in benefiting from the power that God can wield. He minimizes the degree of problem that his substance abuse is causing, and his own role in driving away his former girlfriend. The recent incident with a college woman may also reflect a high level of defense and denial on Jake's part, though the circumstances of that event are not clear.

Highly defensive clients are generally not good candidates for counseling or psychotherapy. While it is important for his counselor to offer Jake hope, I would ask the counselor to avoid making assurances that counseling will bring about dramatic changes in Jake's life. Counseling may or may not be helpful for him, depending to a great extent on whether Jake ever feels safe enough to let down his guard and begin looking honestly at himself.

Relationships. The good news is that Jake yearns for relationships. He feels isolated at school, looks back to the "good old days" when he had a tight-knit squad in the military, and desires to be reconnected with his former girlfriend. Also, he reached out for counseling. All these suggest that he sees himself as a relational being and that he wants to find meaningful connections with others.

However, we don't see much evidence that Jake is skilled at deep, meaningful relationships. From the information available at this point, it seems that his past friendships have revolved around pleasure seeking, and he appears to be quite self-focused in how he perceives God and others. He may be manipulative at times to get his way, such as when he wanted Cheryl, his counselor, to contact his former girlfriend's family, and then became morose when Cheryl hesitated. The most wholesome relationships require that both parties have developed a sense of self and are able to see themselves as flawed, broken human beings. These are areas of struggle for Jake, so it is not surprising that most of the relationships in his life seem to be fleeting and relatively superficial.

Further assessment. My views of Jake's health should, at this point, be considered musings based on a limited case study. If I were consulting in Jake's care, I would want to do a more systematic assessment, remaining open to alternative ways of viewing Jake and his circumstances. Thorough assessment would involve a sincere and sustained effort to get past medical records, referring him for a neuropsychological evaluation, personality testing, understanding diversity, and assessment of spiritual and religious identity.

The case description states, "Jake has not been cooperative with ob-taining any medical or psychiatric records." These records need to be ob-tained, and getting them should probably not have been Jake's responsi-bility in the first place. The counselor needs to have Jake sign an authorization form to request the records, and then the counselor should contact former providers to get records. This is an urgent matter because it is essential to know about past test results, diagnoses and treatment out-comes for Jake.

One reason for obtaining records is to determine which tests have al-ready been conducted since the time of his head injury. Has he already had a careful medical workup? Has he had a neuropsychological evaluation to determine the functional deficits of his injury? If not, he should be referred for a neuropsychological evaluation now to determine his current intel-lectual abilities as well as lasting effects his injury may be having on the skills required to succeed in school and in social relationships.

Throughout the centuries Christians have sometimes been guilty of gnostic views of the world. That is, we elevate immaterial spiritual knowledge above the material nature of our existence. Recently I passed by a church that had this sign out front: "We are not human beings on a spiritual journey; we are spirits on a human journey." Inwardly, I muttered about the heresy inherent in such a message. We are indeed human beings, embodied souls whose physicality matters, looking forward to a day when we have new bodies and live in a new heaven and new earth. The incar-nation—and indeed, all of Scripture—argues against gnostic views. Ma-teriality matters. Jake's brain function is important to understand.

I would also like to see some personality testing with Jake. If he has not had a personality evaluation in the recent past, I would administer the Minnesota Multiphasic Personality Inventory, second edition, restructured format (MMPI-2-RF); the Rotter Incomplete Sentence Blank (RISB); the Young Schema Questionnaire, third edition (YSQ-3); the Beck Depression Inventory, second edition (BDI-II); and the Beck Anxiety Inventory (BAI). I would also conduct a careful diagnostic interview.

Regarding diversity, I wonder what it feels like for Jake to be "dif-ferent" in the context of a Christian college. As rapport develops in counseling, I would ask his counselor to pursue this. What does it feel like for Jake to be older than other students? What sort of socioeconomic background does Jake have, and how does that feel to him in relation to students who presumably come from relative affluence? If Jake's counselor is a person of color, it would also be good to explore how the ethnic differences between counselor and client might feel to Jake as he grows to trust the counseling process.

In addition to personality testing and understanding diversity, I would like to know about his religious and spiritual perspectives on life. He expresses some faith commitment, but it appears to be nominal and relatively superficial. It would be useful to administer the Religious Commitment Inventory (Worthington et al., 2003) and the Spiritual Assessment Inventory (Hall & Edwards, 2002) in order to determine the depth of his faith commitments and the way he views God.

Case Conceptualization

In *Integrative Psychotherapy* (McMinn & Campbell, 2007), Clark Campbell and I discuss the relationship between assessment and case conceptualization, as illustrated in figure 4.1. Assessment is a set of activities designed to learn more about the client, and is less theoretically bound than case conceptualization. The counselor views the information gleaned from the assessment through his or her theoretical lens, and then conceptualizes the case. Notice also the backward arrow in figure 4.1, which indicates that no counselor can be completely objective in assessing clients. Our theoretical assumptions influence the questions we ask and the assessment methods we use. Still, it is safe to say that assessment is less theory-bound than case conceptualization.

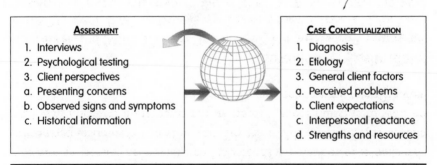

Figure 4.1. Assessment, Theory and Case Conceptualization.
Adapted from McMinn & Campbell (2007). Used by permission.

Because case conceptualization is theory-bound, the next portion of this chapter introduces my theoretical perspective on counseling and psychotherapy. In doing this, I am offering only one theoretical perspective on how integration looks. Others in the integration tradition may have very different ways of conceptualizing Jake.

Integrative Psychotherapy

Integrative Psychotherapy (McMinn & Campbell, 2007) begins with the theological assertion that humans are created in God's image (Genesis 1:26-28), the imago Dei. Philosophers, biblical scholars and theologians have typically understood the imago Dei in one or more of three ways (Erickson, 1985). Jones (2010) refers to these in his *Five Views* chapter, correctly noting that these are not mutually exclusive and that all have merit.

Functional. Functional perspectives on the image of God emphasize that humans are given certain responsibilities that the rest of the animal kingdom does not share. After creating humans, "God blessed them and told them, 'Multiply and fill the earth and subdue it. Be masters over the fish and birds and all the animals'" (Genesis 1:28 NLT). Humans do a better job managing the world around them than dogs would do, or chimpanzees or any other living creature. This managerial capacity that humans have reflects—however faintly—the image of God.

Jake, created in God's image, manages tasks in his daily life. He needs to function in particular ways, and as one created in God's image he is capable of doing so. For example, he needs to figure out how to manage the demands of school, how to cope with his feelings of anxiety and depression, how to deal with urges for alcohol and illegal substances, how to form cooperative relationships with others. Jake is not merely a victim to his impulses; he is an image bearer, one who is capable of functioning in a more effective way than he is currently functioning.

In *Integrative Psychotherapy* (McMinn & Campbell, 2007), functional interventions are typically aimed at changing symptoms, and are therefore called *symptom-focused strategies*. Behavioral and cognitive-behavioral strategies in psychology are often valuable tools in helping people function more effectively and responsibly. I discuss symptom-focused strategies for working with Jake later in the chapter.

Structural or substantive. Another tradition emphasizes the ontological nature of the imago Dei. There is something about being human that is fundamentally different from being a cat or a gopher or a deer. Most often philosophers and theologians emphasize our human capacity to be rational and to make moral choices. It would do little good for a cat to become convicted about eating food from the dog's food bowl and try to make a change in behavior, because cats lack the rational and moral capacity to do such a thing. But Jake, made in God's image, can make deliberate changes in his life if he chooses to do so.

More than just having rational and moral capacity, we humans actively make meaning of our lives. We each tell our story even as we live it. Only humans reminisce about childhood days, set goals for the future, place their faith in a divine being and anticipate their own death. How we make meaning in life has both spiritual and psychological implications.

Jake is living out a particular story, no doubt influenced by past trauma. In counseling, it will be important to explore how he tells the story of his life, with the goal of helping him restructure his story into one with deeper faith experiences, more hope for the future and healthier relationships. Because structural interventions in integrative psychotherapy (McMinn & Campbell, 2007) consider the schemas (i.e., meaning-making structures) used by the client, they are called *schema-focused strategies.*

Relational. A relational view of the imago Dei is strikingly different from either the functional or structural view. With functional and structural views, a human individual carries the image of God—the image is contained within a person. But the relational view, which emerges out of the work of twentieth-century Swiss theologian Karl Barth (1958) and others in the neo-orthodox movement, suggests that the image is not contained in an individual, but in relationship. It's not so much that Jake carries the image, or that his counselor carries the image, but rather when Jake and his counselor interact, they reflect God's relational image.

The relational view of the imago Dei has clear implications for counseling. The intimate, caring, genuine, confiding, accepting nature of a counseling relationship reveals something of God's abiding, steady, loving presence with humanity. From this perspective, Jake will change not because of therapeutic techniques or strategies but because of his relationship with his counselor.

A theological view of health. One might ask why I, a psychologist, suggest the theological notion of the imago Dei for understanding psychological health. Every theory in psychology asserts some state of health and un-health, and it seems reasonable for Christians to look to biblical and theo-logical wisdom for this. If brilliant Christian philosophers and theologians have mused over the imago Dei for all these centuries, then we ought to pay attention to what they have to offer. My assumption is that God is bigger than every human system, including functional, structural and relational views of the imago Dei, but that these formulations of God's image reflect our best Christian efforts to know what a fully functioning human looks like. So in the counseling office, as I attempt to help people come to a place of well-being, I ought to pay attention to what our Christian tradition has to offer in defining health. Many of the treatment methods I use come from psychology, and I find the *DSM* a useful way to communicate with other professionals who may not share my faith beliefs, but I believe the essence of health is best understood from this theological vantage point.

It is interesting to see that psychology also has functional, structural and relational perspectives on treatment. This does not surprise me because one does not need to profess Christianity to discover parts of God's truth.

The process of addressing functional, structural and relational issues. Initial efforts in counseling with Jake should be functional, symptom-fo-cused strategies. Like most clients, Jake came with particular problems he wants to have addressed. He is concerned about his class performance, fitting in at college and perhaps about feelings of depression. I am con-cerned about trauma and patterns of substance use, though it is not clear if Jake is concerned about this or not. These are all functional concerns, and will be the primary focus early in treatment.

Beyond these functional issues, pressing structural issues call for schema-focused methods if Jake persists long enough. How does he tell his story—where he has been, and where he is going? Although we do not yet know much about Jake's schemas (his ways of understanding and making meaning of life), it seems likely that he feels quite alone and isolated. Imagine a 10-year-old wandering through the house after a day at school, looking for his father, and then seeing the horrifying sight of his father dead on the bathroom floor, blood streaming from his mouth and nose. At that moment, Jake must have felt profoundly alone, left to survive in a complex world without substantial connection with other family members. It is telling that his mother left Jake alone and let him make his own decisions after his father's death. She was probably traumatized herself and didn't know how to handle a rambunctious 10-year-old son, but her aloofness no doubt contributed to Jake's feeling isolated in a complicated and unpredictable world. In high school he made connections through partying, and he had at least one meaningful relationship with his girlfriend, Missy, but that relationship has now disappeared, and Jake has not even met the child that he may have fathered. Even his understanding of God seems to presume that God is distant and uncaring, evidenced in his mind by God's not giving Jake the life he wants.

Jake may not want to talk about his schemas in the early parts of counseling, both because it requires a good deal of trust to be this vulnerable with his counselor, and because he may not be fully aware of his underlying schemas. It will take time, trust and an effective counselor for Jake to open up to these structural issues in counseling. Sometimes clients start feeling better after the functional issues are addressed, and then they stop coming to sessions. Jake will be prone to do this because he is quite alone in the world, and it will be hard for him to trust another person with the experiences and perceptions that make him feel most vulnerable. If the counselor is able to engage Jake beyond the first few sessions of counseling, then they are likely to move into this structural realm of intervention.

The relational domain of intervention needs to be considered throughout the entire treatment process. Jake is likely to participate in relational patterns that occur time and time again, known as Cyclical Maladaptive Patterns (Levenson, 1995). These patterns may occur without Jake's conscious awareness. As with the structural domain, this will require some good clinical perception on the part of the counselor to figure out what these relational patterns are, and then to engage in a relationship that forces Jake out of his typical cycle. We do not know enough to be certain about his relational patterns, but I suspect that he has a knack for disengaging, or even pushing people away, when he starts to feel vulnerably close. Jake's father was gone or emotionally absent at first, and then dead. His mother was aloof, especially after Jake's father died. Jake longed for intimacy, but ended up feeling abandoned. However painful this felt, it became familiar for Jake, and now he may avoid the fear of abandonment by keeping people at a distance.

When he had an intimate relationship in high school, he risked his relationship with Missy—and eventually sabotaged it—by leading a duplicitous life. His relationship with his bunkmate in the Army is not clear, but it will be important to see what sort of relational dynamics occurred there. Do his inaccurate flashbacks of his buddy being in the helicopter have something to do with fears of his friend abandoning him too? Even his relationship with Cheryl, his first counselor, seems to fit this same pattern. Cheryl seemed happy providing counseling for him when she thought Jake would just be another case of the college blues, but soon Jake started making unrealistic requests (e.g., his request for Cheryl to contact Missy's family) and revealing what a difficult client he could be (e.g., substance abuse, a thinly veiled suicidal threat, allegations of sexual inappropriateness with a college woman). Shortly thereafter, Cheryl had a shift in responsibilities, abandoning Jake again. Jake's next counselor needs to recognize the relational dynamics at play and remain available to Jake throughout the entire course of counseling.

Treatment Plan and Techniques

Treatment relationship. Whatever treatment plan is used with Jake, it is important in working with him to first emphasize the role of empathy, genuineness and positive regard. Most psychotherapists and counselors no longer perceive these to be sufficient for effective counseling, as Carl Rogers (1957) did, but they are necessary. Jake has some behavioral and cognitive patterns that might easily annoy a counselor, such as downplaying his substance abuse problems, not taking full responsibility for his moral shortcomings, making derogatory and unfair comments about God, and so on. Is the counselor able to overcome these annoyances and genuinely like and care about Jake? If not, counseling is not likely to be successful. Romans 15:7 reads, "So accept each other just as Christ has accepted you; then God will be glorified" (NLT). This is our mandate as Christians, and even if none of us is fully able to accept another as thoroughly as Christ has accepted us, counseling is not effective if we do not aspire toward this goal.

Functional perspectives. As mentioned earlier, the treatment plan should begin with Jake's functional concerns. He initially came for help because of troubles completing his class assignments. Some combination of behavioral and cognitive-behavioral strategies may be helpful to Jake. Before introducing these strategies, though, his counselor should receive and review his medical records. It is possible that neurological impairment is affecting his classroom performance, in which case he will benefit from cognitive rehabilitation as well as psychotherapy. He should also be referred to a psychiatrist for a consultation because he has been prescribed medications that he is not taking regularly. This irregular use of medications might be affecting his mood, thoughts and behavior. The counselor should have a direct conversation with the psychiatrist, after getting Jake's authorization to do so.

Several functional strategies emerging from scientific psychology may be useful for Jake. The Premack Principle holds that low-probability behaviors (studying, in Jake's case) can be paired with high-probability behaviors (computer games, for example) to increase the likelihood of low-probability behaviors (Premack, 1959). So, for example, he might try studying for an hour before giving himself permission to play an online game. Over time, the study time might be increased to two hours. This will require compliance and motivation on Jake's part, which could be a challenge.

He might also try writing down a summary of his activities throughout a typical week, with the goal of monitoring how much he studies. Even the act of monitoring tends to increase the target behavior (studying, in this case). Once he has monitored for a week or two, he might then set goals for increasing study time in future weeks.

At this point, it is not clear how much motivation Jake has to make changes in his life. Motivational interviewing might be used to help prepare him for change (Miller & Rollnick, 2002). In motivational interviewing, the counselor helps Jake confront his ambivalence for change, perhaps by thinking through the consequences of how he is currently living, and then to consider how a different set of choices might impact his life.

Jake's trauma also needs to be treated. Though addressing trauma was not his explicit goal when coming for counseling, Jake talked a fair amount about trauma and the implications of trauma in his five sessions with Cheryl. His difficulty sleeping, for example, seems clearly related to efforts to avoid traumatic memories. It is also possible that much of his substance abuse might be related to trauma—both recently and in the distant past. Sometimes people turn to substances to escape from the pain of past memories, making it especially difficult to change the substance abuse behaviors if the trauma is untreated. There are several effective ways to treat trauma, with two of the best being Prolonged Exposure (PE) and Cognitive Processing Therapy (CPT) (Resick, Monson & Rizvi, 2008). In PE, just as the name implies, the client is asked to recount the details of past events in great detail after first learning systematic breathing and relaxation skills. The idea is to relive the experiences as if they are currently happening. Rather than pushing back the images and memories, as Jake is now doing, he would be encouraged to let them come forward in his consciousness, to remember them as fully as possible. Though this deliberate exposure to trauma can be difficult for clients, it can also help free them from the frantic efforts to push back the memories. CPT also involves exposure, but by writing about the trauma more than speaking about it. The client and counselor then consider how the trauma may have affected the client's way of looking at the world. Does Jake blame himself for his father's death? Does he experience guilt that he was not on that helicopter? The point of CPT is to make cognitive and emotional connections as the client reevaluates traumatic experiences.

An additional functional concern is his suicide risk. This needs to be assessed early and often in the treatment relationship. One tool used to assess risk is an acronym known as SAD PERSONS (Patterson, Dohn, Bird & Patterson, 1983).

S = Sex (males are at more risk than females). Jake is, of course, male.

A = Age (some age groups are at more risk than others). At age 22, Jake is in an age group with elevated risk.

D = Depression (depressed individuals are at a much higher risk than others). We do not know if Jake has been diagnosed with depression because we have not seen his medical records, but this seems likely in terms of his current symptom patterns.

P = Prior History (most suicides are preceded by an unsuccessful attempt). We do not know if Jake has attempted suicide, but this should be assessed.

E = Ethanol Abuse (those who use alcohol in excess are at an elevated risk). This is clearly a warning sign for Jake.

R = Rational Thinking Loss (psychotic individuals are at high risk for suicide). Jake does not appear to have any signs of psychosis.

S = Support System Loss (a loss of a significant relationship can precipitate suicide attempts). Jake seems quite alone and feels a poignant
sense of loss in his relationship with Missy.

O = Organized Plan (those with a plan are at higher risk than others).
This is not clear in Jake's case, but it is important to ask what he
meant when he said that he "might as well get blown into oblivion."
Does he have access to explosives? Has he considered a plan for how
he might kill himself or others?

N = No Significant Other (those who feel all alone are at greater risk for
suicide). It is difficult to know what sort of connections Jake has
maintained with Army buddies, but otherwise it appears that he is
quite isolated from others. His relationship with his counselor might
be essential for him to maintain some sense of hope.

S = Sickness (those with chronic illness are much more likely to commit
suicide than others). Jake's head injury is a sort of chronic illness that
may hinder his sense of hope for the future.

Based on the SAD PERSONS test, Jake appears to be at risk for suicide.
This should be discussed explicitly in counseling and assessed routinely.
It is possible that Jake will need to be hospitalized if the risk of suicide
seems imminent.

Structural perspectives. If Jake and his counselor are able to establish
rapport, and if the functional interventions help to relieve some of Jake's
immediate symptoms, then it is likely the treatment focus will shift toward
the ways Jake interprets and makes meaning of the world. We cannot
know exactly how this might look in therapy, of course, but for the sake of
illustration I will proceed with the assumption that he feels quite isolated
and alone in the world, expecting to be abandoned by those closest to him.

It is beyond the scope of this chapter to describe schema-focused therapy
in detail, but the general strategy used in *Integrative Psychotherapy*
(McMinn & Campbell, 2007) is called Recursive Schema Activation
(RSA). Whereas the earlier generations of behavioral and cognitive-
behavioral therapy tended to assume that faulty schemas could be identified
and replaced with more adaptive schemas, the so-called third wave of
cognitive-behavior therapy calls for greater acceptance and understanding
of the schemas that are most persistent and troubling (McMinn, Jones,

Vogel & Butman, 2011). Rather than trying to utterly obliterate a troubling schema, perhaps it is better to learn from it. With time, the client gains some critical distance from the old schema and learns to view life through a different set of lenses.

Jake seems to have a belief that he is alone and bound to be abandoned. Rather than trying to convince Jake that this is not the case—that people really do love and care about him, after all—perhaps it is better to listen and learn from Jake's life. How did he come to view life in this way? What was it like for him to grow up in a home with marital strife, and then his father's premature death? How did his mother's zeal for faith affect Jake and his way of understanding himself in relation to a complex world? How did his military experience feel to him with regard to social connections and isolation? To what extent has his socioeconomic background influenced his connections with others at the Christian college? What sort of relational future does Jake anticipate? What does he hope for? Rather than simply trying to rid Jake of his schema, the notion of RSA is to help Jake understand and evaluate the schemas that influence how he makes meaning of the world.

RSA is recursive in that the counselor repeatedly brings the client back to the same schema to explore and discover its meaning. Schemas are resistant to change, and they operate both consciously and unconsciously, making it important for the counselor and client to return to the schemas over and over again. This requires a degree of creativity so that it does not seem that every session is the same. Rather, the counselor helps Jake take the material from the present moment and connect it with the underlying schemas that are being considered. For example:

SESSION 1 (EARLY IN THE SESSION)

Jake: I don't know why, but Cheryl said she couldn't see me anymore. She sent me to talk to you instead.

Counselor: That must have felt disappointing.

Here the counselor offers a statement sometimes referred to as "advanced accurate empathy," while also hinting at Jake's underlying schema—that he will be abandoned.

SESSION 1 (LATER IN THE SESSION)

Jake: There is so much religion in this school, which is cool, I guess, but I don't understand why everyone acts like God will hold their hands and take care of everything. These guys haven't seen how awful the world can be.

Counselor: It feels like God has left you to figure everything out on your own.

This is a simple reflection, but it points toward Jake's underlying schema. Rather than trying to engage in a theological conversation here, it is better to simply place Jake's schema in front of him so he can see how it operates in his life.

SESSION 2

Counselor: How is dorm life going?

Jake: About the same. Mostly I keep to myself, you know, play video games and stuff.

Counselor: I wonder if keeping to yourself feels safer than relationships feel.

This is a more direct reference to Jake's schema, but again one to keep him thinking about how he interprets the world.

SESSION 6

Jake: You seem to think that I like being alone.

Counselor: That's an interesting observation. Tell me more.

Jake: Well, you keep saying that I'm scared of relationships and stuff.

Counselor: How would that relate to being alone?

Jake: You know, like I keep to myself because others will hurt me or something.

Counselor: Let's sit with that a minute. How does it feel when you say it?

Jake: I don't know. I've been thinking about it though. Sometimes I wish I had better friends, or like a close relationship with a parent or something. Missy means so much to me, but she won't even return my calls. No one on my floor even cares if I'm alive or dead.

Counselor: This feeling you're having right now—feeling alone—is that new or old? Is that a feeling that you remember having years ago?

Jake: I guess.

Counselor: [Sits silently.]

Jake: [Tears in eyes.] I've been alone for a long time.

Counselor: [Nods. Continues sitting silently.]

Again, the counselor is returning to the schema. Rather than chasing the suicide threat, which will need to be discussed in a few moments, the counselor brings Jake back to his schema. Jake's tears indicate the schema is fully activated.

Schema activation in RSA means that the client is engaged affectively and relationally as well as cognitively. The goal of schema-oriented counseling, then, is to identify and activate schemas over and over until the client can begin to construct a new way of understanding life.

It is important to recognize that schemas exist because they once worked well. They now cause problems because they are no longer working well. In Jake's situation, his self-protective schema of anticipating abandonment may have been a useful way to cope after finding his dead father, but now in his early 20s, faced with the developmental task of forming lasting, intimate relationships, his schema is not working well. It will be helpful for him to discover this in counseling, recognizing that his old schema is not foolish or stupid, but that the time of its usefulness has passed.

I find the Pauline notion of an old self and a new self a useful metaphor when thinking of RSA (e.g., Ephesians 4; 6; Colossians 3). The idea is for Jake to develop a new vantage point for looking at his life: the new self views the old self. The old self may never be entirely removed, but as the new self grows in strength and confidence, Jake will be able to make better decisions and grow toward psychological and spiritual health.

Relational perspectives. The relational dimension of integrative psychotherapy (McMinn & Campbell, 2007) informs the way the counselor interacts with Jake. This is closely related to the notion of schemas because the counselor should treat Jake in ways that cause him to reevaluate old schemas. If Jake fears abandonment, it will be important for the counselor to communicate stability in the counseling relationship. In order to move forward, Jake needs to feel safe, to know that he can come to counseling as long as he desires.

Jake's past and current relationships with others are also considered in the relational domain. As Jake starts to make improvements and develop friendships with his peers and mentors, to what extent do these relationships replay his roles in prior relationships, and with what effect? Ideally, Jake will learn to be a student of how he relates to others, and to find ways of establishing healthy, mutually satisfying relationships. In the process, he may also come to see God differently. Rather than God being distant and aloof, Jake may eventually come to see God as loving and present amid the messy and difficult parts of life. If so, this could become an enormous source of hope and resilience for Jake while also helping him understand God better.

Evaluation and Follow-Up Care

There are three potential exit points in integrative psychotherapy (McMinn & Campbell, 2007). Some clients decide to stop counseling after functional concerns are addressed. This is a legitimate endpoint in counseling, even if deeper issues of schemas and spiritual matters are never addressed explicitly. Just as Christ devoted a good deal of his ministry to the physical and health needs of individuals, health care providers can legitimately treat the emotional and psychological needs of clients. Jake may choose to stop counseling once he feels less depressed and is doing better in school.

Perhaps in the process of addressing functional concerns, Jake will become engaged enough in counseling that he persists through a schema-focused phase of treatment. If so, it may well have positive implications for how he understands himself and others. Beyond treating his present symptoms, a schema-based intervention will help him gain insight into his areas of vulnerability and be more intentional about his life choices. This, in turn, may help him live a life more pleasing to God, and one that brings greater hope for his future. Once this schema-focused work has proven effective, Jake and his counselor may elect to stop counseling.

If symptom-focused work takes weeks, and schema-focused work takes months, some clients decide to engage in longer-term relational work that may take many months or several years. This involves a more intensive look at past and present relationships in the client's life as the client builds bridges between past and present relational patterns and works toward enhanced self-understanding in the process. Long-term therapy is unusual in a college counseling center context, and at least at first glance Jake does not appear to be introspective and insightful enough to be interested in long-term therapy. Still, it may be therapeutic for Jake to know up front that long-term counseling is available to him, because knowing this might help him relax his fears of abandonment from the counselor. It seems unlikely he will engage in long-term counseling, but just knowing it is available may help him do better in short- or moderate-term counseling.

It is wise to enter a maintenance phase in counseling before termination. If Jake is being seen weekly for most of the counseling, then he might be scheduled for every second or third week during the maintenance phase. After several maintenance sessions, it would be good to schedule a follow-up appointment in two or three months to see how he is doing.

It should also be noted that counseling is not the only option for Jake. Becoming involved in a church-based support group, a campus ministry or a mentoring relationship may be alternatives and/or adjuncts to counseling. There are various ways to grow emotionally and spiritually, with counseling being only one of them.

Conclusion

This approach to counseling and psychotherapy is described more fully in *Integrative Psychotherapy* (McMinn & Campbell, 2007) and demonstrated in a DVD published by the American Psychological Association (Carlson, 2006). As with any approach to counseling or psychotherapy, it requires graduate-level training and advanced supervision before a counselor should be considered qualified. Counseling can bring great hope and healing to a person's life, but it can also do substantial damage; therefore, it is important to receive excellent education and supervision prior to launching a counseling career.

I appreciate the case-oriented nature of this book, in part because it offers a practical glimpse into the work of Christian counselors and psychotherapists. Jake would be a challenging client, but his is a good case for this book because of the multifaceted nature of his presenting problems. Readers have opportunity to see different counseling approaches applied to clinical issues such as substance abuse, trauma, perceptions of God, depression, suicide, childhood relationships and so on.

That said, I also find it difficult to describe my approach to counseling with any particular case, especially in a single chapter of a book. Counseling is art as well as science, and as art it takes many years to master. Several months ago I spent 10 minutes in silence with a client because words simply seemed cheap amid the depth of pain he was experiencing. Those 10 minutes became pivotal in therapy, as he settled into a place of safety with me, knowing that I wasn't going to trivialize his pain or imply that I could fix him with five new principles for living. Even as an experienced writer, I'm not sure such a counseling experience could be captured in a book chapter or a book or even a series of books. Some things that happen in the counseling office defy theoretical description. They come from the movement of the Holy Spirit, stirring in the lives of counselor and client. May all our theories and book chapters and musings about what makes counseling work always leave room for the work of the Spirit.

References

American Psychiatric Association. (2000). *Diagnostic and statistical manual of mental disorders* (4th ed., text rev.). Washington, DC: American Psychiatric Association.

Barth, K. (1958). *Church dogmatics* (Vol. 3, Part 1; J. W. Edwards, O. Bussey & H. Knight, Trans.). Edinburgh: T & T Clark.

Carlson, J. (2006). *Christian counseling with Mark R. McMinn* [DVD in APA Psychotherapy Video Series]. Washington, DC: American Psychological Association.

Erickson, M. J. (1985). *Christian theology*. Grand Rapids: Baker.

Hall, T. W., & Edwards, K. J. (2002). The spiritual assessment inventory: A theistic model and measure for assessing spiritual development. *Journal for the Scientific Study of Religion, 41,* 341-57.

Jones, S. (2010). An integration approach. In E. L. Johnson (Ed.), *Psychology & Christianity: Five views* (2nd ed., pp. 101-28). Downers Grove, IL: IVP Academic.

Jones, S., & Butman, R. (1991). *Modern psychotherapies: A comprehensive Christian appraisal*. Downers Grove, IL: IVP Academic.

Levenson, H. (1995). *Time-limited dynamic psychotherapy: A guide to clinical practice*. New York: Basic Books.

McMinn, M. R. (2011). *Psychology, theology, and spirituality in Christian counseling* (updated edition). Wheaton, IL: Tyndale.

McMinn, M. R., & Campbell, C. D. (2007). *Integrative psychotherapy: Toward a comprehensive Christian approach*. Downers Grove, IL: IVP Academic.

McMinn, M. R., Jones, S. L., Vogel, M. J., & Butman, R. E. (2011). Cognitive Therapy. In S. L. Jones & R. E. Butman, *Modern psychotherapies: A comprehensive Christian appraisal* (2nd ed., pp. 201-60). Downers Grove, IL: IVP Academic.

Miller, W. R., & Rollnick, S. (2002). *Motivational interviewing: Preparing people for change*. New York: Guilford.

Patterson, W. M., Dohn, H. H., Bird, J., & Patterson, G. A. (1983). Evaluation of suicidal patients: The SAD PERSONS scale. *Psychosomatics, 24,* 343-49.

Premack, D. (1959). Toward empirical behavioral laws: I. Positive reinforcement. *Psychological Review, 66,* 219-33.

Resick, P. A., Monson, C. M., & Rizvi, S. L. (2008). Posttraumatic stress disorder. In D. H. Barlow (Ed.), *Clinical handbook of psychological disorders* (4th ed., pp. 65-122). New York: Guilford.

Rogers, C. R. (1957). The necessary and sufficient conditions of therapeutic personality change. *Journal of Consulting Psychology, 21,* 95-103.

Smith, C., & Denton, M. L. (2005). *Soul searching: The religious and spiritual lives of American teenagers*. New York: Oxford University Press.

Worthington, E. L., Jr., Wade, N. G., Hight, T. R., Ripley, J. S., McCullough, M. E., Berry, J. W., . . . O'Connor, L. (2003). The Religious Commitment Inventory-10: Development, refinement, and validation of a brief scale for research and counseling. *Journal of Counseling and Psychology, 50,* 84-96.

5

A Christian Psychology Approach

Diane Langberg

LEARNING OBJECTIVES

- *Describe how the priority of representing the character of Christ guides the practice of the therapist and the overall helping relationship.*
- *Analyze how clinical research and the three-phase model for working with victims of trauma are used in treatment aimed to enhance Jake's Christian faith.*
- *Ponder the admonition that the Spirit of God and his Word must be vibrant and operational on both sides of the helping relationship for the helping to be therapeutic.*

In formulating a response to the case of Jake, it seemed advisable to lay out a couple of presuppositions that are not explicitly stated in most Christian psychology writings. In *Psychology & Christianity: Five Views*, Roberts and Watson (2010) state, "All Christians who work as professionals in psychology should at least be as well versed in the thought of some great Christian psychologist as they are in their own corner of establishment psychology" (p. 174). Recently, McMinn, Staley, Webb and Seegobin (2010), referring to Christian psychologists (members of the Society for Christian Psychology [SCP]), observed: "SCP members seek to uncover the psychology implicit in historic Christian writings, including the Bible. . . . SCP members are interested in psychology, albeit mainly the psychology of the Bible and other Christian historical sources" (p. 394).

Christian psychologists seek to draw their understanding more from these uniquely Christian categories than from modern psychology, though valuing the latter and its methods. The focus is on the philosophy, theology, theory, research, and clinical skills and techniques that constitute a Christian psychology. These are, in fact, all vital components of a Christian psychology. But there is an additional arena worthy of focus and that is the person who is doing the work of a mental health professional (MHP)—a concept I believe to be distinctively Christian and also quite central to the development of a Christian psychology. This holds true whether the MHP is building a theory, formulating a research problem, teaching students or entering into a therapeutic relationship. The therapist is the human tool in the counseling relationship, and it is paramount that the tool be deeply rooted in both God and his Word so that the character demonstrated in the counseling dyad reflects him well.

It is also true that, when engaged in the work of therapy, not only does the person of the therapist assume a central place, but the model that therapist holds of health and wholeness becomes a significant factor in the ensuing interactions. I believe that a true *Christian* psychology is based ultimately on the knowledge and understanding of the personality of the Son of Man, Jesus Christ. We have, in the study of Christ, a rich picture of a whole and healthy human person. We have a study of humans as they are meant to be in this world. My understanding of the human beings who enter my office must be informed by my study of the person of the Son of Man. And if I have studied rightly, then that study should also result in an ongoing transformation into that likeness in me and be evidenced in the actual work of counseling.

One factor involved in this that is so germane to the work of therapy is self-awareness, or truth about oneself. What is seen and known about the self must be daily brought into submission to the person and work of Christ. He alone is truth, wisdom, kindness, patience, justice and mercy. It would be an oxymoron to call oneself a *Christian* psychologist if these characteristics were not developing and seen in the therapist over time. Christian psychologists ought to bear in their person a representation of the character of Christ, and that character must shape the therapist, the client and the relationship between them. Such character traits are fed by such things as worship, study and prayer (for elaboration see Langberg, 1997, especially chapters 24 and 25).

These factors, central to a Christian psychology and its clinical applications, mean first of all that any Christian clinician should be steeped in the knowledge of the Word of God, both written and made flesh in Jesus Christ. He is not only the model of what we are to be; he is also God in the flesh ministering to wounded humanity. Saturation in this eternally living Person, his Word and his life—so that who he is, is worked out into the character, thoughts and life of the clinician—is vital if therapy is to be fully Christian. *That* Christian psychologist then carefully gleans from secular theories, techniques and skills. *That* psychologist reads the historic Christian literature and engages in research. *That* Christian psychologist enters into a therapeutic alliance, listening, waiting, sifting, discerning, asking and responding. *That* Christian psychologist brings the mind of Christ to bear first on one's own self and subsequently on the client in the consulting room, on his or her life story and its difficult places, and the way forward in growth, healing and hopefully an ongoing likeness to Christ. And from this foundation, we turn now to its application in the case of Jake.

Introduction

The primary focus in the beginning of therapy with a new patient is to form an alliance. As I have previously observed (Langberg, 1997, p. 31), "Therapy is first and foremost a relationship." Without that alliance the client is not attached to either the therapist or the therapy process and will probably not stay engaged when things get difficult or feel overwhelming. Forming a relational alliance requires initially hearing the narrative of the client and actively searching for ways to enter into the life and mind of the one before you in an understanding, empathic way. At the outset, therapy is not about diagnosis of difficulties or sin, or simply giving directives for stated problems and expecting the client to come to you actively engaged in dealing with the issues they most want to avoid or eliminate. The therapist must "go in" and sit with and connect with the client so the alliance is experienced as a team of two people on the client's side, facing the issues and finding constructive ways of understanding them and then dealing with them. It is, frankly, incarnational work.

The Word made flesh is God in a body on the ground. He became like us. That is how we know he understands, and that is how we begin to grasp the truths he came to teach us. That is also the beginning point of all therapy. The sitting down with, the listening so as to understand one both like and different from ourselves, the forming hour by hour of a safe and trustworthy relationship is absolutely foundational to the often difficult work of counseling. Without that, we become simply a stranger with academic degrees, knowledge and some level of skill who instructs another human being in how he or she might change. Like our pursuing God, we pursue through listening, through empathy and deep understanding of the person before us. We enter into the client's suffering in a manner similar to Jesus' entering the life and suffering of humanity.

In consulting with the counselor in Jake's case, we note that early on an assumption was made ("a simple case of adjustment to college life"), but there were many clues given from the outset that this was not so simple. It is my experience that young therapists often fail to ask sufficient questions and tend to assume they understand. However, words can be used to camouflage or cloud issues. Clients often want to hide things from themselves. A client may say they feel sad, but without gentle exploration we might never come to understand that "sad" really indicates significant, mind-numbing grief and depression. We need to discover what the words mean experientially to the person using them, and so we ask things like, "What is sadness like for you?"

In considering the counseling relationship with Jake, we see that from the very beginning he is informing us about himself and what we might expect from him. He let us know in the initial session that the stated intention—seeking assistance in getting assignments completed—is in fact not likely to be the central issue, as we shall soon see. In fact, the presenting problem is rarely the central issue in counseling, but merely what the client is comfortable saying out loud to a yet unknown person. Let us look at the important information Jake gave us in his first few sessions.

Initial Impressions

First, Jake made his original appointment with reluctance, so we know from the outset that we have an ambivalent client. We also note ambivalence in the gap between his stated issue and his hints at other issues, such as the cause of a medical discharge and a "history that is messed up." A strong alliance will be critical lest the therapist get caught in the crossfire of his ambivalence. The push-pull of the client will stall treatment as the therapist attempts to explore the competing aspects of the ambivalence unless a strong and viable alliance is created to help override the fears that result in such stuck places. Further, Jake let his counselor know that the "Jesus thing" feels phony, so here is another relationship about which he is expressing ambivalence.

Second, we know from the outset that Jake is a veteran who was medically discharged and needed a long recovery. That information raises many questions: What was his war experience? What degree of trauma was involved? How might that still be affecting him? Why the medical discharge? Is he still struggling with limitations due to injuries received? If so, how might those limitations affect his functioning or his thinking?

Third, in the initial consultation Jake said that "his personal saga was 'pretty messed up.'" That is a very vague way of letting us know there are aspects of his history, prior to his time in the Army, that were complicated and difficult. We will need to know what those factors are, how they impacted and continue to impact him, and what choices he made and is making to cope with them.

Fourth, in his first session he also emphatically informed the counselor that there was no way he would fit in with other students. Jake has let us know he is feeling different, isolated and disconnected. This makes the formation of a therapeutic alliance even more critical as Jake has no current relational base from which to draw. Clearly, many questions must be answered before we have a good understanding of Jake, his struggles, his weaknesses and his strengths. These are not questions with which to barrage him, but rather are ones to be carefully woven into the clinical hours, paced according to his level of comfort and encouraging him to gradually unfold himself to us so we understand something of what it means to be Jake.

The fifth thing we learned is that Jake's stated goal for counseling is to get help completing class assignments. We do not yet know the reasons for his spotty academic history. Though we are beginning to grasp the complexity of this case, we want to affirm his goal and enter into it with him. We also want to communicate our desire for a greater understanding of his life experiences and who he is so that we can, in the best possible way, assist him toward achieving his goals. And finally, Jake has told the counselor he is having great difficulty sitting still in order to study. We do not yet know if this might be anxiety, possible posttraumatic stress disorder

(PTSD), a simple lack of discipline in his life, attention deficit hyperactivity disorder (ADHD) or a traumatic brain injury (TBI). We do know that Jake has exhibited great difficulty staying on task in his counseling. He has talked about many significant issues in his life that have no obvious connection to his stated goal. Clearly, those issues need attention.

In reviewing Cheryl's first session with Jake we realize that the conclusion that this is a simple adjustment to college life is not likely accurate. As we peruse Cheryl's notes further we read about suicidal ideation, impulsivity, significant loss, insomnia, flashbacks, nightmares and substance abuse. We begin to raise questions about possible PTSD. Jake gives some evidence of secondary stress due to the vivid accounts he heard from other vets in the hospital. He speaks of witnessing a horrific accident, the loss of his best buddy and the survivor guilt he carries. His substance abuse increased substantially after that accident, resulting in a brawl and life-threatening head injury, raising questions for us about possible traumatic brain injury. His recall capacity seems compromised, and he has fears about his ability to perform in college, a goal he has chosen in honor of the buddy he lost, so possibly college is in part a way of assuaging his guilt.

Sixth, Jake also talks about attending an Alcoholics Anonymous group as part of his rehabilitation process. He stayed with it, not because he believed he had a substance abuse problem but simply because he liked the chaplain who ran it. This piece of information informs us that Jake was able to do something he initially resisted because of his attachment to the chaplain. It will be important to discover what it was about the man and the relationship that fostered such a bond, and to use that to help build a new therapeutic relationship.

Lastly, in further sessions we learn from Jake's counselor that he grew up in a violent neighborhood, so it is likely he may have witnessed brutality prior to the Army. He lost his alcoholic father at 10, finding him dead on the floor. Jake does not know the cause of death, nor does he tell us of the impact of that death on his life. It seems likely that his father also abused drugs, and Jake probably carries a great sense of shame as he was often told by his mother that he acted like his father. In middle school his academic performance changed dramatically, probably impacted by the death of his father. Jake also has a child he has never seen or supported—another fatherless child.

Here is a summary of initial impressions with Jake. Grief and loss are major themes as he has witnessed death and violence several times in his life. He has had a severe brain injury with probable ongoing effects. He is impulsive, insomniac and inconsistent. He cannot focus or follow through. He seems somewhat concrete in his thinking and demonstrates little insight. Thus, Jake needs to be carefully evaluated for possible posttraumatic stress disorder, traumatic brain injury, substance abuse, depression and anxiety. Jake is highly ambivalent and avoidant. He may be a difficult and erratic client, which again means that a strong alliance is vital. Jake needs to sense that his counselor understands him and is on his side. He has hard work to do if his life is to change. He has many obstacles, and some of those may be irreversible (such as a TBI). His major coping mechanism has been avoidance, both literally and also through the abuse of substances. He appears to be using "religion" in an avoidant way as well, seeming certain he has been healed and so does not have to face the possibility of any limitations from his injury.

Counseling Jake

Jake presents us with a complex case. He is compromised physically, cognitively, relationally, emotionally and spiritually. He is in a tenuous place regarding his position at college. Yet he has also expressed determination to cooperate and progress in counseling. The first few sessions are critical. We will want to join with Jake, letting him know we want to assist him toward his goals and a healthy, productive life. We want to understand what obstacles get in his way and what it is like to be him.

We can also commend him. He has suffered a great deal and is still standing. He was not expected to live, let alone get up and function after the head trauma. He cannot sleep and lives with ongoing nightmares and is still determined to get an education. Jake also has strengths that need to be mustered for progress. We will want to ask him what he thinks those are and how he uses them. We want to find ways to build him up, nurturing what is good and what works for him. Jake is due respect for his commitment to his buddy, his hard work to get back on his feet, his willingness to come for help in achieving his goals. It will be important not to just focus on his pathology. His strengths and limitations *both* need to be understood—his strengths so they can be buttressed and actively used; his limitations so they can be understood and either compensated for or eliminated.

Commending, understanding and bolstering Jake's strengths are particularly important due to his tendency to avoid emotional pain. Whatever resiliency he has will be needed to enable him to face that pain with new ways of coping constructively, otherwise therapy will simply increase his need for and use of avoidance behaviors and the substances he uses to numb himself. We now have a rough outline of categories to pursue in knowing Jake more fully, and more questions than answers to aid us in that pursuit.

Initial Steps

Forming a treatment team. For many clients, a treatment team approach is most profitable. In part, that ensures that the psychotherapist is not the only person walking alongside a struggling human being. The more complex the case, the greater the need for such a team. In Jake's case, a team approach is warranted. In order to set up appropriate care for Jake we need more information, yet Jake has found it difficult to follow through on previous requests for release of that information. We need his records, both medical and psychological, to coordinate with other potential team members. Getting Jake to sign a release and pursuing those records ourselves is likely to be more productive than leaving it to Jake. The university can probably help us discover what assistance is available to Jake as a veteran. The Veterans Administration (VA) will also likely be able to provide support for Jake in covering his care by a psychiatrist, a primary care physician and possibly a neurologist. The VA may also provide financial aid for a tutor who can give him ongoing study support. We will also need to find out if the VA has any nearby support or treatment groups for returning vets, given that Jake lacks community yet bonded intensely with some of his fellow soldiers. Many vets find it helpful to process some of their war experiences in a group with other soldiers. Jake may find this to be a more like-minded group than young college students. The camaraderie may serve as a strengthening influence.

Jake attends a Christian school, and we know he bonded with a chaplain during rehabilitation. Perhaps there is a campus pastor or chaplain who might come alongside Jake as well. He has expressed ambivalence about his faith, and his theology is meager, unclear and somewhat self-serving. It would be hoped that he might connect with another man, such as the chaplain, who could provide support and connection as well as ongoing spiritual nurture that is grounded in the Word of God. Jake is a fatherless man, and the support, encouragement and connection of a stable man of faith will be an excellent supplement to the therapeutic relationship and enable him to persevere in the difficult work of treatment he is facing. It will also nurture his immature faith, as the Christian psychology approach values the biblical stress on community. In addition, it would be likely that the campus pastor might be able to help Jake find a solid local church, perhaps one that has other veterans or retired military among its members. Jake is more likely to find community with others more like him than with college freshmen. If one or more mature Christian men were to come alongside Jake and provide relationship, support and camaraderie, Jake would be much more likely to continue in counseling and profit from it. This would also provide insight for Jake into what it means to be a father, a husband, a man of integrity and a Christian man in real-time relationships.

Trauma history. Jake certainly meets diagnostic criteria for posttraumatic stress disorder (APA, 2000)—he has witnessed more than one event in which the life of someone was threatened and/or destroyed. He has felt fear, helplessness and horror. He continues to experience the trauma anew through nightmares, flashbacks, and psychological and physiological distress. He seeks to defend against reminders through avoidance and the abuse of substances. He shows signs of persistent arousal such as difficulty with sleep, as well as difficulty with concentrating and regulating his anger.

Psychological literature contains a growing amount of information about complex trauma (e.g., Herman, 1992; Luxenberg, Spinazzola & van der Kolk, 2001; Luxenberg, Spinazzola, Hidalgo, Hunt & van der Kolk, 2001). While the biblical framework described above is vital, Jake's therapist also needs to read and understand such empirical literature to offer him the kind of care he needs. Complex trauma involves multiple traumatic events or interpersonal trauma or events of prolonged duration. Jake lived in a violent neighborhood, found his father dead on the floor and experienced war trauma. As Luxenberg et al. (2001 Part I) indicate, complex trauma includes alterations in affect, consciousness, self-perception, relationships and systems of meaning. Jake has experienced all of these. He has also experienced the physical trauma of his head injury.[1]

---

[1]Symptom information may be found at <www.traumaticbraininjury.com>.

Trauma has been a factor of his life in both childhood and adulthood. It has likely had a significant shaping influence.

Jake also appears to exhibit signs of a traumatic brain injury. His reported symptoms consistent with this include anxiety and nervousness, difficulty controlling urges (disinhibition), and impulsivity and irritability. He also has difficulty concentrating and trouble sleeping. Jake was told he might experience memory problems. Depression and difficulty interacting appropriately in social settings can also result from TBI. There is obviously overlap symptomatically with PTSD or complex trauma, and until we see the medical records it will be hard to discern all that might be affecting Jake. Caution is in order here as we need to grasp exactly what impact Jake has suffered from his various traumas and which symptoms need attention. The treatment team should then minimally include a primary care physician, neurologist, psychiatrist and other resources through the VA.

Another possible diagnosis is some form of depression. Jake demonstrates symptoms in this area as well: insomnia, inability to concentrate, sense of hopelessness and suicidal ideation. Jake clearly feels isolated and alone in his current setting. Finally, due to Jake's long history of abusing substances, the school's concern about his drinking episode, and his chronic minimization, we need to evaluate Jake regarding his apparent addictions and incorporate treatment of these into the counseling plan.

These may all be seen as separate diagnoses or as covered under the larger rubric of complex trauma. Kessler, Sonnega, Bromet, Hughes and Nelson (1995) found that persons with PTSD were eight times more likely to have three or more additional disorders than those without the diagnosis of PTSD. The study found that 79% met criteria for one additional disorder and 44% for at least three other disorders. Some of the most common found to co-occur with PTSD were other anxiety disorders, depression and substance abuse. Rather than categorizing this as comorbidity, many have concluded that a separate category of complex trauma is warranted (Luxenberg et al., 2001 Part I).

Treatment Phase One

Much research demonstrates the effectiveness of a three-phase model for working with trauma (Brown, Sheflin & Hammond, 1998; Langberg, 1997; van der Kolk, MacFarlane & Weisaeth, 1996). Christian psychology draws from all areas of study that illuminate truth. Research in trauma has consistently documented many helpful things worthy of incorporating into the discipline. One of the things we know from the trauma literature is that the first stage of treatment is focused on safety and stabilization. Jake has experienced multiple kinds of trauma throughout his life and, as a result, is not stable. Given Jake's difficulty with affect regulation, night-mares and insomnia, modulating anger, his sense of shame, his guilt and passive suicidal ideation, his disconnection and loss of faith, it seems clear that Jake needs to find safety in the therapeutic relationship. The first order of business is to stabilize him so that he can function more effec-tively and begin the hard work of dealing with some of the issues and choices in his life that are damaging him.

Initially, in conjunction with forming a strong alliance, therapy needs to be psychoeducational and rather concrete in nature. Jake needs us to assist him to make sense of himself and his life experiences. He needs help understanding the long-term impact of those experiences and how his current world is exacerbating some of those issues. Clients with a trauma history often do not make sense to themselves, and having their symptoms and struggles normalized provides great relief. One of the initial tools Jake will need is an understanding of how to ground himself when he has flash-backs or intrusive thoughts or images. Grounding simply involves methods of establishing a person in the present when intrusive thoughts and affect are overwhelming. Teaching Jake how to use his senses to focus on objects or sounds or color, reminding himself where he is and what is happening (or not happening), will enable Jake to modulate his reactions and gain some sense of control. The exercise literally means keeping yourself on the ground where you are. Learning this skill gives trauma survivors a sense of control when affect and intrusive images feel uncontrollable.

A second area of initial focus is the physical well-being of the client. Regu-lating Jake's sleeping, eating and exercise will help stabilize him, lay a foun-dation for the later work of affect regulation, give him a sense of control and well-being, and increase cognitive clarity. Here is where the physicians on the treatment team will be important. Medication may be helpful or necessary for his insomnia and perhaps his depression, but it needs to be prescribed with knowledge of Jake's history of substance abuse. It is easy to see why the team approach mentioned earlier could prove not only effective, but necessary.

Gaining stabilization and constructive coping mechanisms will require a significant amount of time and clearly need the development of the support network described above. Any rush to focus on the trauma work will destabilize Jake and throw him further into affect dysregulation, insomnia and substance abuse. This phase requires the therapist to take a more active and direct role, *suggesting* positive coping mechanisms and guidelines. Many of Jake's physiological symptoms and some of his mood might be made more manageable with sleep, regular aerobic exercise, learning deep breathing and relaxation techniques. Engaging in these with the resulting calming effect will contribute to his sense of being able to manage himself. It is crucial for Jake to begin to take charge of his affect and his choices so he is assuming responsibility for himself. It is also likely that Jake will respond with opposition if he is simply told what to do, so suggestions and partnering together with him regarding his care are likely to be more effective. This phase is often full of crises as new ways are slowly built up and developed. The therapist will need to have clear boundaries, be patient with regressions, and continue nurturing the alliance and teaching the client new ways to handle himself little by little.

It will be important to work toward Jake's admitting his need for ongoing help for his substance abuse. Two things may assist us at the beginning. The first is his positive relationship with the chaplain who ran the Alcoholics Anonymous group in which he participated. Jake may be willing to attend another AA group because it is familiar, or perhaps a Celebrate Recovery Group in a local church, a great option for nurturing his faith in healthy ways. Finding a supportive facilitator will be critical since that is what enabled Jake to persist before. Second, we know that Jake bonded with his fellow soldiers, which might be a useful metaphor in encouraging him to try a group dealing with addictions. He might be able to see such a group as working side by side with fellow soldiers in a different sort of war. An early start in such a group will be helpful in keeping Jake from relapsing. However, Jake denies having a problem, and his coping mechanisms may have to fail before he will be willing to attend the group meetings. In any case, relapses in addictions are part of the process and should not come as a surprise if they occur.

Learning how to self-soothe or manage his own feelings is a crucial part of the first phase. Jake seems to have little emotional tolerance. It is possible this extends back to childhood and growing up in a home full of anger and alcoholism where no role models for managing feelings were available. He retreats into substance abuse or his computer when his feelings overwhelm him. When working with someone who may respond negatively to directives, it is often helpful to suggest they attempt a new behavior as a short-term experiment. Keep in mind that these are areas of feeling overwhelmed and incompetent. To suggest a coping method can also feel overwhelming unless it is given as something to try for a short time. For example, Jake may find engaging in physical activity helpful for his distress and anger, so we might suggest he try this in a scheduled way for one week and then report back as to its helpfulness. One week feels doable, and he is given a voice in the process as it moves along. Learning muscle relaxation and deep breathing may help give Jake a sense of control when he feels wound up. Connecting with men in his support network or listening to calming music may be other options to try. It would probably be helpful for Jake to begin a log of his feelings of distress so he can begin to predict when stressful points might occur. This will lead to a greater sense of mastery that will be important to Jake.

We will have to explore Jake's faith and relationship to God to see whether or not that can contribute to his stability at this time. Often if the client's faith is weak or distorted at the beginning of treatment, any attempt to incorporate it creates more anxiety and agitation or encourages "using" faith in wrong ways (e.g., to get what the client wants). It is sometimes better, once some of the work of therapy has been done, to do more focused work in the area of faith and nurture a healthy relationship with God, grounded in the Scriptures, at a point when the client has known good relationships, has developed clearer thinking and has seen Christianity lived out by others in a way that is true to the character of God. The client is less likely to be resistant at this point and also not as liable to "use" faith in distorted ways as his patterns of thinking have significantly changed.

Initially, in this case, we are not emphasizing faith issues because of the obvious distortions in Jake's theology and his use of faith in an attempt to get what he wants. Focusing on more concrete arenas will help stabilize him while forming a strong alliance as he experiences his therapist meeting him where he is, helping him to manage what is overwhelming and giving him a sense of hope for change. It involves a therapist entering into the human life of another in ordinary, functional ways to show empathy and gain trust. When faith issues are later considered more overtly, Jake will be far more open to hearing new truths, laying aside his distortions and not using his faith as if it were another substance available to bring relief in destructive ways.

We can expect issues of trust to arise during treatment with Jake. He has had broken relationships; he has experienced the loss of his father, the shaming of his mother, and the rejection of his girlfriend; he feels isolated and different; he seems to use either substances or technology rather than healthy means to self-soothe. He may be very cautious, vigilant and self-protective. Those feelings will need to be understood, expected and carefully worked with so that Jake feels respected and is given the time to develop trust. Though perhaps unknown to Jake, he will be experiencing the care of someone who is truthful, trustworthy, kind and focused on nurturing his growth. This will eventually give him a small taste of the character of God and his work in Jake's life, even though they may not be addressed overtly. The focus of this initial phase is *not* the trauma and distressing life experiences Jake has endured in the past, but rather a sense of stability, mastery and safety in relationship. These will form the foundational building blocks for the later work.

Treatment Phase Two

The second phase of treatment for Jake will involve exploring the grief and trauma of his life and how those events have shaped him. The purpose of this is to explore the truth of his life, the truth of his responses—both reactive and chosen—and the story that tells. As he begins to face what he avoids and recognize the negative feelings and confused or distorted thoughts that he experiences, he can begin to make different choices and see himself in a larger context than simply the sum of his tragedies and his avoidant choices.

There seem to be three aspects of this work for Jake. These are not listed in the order of importance. In fact, having Jake involved in the decision regarding the order of importance may increase his involvement and commitment to this difficult work. The first aspect would focus on his growing-up years, which include the loss of his father first to alcohol and then to death, the shame from his mother because he reminded her of his father, the violence in his neighborhood, and what he learned about faith in God from his mother who "tends to get a little wacky about religion." Jake's formative years were full of instances that would lead to great grief, fear, anger and confusion. Helping Jake articulate those experiences, their impact and how he wants to respond now as an adult will be important. Returning to those memories will likely upset and agitate Jake, and the processing will need to be broken up with intervals of safety and stabilization so Jake finds out how to practically use what he learned in the first phase and does not derail by abusing alcohol or other substances. This will also give opportunity for his support network to step up and be with him outside the therapy hour to encourage and nurture him.

The second aspect of this phase would be a focus on Jake's war experiences and his PTSD. The story that is creating flashbacks needs to be considered multiple times so Jake can acknowledge, normalize and experience both the emotions and cognitions related to the helicopter incident. Trauma is by definition unspeakable. Processing those experiences allows clients to put the unspeakable into words and tends to disrupt the intrusive nature of PTSD symptoms. Exposure to the trauma needs to be done in small pieces so as not to overwhelm Jake in the same way he was during the original event. We want him to learn, little by little, to tolerate the emotions that accompany the traumatic memory. Again, this is done with intervals of self-care and respite so as not to destabilize him. Eventually, we will also consider the beliefs Jake has carried that are rooted in this experience, such as the heavy load of false guilt. Since this event is what propelled Jake back into abusing substances, we will have to watch very carefully and enlist the support of his team to actively assist him to constructively care for himself.

The third part of this phase would be to gain a fuller understanding of the ramifications of Jake's head trauma and its residual effects. Jake needs a clear understanding of any ensuing limitations so that he can actively participate in getting the support he needs in order to accomplish his goals. He is likely to need adjunctive assistance in order to deal with any memory or learning difficulties. If those limitations are to be lifelong, these patterns will need to be established so that he learns constructive ways of compensating and can predict where he might encounter future difficulties. Collaboration with a psychiatrist and a neurologist will be vital in this pursuit. It is also probable that Jake will need to face and come to terms with the fact that his head injury is a consequence of his own bad decisions. He is likely to struggle with guilt and self-blame and even some embarrassment over his choices.

During this phase, as Jake is facing the truths about the past—those both chosen and forced on him—the relationship with the therapist is critical. Not only is the therapist called to live out in the flesh the character of God throughout the process, but also now must become more active in speaking truth to the client. This certainly involves the truths of the past. For example, finding your father dead on the floor has a huge impact and is not "no big deal" as many might attempt to say to themselves. Or, having PTSD as a result of war trauma is not a sign of weakness but is in fact what happens to human beings who experience horrific things. It also means assisting Jake to speak the truth about his own choices and the consequences with which he now must live. Clients often hold themselves responsible when they are not and tend to blame others when in fact they are at fault. Jake feels guilty about the helicopter accident over which he had no control, and yet does not seem to accept responsibility for his addictions or his own child.

This part of the work also allows for a more explicitly Christian component as many of the lies that the client has held need to be gently but repeatedly exposed to the truths of the Word of God. Jake is his father's son, but he is not "just like his father." He is a man created in the image of God, loved by his eternal Father who wants to grow him into the likeness of God's Son. He has eternal value, and he has been gifted by God for good work. He matters, and therefore his choices do too. His suffering and grief have not gone unnoticed but in fact have been borne by Christ himself. The truths are easier to assimilate after experiencing a significant therapeutic relationship where such truths have been lived out before him. If Jake has been connected to a pastor and/or chaplain and a church community, then he has seen that lived out in multiple arenas by both men and women. They will have treated him with respect, encouraged him, and been supportive of his strengths and gifting. They will have entered into his suffering and grief and loved him enough to hold him to the highest when he struggles or fails.

It is very common during this second phase of treatment for safety and stabilization needs to resurface. When this happens, the counselor must hit the pause button to readdress safety needs and regain stability before returning to the work of dealing with history and its attendant emotions and cognitions. This stabilizing may take several sessions or only one. It is very important for the therapist to pay attention to any indicators that the client is getting overwhelmed. Should this happen, Jake would be vulnerable to returning to old coping mechanisms, just as he did after the death of his friend—"I went back to my old ways and started drugging." It is much more effective to slow the treatment down and ensure stability than to attempt to process quickly with the result that the client experiences yet another failure. It is helpful to ask clients during this phase how they did after leaving the previous session. Did they experience anxiety? Were they able to sleep that night? How did they handle their emotions? While processing history is important when dealing with trauma, it must be balanced with a careful attendance to affect regulation. Otherwise the client feels continually overwhelmed and incapacitated, which merely repeats those feelings that accompanied the original trauma and leads to a descent into destructive coping mechanisms. This balance is vital to productive therapy.

Treatment Phase Three

Having learned safety and stability, having come to terms with his history and been saturated in the truth about himself, his life, his choices and his God, Jake is now ready to look forward with hope, focus on current relationships and forge a future for himself. His old beliefs about himself, relationships, coping, suffering and God have been challenged. The third phase is about newness of life. This is the phase of greater pursuit of educational and occupational goals. Jake will also hopefully find other interests and hobbies he has not been free to pursue. This is where he focuses on developing healthy relationships with family, friends, fellow students or coworkers.

Jake has a mother and a sister, and those relationships need careful thought and some repair work. Jake has a son who has, to date, lived a fatherless life. Jake will need to grapple with his responsibility to the child while letting go of his demands that the mother do what he wants.

He will need to face the consequences of his old choices, grieve those losses and accept responsibility for helping with the child he brought into this world. Hopefully, having experienced empathy repeatedly throughout the course of therapy, Jake will be able to demonstrate some of that for the mother of his son and her family as he grapples with the impact his previous choices and behavior have had. Once the bulk of the trauma-focused work has been done, it is usually true that a more direct and forthright approach can be taken with regard to spiritual matters. Once Jake has faced his life, its impact, his choices and their consequences, and has lessened the governing influence of the various traumas, he will be freer to wrestle more fully with the truths of God's Word and the application of those truths to his heart, his person, his relationships and his goals. Prior to doing that work, Jake is more likely to "use" God the same way he uses substances and people (i.e., to get what he wants or to feel better). He will have little understanding of himself and the shaping influences in his life. Once he has done the work of therapy he will be able to hear truth with more clarity, understand his capacities for deception more fully, and have found safe relationships where he is both loved and held accountable. That means a more directive approach to God's Word can be used to think through his survivor guilt, his responsibility for his child, his need to ask the mother of his son for forgiveness (rather than the other way around), a godly understanding of anger, his responsibility for his avoidant choices, and what it means to draw on the power of the Spirit in his life to make godly choices and form godly relationships. These are not things I simply teach the client; rather, I direct them to specific Scriptures that speak to their struggles and have them study and come back to me with their wrestling and new understanding. It is far more effective to have the client actively do the work of grappling with the Word of God than to just spoon-feed them what you think they need to know. Their thinking is gradually transformed, and they learn new skills for study and thought that impact the rest of their lives.

It is hoped that Jake would, through his greater understanding of God and his own hard work in therapy, begin to grasp that God can gather up the old places, the bad choices, the suffering and grief of his life, and use them in a redemptive way in the lives of others. Nothing Jake has done and nothing that has happened to him is beyond the reach of the grace of God to redeem. Jake has yet to find his vocation, his ministry and his ways of contributing to others. That vocation will probably look quite different having done the hard work of counseling. It is not uncommon for clients, having done such work, to seek out something missional in which to invest themselves, either vocationally or avocationally. Judith Herman (1992) writes about how those who find "survivor mission" tend to make the best recoveries. It involves seeing the events of one's life in larger context and using the events to form meaningful and purposeful connections with others. This greatly enables clients to see themselves in a new light, alter their negative thinking and life expectations, and begin to see themselves as productive, contributing people whose choices have eternal value. What greater survivor mission than serving the God who gives each of his children a vital calling in life.

Termination

Jake will show signs of readiness to terminate therapy when he is able to focus more significantly and productively on his present life, manage his affect without harm to self or others, and have a safe and supportive network of people who will continue to walk with him and nurture his new life. Termination is usually best done in increments. Assuming Jake has had weekly sessions, the therapist and Jake might agree together to meet twice a month for a while, and then once a month, monitoring Jake's life for ongoing signs of health and growth. After three to six months of titrating down, visits may then be extended to three months later, six months later and then finally a year later. It is critical to encourage Jake to continue with his relationships and support networks in the body of Christ as that will be the circle from which he draws assistance, and now hopefully gives such assistance in return. If Jake is in distress such that his support networks and relationships are not sufficient, a few consecutive sessions may be instituted. We will want him to have a strong network for care and for giving back before he terminates altogether. If things continue well for Jake, then these "maintenance checkups" are times of review, catch-up and hope for the future, as counselor and client rejoice together in the fruit of their mutual labors and the ongoing work of God in a redeemed life.

Summary and Conclusion

There is obviously much that cannot be said about the specifics of Jake's counseling. When and how to speak with Jake about his grief, his choices, his sin or his sorrows; where to show gentleness and where to be firm; where repetition is necessary; when to confront him with the truths of Scripture and when to simply live them out—these are all questions that must be answered as treatment progresses and Jake responds. Such variables are an invitation to the therapist to dialogue with and rely on the Spirit of God as the work proceeds. It is he who is the true Comforter (John 15), the one who leads us into truth and is the indwelling Wonderful Counselor (Isaiah 9:6). The difficulties and challenges of a complex case will result in growth and deepening faith for the counselor, which will in fact be part of Jake's legacy to future counselees!

Jake's treatment is a three-phase plan, with the first being safety and stabilization; the second, trauma processing; and the third, a connection with his world and his future that is based now on a more solid foundation and hope for a more godly and productive life. Elasticity of movement back and forth between the phases is important in working with trauma. It is also important to note that Jake's case is complex and involves many needs and difficulties and will therefore certainly not be a linear process. This case requires an understanding of the trauma literature, good clinical skills, a grasp of the research bearing on these matters, a wise involvement of the Christian community for support and a vibrant faith, clear understanding of the Scriptures, and reliance on the Spirit of God—all of which constitute the facets of a Christian psychologist.

In conclusion, if the work of therapy is done in a manner consistent with the two presuppositions mentioned at the beginning of the chapter, the outcome of that work will be visible redemptive work in two lives, not just one. The eternal pursuit of our God is always that of making us like his Son. In the initial stages of counseling, that work is often being intensively done in the life of the counselor in contending with denial, deception, resistance, confusion, fear, relapses and outright opposition. The discernment, wisdom, patience, gentleness, mercy and compassion that are needed are only found in the person of Jesus Christ and his work in a human life. That means that in the early stages of this Christian psychology approach, the evidence of Christ in the room and in the relationship is seen (or should be seen) in the responses, both verbal and non-verbal, of the therapist. Wherever the therapist comes up short in responding to a difficulty with the client, that is the place where, rather than pushing on the client to change, the therapist must continually go before God and his Word for his perspective and his character to be worked out in the counselor's person. Over time, the living, visible presence of the character of God in the flesh will begin to bring about hunger for change and then change itself, until in the later stages that character begins to be visible in small choices and behaviors in the client. It is my experience that God is always working both sides of the equation and most frequently begins in the life and character of the therapist rather than the stated client. For those who adopt a Christian psychology approach to counseling, this is not surprising. God-dependence is a therapeutic requirement for the therapist before the client even enters the office. Modeling this is a vital part of the counseling process.

This is a work that is a great privilege to do. It is a call to immerse oneself in the life and person of Jesus Christ, become his disciple in the school of Christlikeness, and then watch his remarkable redemptive power restore a broken and wounded life to one that begins to reflect his image out into the world.

References

American Psychiatric Association. (2000). *Diagnostic and statistical manual of mental disorders* (4th ed., text rev.). Washington, DC: American Psychiatric Association.

Brown, D., Scheflin, A.W., & Hammond, D. C. (1998). *Memory, trauma treatment and the law: An essential reference on memory for clinicians, researchers, attorneys and judges*. New York: W.W. Norton.

Herman, J. L. (1992). *Trauma and recovery*. New York: Basic Books.

Kessler, R., Sonnega, A., Bromet, E., Hughes, M., & Nelson, C. (1995). Post-traumatic stress disorder in the national comorbidity survey. *Archives of General Psychiatry, 52*, 1048-60.

Langberg, D. M. (1997). *Counseling survivors of sexual abuse*. Wheaton, IL: Tyndale House.

Luxenberg, T., Spinazzola, J., & van der Kolk, B. A. (2001). Complex trauma and disorders of extreme stress (DESNOS): Diagnosis, part I. *Directions in Psychiatry, 21*, 373-93.

Luxenberg, T., Spinazzola, J., Hidalgo, J., Hunt, C., & van der Kolk, B. A.

(2001). Complex trauma and disorders of extreme stress (DESNOS): Diagnosis, part II. *Directions in Psychiatry, 21*, 395-415.

McMinn, M. R., Staley, R. C., Webb, K. C., and Seegobin, W. (2010). Just what is Christian counseling anyway? *Professional Psychology: Research and Practice, 41*(5), 391-97.

Roberts, R. C., & Watson, P. J. (2010). A Christian psychology view. In E. L. Johnson (Ed.), *Psychology & Christianity: Five views* (pp. 149-78). Downers Grove, IL: IVP Academic.

van der Kolk, B. A., MacFarlane, A., & Weisaeth, L. (Eds.). (1996). *Traumatic stress: The effects of overwhelming experience on mind, body and society*. New York: Guilford Press.

6

A Transformational Approach

Gary W. Moon

LEARNING OBJECTIVES

- *List the unique features of this spiritually sensitive approach to client care.*
- *Identify and explore the methods applied to further the client's experience of "Christ within" and "union with God" (i.e., daily examen, lectio divina, Scripture memorization, solitude and imagery restructuring).*
- *Reflect on how the spiritual formation premises of this approach are as relevant for counselors as clients, and evaluate personal priorities.*

The task in this chapter is to present a "behind closed doors" view of one of the five major counseling perspectives at the interface of Christianity and psychology—transformational psychology. This will be accomplished by displaying its distinctives when applied to the case of Jake as presented earlier. While this sounds fascinating, I need to ask the reader to be patient with my attempts to make transformational psychology more concrete. There are numerous reasons for this request. I will highlight the three most obvious: (1) Transformational psychology is the most recent invitee to this multiview discussion; (2) in fact, this "approach" to the relationship between the social sciences and Christianity that I will be attempting to represent was not formally recognized until the authors—and my friends— John Coe and Todd Hall (2010), labeled it in *Psychology & Christianity:*

Five Views; and (3) while my own approach to relating Christian spiritual formation with the professional practice of counseling and psychotherapy shares much in common with that of Coe and Hall, the reader will observe many dissimilarities—and a few occasions of outright disagreement. Indeed, for reasons that I will soon explain, I would be more comfortable simply presenting an approach that views matters of soul and spirit as integral or essential to working with the person. With those confessions on the table, we will begin.

Introduction

For more than 20 years I have taught in two seminaries and two "integration" programs. My primary teaching has been in the area of merging professional practice with a Christian worldview. In addition, I have been somewhat obsessed with looking for professionally appropriate ways to incorporate insights from the long history of spiritual direction literature into a counseling setting (McMinn, Moon & McCormick, 2009; Moon, 1993, 1994, 1996, 2003a, 2007, 2009, 2010b; Moon & Fantuzzo, 1982; Moon, Bailey, Kwasny & Willis, 1993; Moon, Willis, Bailey & Kwasny, 1993).

I read Johnson's (2010) wonderful book *Psychology & Christianity: Five Views* with much pride in this new "discipline" of relating psychology and Christianity. I was greatly impressed by the wisdom and professionalism expressed by the contributors and by how far the "movement" has traveled in such a short time. But I also read the book with a tinge of sadness over what sometimes appears as silo construction—building somewhat insulated views—which I believe must eventually come down if significant advancement is to be made in this important endeavor. I am riveted to the possibilities of attempting to see almost everything in terms of both/and as opposed to either/or, and for me this even applies to the notion of assimilating modern, postmodern and premodern views.

As you recall from the first chapter of this book and from Warren Brown's (2004) "Resonance Model," John Wesley talked about the church deriving its stability from a dynamic interplay of four forces: Scripture, tradition, reason and spiritual experience. I was delighted to see these references, and a fifth force—the "integration"—implied. I also think Wesley was on to something quite profound. I am certainly very glad he did not pit one member of that quartet against the others. Indeed, I believe that it is only through such a dynamic interplay that eventually a sixth view—an "integral" view, an integration of radical inclusivism—can be discovered. But in the meantime I will try to describe an approach to counseling that lives somewhere between explicit integration and "transformational psychology."

Five Views/Five Factors

I learned something from my mentor and expert in the area of factor analysis, Richard Gorsuch. Most things that psychologists examine are far too complex to be explained by a single variable or even a single cluster of variables, a factor. Gorsuch's book *Factor Analysis* (1983) was very well received, and may be the only serious tome on that topic to examine the Pentateuch using a factor analytic approach for investigating the sources of the text. But what has stuck with me from spending time with both text and author is the need for multiple factors to account for the maximum variance among variables.

Given the enormous complexity of the present "y" in question in our discussion—improved functioning of a human being—I (along with several of my colleagues in this text) believe that a far better approach than picking a "winner" among the five views we are studying would be to work toward a deeper understanding of how each of these five approaches might represent a different factor of predictability and help. To consider this analogy, what if accounting for our desired changes in "y" might best be served examining the additive role that each of our approaches can play? Consider the following equation: $(y) = a + b_1x_1 + b_2x_2 + b_3x_3 + b_4x_4 + b_5x_5$; positive changes in "y" may be associated with each of our five approaches (x_1 through x_5) but with different weights or magnitudes (b_1 through b_5) across a variety of different circumstances (e.g., presenting problems, client openness to explicit integration, etc.).

As suggested above, one of the reasons I struggle with the notion of forming a clear allegiance with any one of the approaches—including transformational psychology—is that I have found over time it is the circumstances of the client's situation that suggest when the strengths of a particular approach, or multiple approaches, should be brought in to serve the client. With a nod to Wesley, a variety of variables determine when approaches leaning on Scripture (biblical counseling), tradition (Christian psychology), reason (levels of explanation), spiritual experience (transformational psychology) or synthesis (integration) receive the most weight of emphasis.

However, even with my own leanings toward inclusivism, I have long felt that explicit approaches for incorporating insights from spiritual direction into treatment models (e.g., a transformational approach) have been somewhat neglected from the discussion. So I read John Coe and Todd Hall's (2010) chapter on transformational psychology in *Psychology & Christianity: Five Views* with great interest. For almost 20 years I have felt like somewhat of a voice in the wilderness (Moon, 1997, 2003b, 2004a, 2004b, 2009, 2010a; Moon, Willis, Bailey & Kwasny, 1993; Walker & Moon, 2011). I applaud John Coe and Todd Hall for boldly making a case for: (1) the importance of the spiritual development of the counselor; (2) the potential benefits of learning to live more and more moments of one's life "in Christ"; (3) a biblical view of the person; and (4) underscoring the importance of letting the realities of the object being studied (in this case, the person) dictate the method of study.

However, as presently stated, I find their agenda a bit too ambitious, optimistic and somewhat exclusive of the other four positions. Specifically I am concerned with: (1) the claim to rethink the very nature of science itself; (2) possible leanings toward what may be perceived as elitism in the way it applies the concept of the need for the psychologist to be transformed; and (3) the lack of articulation concerning how it offers a clear, distinctive and practical application to the process of Christian counseling.

A Nuanced Transformational Approach

You may be thinking, is this the transformational psychology chapter or not? That is a fair question. As you have likely discerned, I would feel very comfortable writing from an integration perspective that had a primary focus on the potential interplay between modern applied psychology and spiritual formation in working with certain client populations and certain presenting problems. David G. Benner (1998) might call such a model a spiritually sensitive approach to psychotherapy. I would also be comfortable writing from an integral perspective that would present the soul and spirit as essential to the functioning of a human being.

With that said, let me provide a few nuances to the transformational psychology approach as it relates to how I would work with a client, and then I will actually get down to the intended business of this chapter.

Six streams as an example of inclusivism. I have been deeply impacted by the organization Renovaré in general and the writings of Richard J. Foster and Dallas Willard in particular. The mission of Renovaré is to provide individual churches and their members with a balanced, practical, effective small-group strategy for spiritual growth. Part of this "balanced" approach includes the study and celebration of six of the great traditions of Christian faith: contemplative—the prayer filled life; holiness—the virtuous life; charismatic—the spirit-empowered life; social justice—the compassionate life; evangelical—the word-centered life; and incarnational—the sacramental life. Far from pitting one tradition against another, the aim is to draw from each in a similar way that a nutritionist would encourage a person to eat a balanced diet that takes from each of the major food groups.

For me, in a similar vein of inclusivism, a nuanced transformational psychology approach will maintain a primary focus on personal spiritual transformation—for both the counselor and counselee—while looking for ways to incorporate insights and techniques from each of the five approaches presented in this text: levels of explanation, biblical counseling, Christian psychology, transformational psychology and integration.

Willard's model of the person. In a recent article (Moon, 2010b) I speak of Dallas Willard—a philosopher by training and practice—as my favorite psychologist. One of the reasons for my praise of this sage of spiritual formation as a "psychologist" is the help I have received from his writings for understanding in bringing the entire "person" into sharper focus. *In Renovation of the Heart: Putting on the Character of Christ* (2002), Willard proposes there are six basic aspects of a human being, which together and in interplay make up "human nature" (p. 30). You may find it helpful to think of this model as a "BASIC-ID" (Lazarus, 1989)—but with a soul.

- *Thought* (images, concepts, judgments, inferences)
- *Feeling* (sensations, emotions)
- *Body* (action, interaction with the physical world)
- *Social Context* (personal and structural relations with others)
- *Spirit* (choice, will, heart, decision, CEO of the person)
- *Soul* (the factor that integrates all the above into one life)

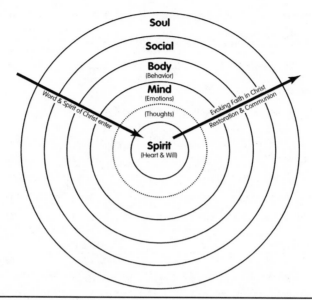

Figure 6.1. Willard's Model of the Person

In this model (see figure 6.1), we are presented with not only the components of the person but also the only five things a human being can do. Humans can think, feel, behave, interact with others and choose. The spirit/will/heart is the center or core of a person's life and may be called the "ego"—especially when functioning separately and apart from God as the source of life.[1] "Choice" is perhaps the best one-word encapsulation for the activity of this spirit/will/heart dimension. It underscores the most fundamental decision faced by humanity. Like their forebears, Christians, I believe, awaken each day to the choice of living in an intimate, conversational and communal relationship with God, or of initiating and maintaining a separate existence. The critical decision for the spirit/will/heart (or CEO of the person) is between willingness, surrender and obedience versus willfulness, autonomy and separation from the Source of life.

According to Willard, the soul, as distinguished from the spirit/will/heart, can be viewed as the invisible computer that keeps everything running and

---

[1]I hope I am not being confusing here; I believe that we both need a healthy ego and that as part of a Christian's journey of experiencing a greater sense of union with God, we need to lay it down. In this sense I am using "ego" to represent what is being called the "false self," or that aspect of the person which is holding on to the notion that a life separate from God is good and desirable. I am not using ego in a technical sense.

integrated into one person. The soul is the aspect that integrates all of the components of the person to form one life. The soul, Willard pens, "is that aspect of your whole being that *correlates*, *integrates*, and *enlivens* everything going on in the various dimensions of the self. It is the life-center of the human being" (Willard, 2002, p. 199).

Willard's model of human functioning provides a holistic way of conceptualizing and working with individuals that easily embraces abnormal psychology, positive psychology and the soul/spirit. That is to say, each component (think "cognitive" aspect as one illustration) can be focused on for the purpose of (1) improving maladaptive functioning (e.g., reframing and restructuring thought patterns that lead to negative outcomes); (2) increasing positive outcomes (e.g., strengthening and enhancing existing thought patterns that support positive functioning); and (3) enhancing Christian spiritual formation (e.g., examining an individual's views and concepts of God for the purpose of facilitating the process of learning to live more moments "with" God). Now, that is a psychology that excites me, and it is certainly one that informs my application of a transformational psychology.

Jesus is very smart. For most of my professional career I created a hierarchy of value for the various "schools" of psychology based on how closely they resembled the natural sciences. Neuropsychology and the biological explanations of behavior were at the top, closely followed by behavioral and cognitive approaches. I gave some credence to person-centered approaches as a safe way to spend time with clients before the "real psychology" could be brought in, and I tolerated the existence of Freudian approaches in a manner similar to the way I would tolerate a beloved, senile grandparent.

At the same time, I came to accept the Western view that the term *knowledge* should be reserved for subjects like math and the natural sciences. Religion—even Christianity—dealt in matters of faith, belief and profession, but not knowledge. Indeed, how could one make a "leap of faith" if one's faith were grounded in actual knowledge?

Recently, however, a slow change in my way of thinking has percolated and now causes me to believe that I have been dramatically shortchanging what Jesus has to offer. I believe it is time for me—and perhaps others who are attempting to relate psychology and theology—to reposition faith in Jesus Christ and the ability to live interactively with him back within the category of knowledge. I am confessing that before encountering Willard's line of thinking on this matter, I had not given Christianity its rightful place at the table as a source of not merely belief and practice, but *knowledge*.

As just one example, consider table 6.1, which presents the four most fundamental worldview questions in the universe: (1) What is real? (2) Who is well off? (3) Who is a good person? and (4) How do I become one? (Willard, 2009).

Table 6.1.

	Jesus' Answer	Skinner's Answer	Freud's Answer
1. The Reality Question The foundational part of a worldview is always what it considers to be real—*What is reality?*	God and his kingdom; that is what you can count on and what you have to come to terms with.	The measurable physical universe.	The physical universe—including the unseen subconscious mind.
2. The Well-Being Question The reality question is joined at the worldview level with the question of well-being—*Who is well off?*	Anyone who is alive in the kingdom; that is, anyone who is interactively engaged with God and the various dynamic dimensions of his reigning. Such engagement with God is *an eternal living, an eternal life.*	Anyone who is able to live with as many pleasant events as possible while living free from physical pain.	The person who is maximally in touch with his or her unconscious and able to live an examined life.
3. The Character Question Who is a really good person?	Anyone who is pervaded with love.	Anyone who, on a personal and corporate level, seeks to minimize pain and maximize pleasure for self and others.	The person who seeks to understand the self and help others do the same.
4. The Development Question How does one become a genuinely good person?	By placing your confidence in Jesus Christ and becoming his student or apprentice in kingdom living. That amounts to progressively entering into the abundance of life he brings to us.	By learning to shape your environment in such a way that you minimize the cause of pain in others.	Analysis.

I have become convinced that Jesus offers a source of exquisite knowledge that answers life's most important questions and that his answers deserve—at minimum—equal attention to that received by psychology's pioneers. I also believe that profound psychological good could be accomplished by moving this knowledge from the academic slums to the ivory towers. The mental health benefits of becoming a person pervaded with love are simply too enormous to ignore, as is the possibility of living more and more moments of each day in firsthand interaction (knowing by acquaintance) with Jesus and his kingdom.

Training implications of a three-legged stool. In a similar fashion as McMinn (1996), I have come to believe that the best training program for producing "transformational psychologists/counselors" would resemble a three-legged stool. That is, I have envisioned the training to be composed of three primary domains with each receiving about one third of the curriculum space. The three areas would be: (1) professionally sound and respected training in a mental health discipline; (2) classic models of spiritual direction (Orthodox, Benedictine, Ignatian, etc.); and (3) the best from a body of modern evangelical thought that presents a high and explicit Christology.

Please understand, I am not saying that the boundaries between these domains should disappear and spiritual directors should start asking questions about a directee's defense mechanisms, prescribing medication and giving personality tests. God forbid. And God forbid a psychiatrist should start assuming that all major depressions are dark nights of the soul or writing prescriptions to pray. However, I have come to believe that a trilingual and tricultural (a person fluent in the language and culture of counseling, classic models of spiritual direction, and Christ-centered approaches to spiritual transformation) could do a stellar job of working with one individual in ways that respect the ethical boundaries of each of those professions while also realizing the holistic nature of the individual. It is time for new training programs that are no longer artificially hamstrung by the confines of modernism.

All the roulette wheels must be considered. In addition to the four nuances for a transformational psychology that I have discussed above, I will offer one final distinction before addressing our case study. The extent to which concepts and techniques from spiritual formation will be integrated into my work with a particular client will be dependent on where at least six "roulette wheels" stop spinning.

1. *It begins with me—training:* The "spiritual interventions" I provide are first and foremost informed by my own level of training in this area of practice.

2. *It begins with me—formation:* I will not attempt to lead a client down roads I have not walked.

3. *Client and setting:* I will only consider "spiritual approaches" for clients who have given informed consent and who are requesting such interventions. Further, I will not go beyond the boundaries appropriate to the setting in which I am practicing.

4. *Presenting problem:* The client's presenting problem will have a huge impact on the decision to offer a spiritual insight or intervention. The diagnosis of enuresis might eliminate—pun intended—such an intervention.

5. *Stage of the relationship:* While I will say more about this, I am inclined to draw from the discipline of spiritual direction in the latter, as opposed to earlier, stage of the therapeutic process.

6. *Empirical "permission" for using techniques from formation field:* I am more inclined toward such explicit integration if I can find supportive evidence in the psychological literature.

Against this backdrop, let's now turn our attention to the case study.

Priorities and Initial Impressions

Consultation with the counselor. In consulting with the new counselor I would affirm that this is not a "simple case of adjustment-to-college-life 'blues,'" nor does it appear to be primarily "a rather severe case of 'academic anxiety.'" I would also let her know that it may take a village of mental, medical and spiritual health professionals to appropriately attend to all the needs Jake presents.

Ideal setting. While I'm uncertain as to whether Jake will need a very intensive outpatient intervention—and possibly a brief inpatient stay for safety and evaluation—we will assume for now that Jake is being seen in a private practice setting in close proximity to his college. We will also assume that in addition to appropriate release-of-information documentation there will be informed consent concerning the fact that Jake will be seen by a licensed mental health professional who is also a Christian and, if the client so chooses, is willing to explore Christian resources as part of the counseling process.

Essential presuppositions and priorities. An immediate priority surpasses all presuppositions: is it safe for Jake to leave the counselor's office? Records indicate that he has made several references to self-harm. While these were, according to the records, "loose and without threatening details such as driving a car into a wall at a high speed," Jake has stated that "he has a recurring desire to no longer live the life he is living" and has made the additional statement, "If I can't make it here I might as well get blown into oblivion." Given these statements, his lack of social engagement, potential indicators of depression and "signs of impulsive tendencies and decisions," my initial recommendation is to do some brief screening measures (a standard suicide assessment checklist and Beck Depression Inventory, second edition [Beck, Steer & Brown, 1996]) to get a better handle on Jake's level of depression and suicide risk. It is not comforting to note the possibility of suicide in the death of Jake's father.

From a more global perspective, my primary presuppositions are captured in Willard's model of the person that has been presented. I am assuming that Jake is a nonceasing spiritual being who will likely benefit greatly from aligning himself with the Creator of the universe in an ongoing and transforming friendship. However, it is likely that such discussion will not be the primary focal point of the initial evaluation process. Jake is also a decaying earthen vessel and appears to have many prominent areas of maladaptive functioning in the other, less ephemeral, aspects of his person.

Assessment

Definition of health and pathology. In the ultimate sense I believe that people are most healthy when they are living in as close an alignment as possible to God. Three helpful ways to describe this process toward ultimate soul health include Jesus' use of the imagery of living in the kingdom of God, the apostle Paul's repeated use of the phrase *Christ in you* and the early church's view of salvation (Ware, 1995) as being on a path toward union with God. In fact, I believe Jesus summarizes this ideal state in John 15:5: "I am the vine; you are the branches. If you remain in me and I in you, you will bear much fruit; apart from me you can do nothing" (NIV).

I further believe that learning to live a life of trusting submission to the will of God on a moment-by-moment basis, alive with the energy, power and presence of God, is a picture of healthy functioning. A life lived in transforming friendship with the Trinity (John 17:3) should have a positive impact on all other aspects of the person—thinking, feeling, behaving, relating, choosing. By contrast, spiritual pathology is living life separate and apart from God. Pathology thus defined—so common, I believe, even among Christians, as to be considered "normal" functioning—is living life out of our false or "ego" self. Pathology is living apart from the Tree of Life.

Having said that, I am doubtful that such lofty language will be very helpful to Jake during the initial sessions. Other pathologies are practically defined by the DSM-IV-TR (APA, 2000) as maladaptive functioning resulting in a disruption of social, vocational or emotional functioning. The first priority for Jake's counselor will be the examination of his health and pathology from this reference point while also considering ways of introducing additional and alternative approaches to healthy functioning.

The need for counseling. Problems need counseling whenever there is maladaptive functioning with any or all aspects of the person. The presenting problem, the scope and nature of the counselor's training, and a variety of client factors—including genuine motivation for change—will help determine if the counselor is equipped to handle working with the client in the domains of maladaptive cognitions, behaviors, emotions and relationship, and also in the domains of spirit (e.g., will, heart, choice) and soul.

Categorizing problems for counseling. With this case study I am concerned with the following questions:

1. Is it safe for Jake to leave the office?

2. What is the diagnosis (conceptualized first in DSM categories)?

3. Is the counselor (and am I) the right person to be working with Jake, and what appropriate referrals may be needed?

4. Does the client have sufficient motivation to enter into counseling in a meaningful way?

5. What are the indications that a "spiritual" intervention (from discussion about Jake's "God view" to more explicit discussion of where Jake is in regard to a transforming friendship with God) may be important to working with Jake?

Distinguishing counseling and spiritual direction. It is tempting to offer the following succinct distinction: (1) Spiritual direction has an emphasis on enhancing one's awareness of God's presence and facilitating a journey toward spiritual health through increasing discernment and the practice of a variety of classic spiritual disciplines toward the end of experiencing union with God; and (2) Counseling has an emphasis on enhancing one's awareness of self and facilitating a journey toward psychological health through the use of classic counseling techniques toward the end of seeing improvements in patterns of thought, behavior and relationship.

However, I have come to view the spiritual aspects of the person as far too integral (essential) to other domains of functioning to continue making that distinction—which now feels artificial. I now believe that distinctions between counseling and spiritual direction are more about training and turf (i.e., professional boundary claims) than about the person.

Conceptualization

What makes a person change? According to one version of the old joke "how many counselors does it take to change a light bulb?" the answer is: "Only one, if the bulb really wants to be changed." I'm afraid there is much truth in that quip. Client motivation to change may be the single most important predictor of positive outcome. I would place that variable just ahead of the counselor's ability to embody key nonspecific therapeutic factors of a warm, genuine and empathetic relationship.

However, if pressed to answer the question "what makes a person change?" I would have to say that the two primary "motivators" are *pain*—when it leads to a willingness to abandon maladaptive and self-defeating patterns of behavior—and *love*—when a client truly believes that another (God, the counselor, a significant person) genuinely desires for him or her what is good. Jake's pain will hopefully increase his motivation to do the hard work of counseling, and I hope that the counselor will be able to model some small measure of the type of love the Trinity feels among its members. I would also hope to encourage Jake's counselor to help him wrestle with the following questions: (1) What can I learn from my pain? (2) Am I at a place of possible *metanoia*—am I ready to start rethinking my thinking? and (3) Can I imagine a God who truly desires for me what is good?

At the risk of sounding grandiose, the goal of a nuanced transformational psychology model is for the client to reconnect with God in a deep and profound way. The ultimate goal is perhaps captured best by the only verse in Scripture where Jesus defines eternal life (John 17:3). The goal is for the client to enter into a transforming friendship with the members of the Trinity, to deeply "know" God, Jesus and the Holy Spirit. To state the obvious, such an explicit spiritual goal does mean that the client must be both informed and desirous of such an intention.

The ultimate hope for Jake is vividly portrayed in the dynamic, pre-Fall relationship of Adam, Eve and God in the Garden of Eden—to be in love with God and others, alive in a community of self-forgetful love. The ultimate goal is nothing short of the experience of union with God, as defined by the client's ability to have an experiential awareness of more and more moments living life *with* God while experiencing love *for* God and others. Prominent among my goals and hopes for Jake will be for him to be able to experience theology in a way that makes a difference in how he lives his life.

Treatment plan and techniques. While the intake process should be very standard—with a focus on presenting problems, history of presenting problems (e.g., onset, impairment to functioning, recent interventions, explanation of causation), psychiatric/counseling history, family history, social history, medical history and a mental status exam—I would encourage the counselor to ask a number of additional questions (of a spiritual nature) if Jake has consented to a method of counseling that would be a blend of professional counseling (with the focus on the client's emotions, thoughts, behaviors and relationships) and spiritual formation or direction (with a sensitivity to matters of the spirit and insights from spiritual theology). For example, I would want to know more about the positive and negative roles religion has played in Jake's life and how he has viewed God at various points in his life. I would also want him to feel free to encourage or veto any "God talk" during the counseling process.

Jake's situation is very complex. In working through the intake and evaluation and considering additional testing, the counselor ought to be very aware that in addition to a potpourri of maladaptive dynamics within Jake's social and family history, there are a number of concerns and diagnoses that will need to be ruled in or out. Among these are: possible suicidal ideation; impulsive actions and decisions; social isolation; possible mood disturbance; substance use/abuse; possible posttraumatic stress disorder; neurological impairment from a significant head injury; mixed personality disorder, which seems to include prominent antisocial traits; and malingering—"the need to keep disability funds flowing."

I will strongly suggest a referral to a neuropsychologist to better understand the severity of Jake's head injury. This referral may also provide information concerning Jake's preferred learning style and potential learning disability. A referral should be made to a psychiatrist both for diagnostic clarity and medication management in the areas of a possible mood disorder and posttraumatic stress, and Jake should continue meeting with a psychiatrist during his counseling. Also Jake will be encouraged to reestablish involvement with an Alcoholics Anonymous (AA) program.

Jake's therapist might follow a classic pattern for counseling developed by Gerald Egan (1975, 2009), moving through various stages that could be labeled *exploration, understanding* and *change strategies.* I would probably add a fourth stage, which may look to some more like traditional spiritual direction than professional counseling. Each of these stages would focus on the aspects of Jake's life and personhood that include his patterns of emotion, thought, behavior, relationships and volition—including how these aspects of his life include God and a spiritual dimension. In sum, the work with Jake will primarily be concerned with journeying with Jake through the numerous individual, community, academic and family issues he is facing, while looking for possibilities for enhancing his relationship with God.

Phase 1: Exploration. Against the backdrop of a solid initial evaluation, and assuming Jake's agreement to and active participation in referral suggestions (a very big assumption), he would settle into an ongoing counseling relationship. During the initial work with Jake, the overarching goal would be to develop a therapeutic relationship and an environment where Jake will feel safe, cared for and free to share openly and transparently. Stress will be placed on the counselor's ability to feel and express the crucial nonspecific factors—warmth, genuineness, acceptance, hope instilling—of a good therapeutic relationship. Spiritual factors are important, but at least initially, these will primarily center upon nurturing the counselor's own relationship with God and, ideally, becoming a better conduit for grace to Jake.

During the time of exploration, I will encourage the counselor to be with Jake and gently foster discussions about the key relationships in his life. The counselor will be encouraged to walk with him as he relives many events from the highlight reel of past times with his father, mother, sister, significant peers, teachers and others who have molded his life. To facilitate this process—by extending the exploration to outside the counseling hour—a memory exercise may be useful. This exercise involves asking Jake if he is willing to do some work outside of our sessions.

If Jake agrees to the task, the counselor will ask him to visit one of his favorite places for being alone (library, park, McDonald's, etc.) at least two times between sessions. He should take a note pad (or laptop) and simply sit in silence and allow memories to come to him from various time periods of his life. In subsequent weeks the counselor will systematically walk through Jake's life, allowing him to progress at a pace that feels comfortable. A portion of these early sessions will be devoted to Jake's leading the counselor through the significant memories of his life, with the counselor simply facilitating a Rogerian (nondirective) exploration. The primary "God views" (the ways that he has come to view the Divine) that have colored his spiritual life will also be explored.

The exploration together will also extend beyond key family and peer relationships in Jake's life to critical themes raised during the intake and evaluation sessions. In addition to monitoring his progress and following through with neuropsychological testing, sessions with his psychiatrist, and attendance at AA meetings, the counselor will explore a variety of themes, including but not limited to: suicidal ideation, including the exploration of the spiritual implications of making a decision to end one's life; mood monitoring; any apparent patterns of impulsive behaviors and decisions; social isolation; and possibilities of secondary gain.

As Jake feels comfortable with the counseling relationship, he and his counselor can explore key religious and spiritual themes that would include his statements about: (1) being "hungry to grow in his faith"; (2) how he feels toward a God who is not readily "fixing" all his problems; (3) how his mother's Holy Roller faith may have colored his own; (4) the positive relationship he had with the Army chaplain; (5) any anger he may be feeling toward God; (6) his feelings for his former girlfriend and young son; and (7) his view of God during what Jake would consider to be the key events of his life.

Concerning these and other key themes, the use of the "empty chair technique" can be helpful to the process of exploration. While Jake may be invited to put any of a number of primary characters in the chair, it may prove particularly helpful for him to have many conversations with God. Particularly whenever Jake makes an emotional reference to God, I would encourage his counselor to have Jake place God in an empty chair and enter into an in-the-present-moment conversation. The counselor will need to avoid putting words in God's mouth and simply facilitate the dialogue. With this simple technique much can be learned about Jake's perceived I-Thou relationship with God—especially as this relates to whether Jake has a healthy or unhealthy view of his Maker.

Phase 2: Understanding. Sometimes a climate of exploration is all that a client needs, though this may not be true for Jake. As is often the case, many clients need help in "unpeeling the onion" of maladaptive patterns of thought, emotion, behavior and relationship. For this reason, as a counselor, I often add dimensions of interacting to my Rogerian core for the purpose of facilitating insight and deeper understanding of the persistent patterns in one's life. During the middle phase of working with a particular client, the emphasis will often shift to the counselor's use of self-disclosure, immediacy, probing questions and some gentle challenges to maladaptive patterns.

In the understanding phase of working with Jake—and assuming a strong therapeutic relationship has been established—I will encourage the counselor to bring a prominent theme into play. Most succinctly stated, I will want the counselor to examine how Jake's current and past patterns of thought, behavior, relationship and choice are working for him. That is, they will examine just how well his "self-protective-ego-self" is doing in running his life. We will also be looking to see if he has picked up any patterns from his past—ways of protecting himself from pain that are often present in his life now but causing more harm than good. In short, it is important here for Jake to understand the narratives he is using to run his life and compare them to the suggested narratives found in Scripture and the life of Jesus.

Before facilitating this comparison of narratives, Jake's counselor has hopefully earned enough trust from Jake for him to be willing to explore themes from "spiritual" theology. Specifically, I will want Jake to reflect on whether he sees *the Trinity* as a creative and compassionate community who is inviting him to join their dance of self-forgetful love—or as something much less than the prodigal's father (a picture of grace and love). The intent is that Jake will come to understand more about the good, the bad and the ugly about *himself*—that is, the fact that he has been created in the very image of God (the good) but is now separated from God (the bad), and that within him there is a great tug of war between his false self (that part that still believes autonomy from God is good and desirable) and true self (that part that believes the best thing that he can possibly do is give up, embrace willingness and surrender, and begin a journey back home to the embrace of his prodigal—"lavish loving"—Father).

I also hope to help the counselor facilitate Jake's view of *Jesus* as the most intelligent Being who ever walked the planet and to experience Jesus' invitation to live life a whole different way—alive to the realities of the kingdom of God and the experience of Christ within. Finally, from the perspective of spiritual theology, I anticipate that part of the counseling work will involve Jake embracing the classic movements of *transformation*—purgation (rejecting God substitutes), illumination (embracing the ideal of union with God and the desire to move toward willingness and surrender) and union (an experiential awareness of that ideal).

I suspect that few if any of those ideals from spiritual theology are true for Jake. So the most important thing that may happen during this phase of understanding will be an examination of his current narratives concerning spiritual theology and a discussion of the aspects of his life that caused them to be written in such a harmful manner.

James Bryan Smith (2009) does a remarkable job of contrasting common core narratives used to navigate life with those of Jesus. To use but one example of this, the counselor might help Jake understand whether he has developed a core narrative of distrust for God because of the negative events in his life. Is he sure that he can trust God? Has his own earthly father colored his perception of God? The counselor might then help Jake begin to understand that when Jesus describes God as "Father," it is important to let Jesus define what this means—not Jake's earthly father. I would hope that this insight would cause enough motivation in Jake for him to be willing to explore—through bibliotherapy—how Jesus rightly defined divine fatherhood and demonstrated trust under extraordinary circumstances.

Phase 3: Change strategies. In the best of worlds, careful attention to evaluation, assessment, case management, creating an environment conducive to exploration, and facilitating deeper understanding and insight would be enough. And sometimes it is. However, for most clients, insights are the necessary but insufficient condition for change. For this reason a third phase in working with Jake would involve a shift of focus to the development of change strategies.

Some of these change strategies might look a lot like what my levels-of-explanation and integrationist friends might prescribe. It is likely that I would assist Jake's counselor in working with Jake both in session and via homework in developing plans for monitoring and modifying maladaptive patterns of thought, behavior, choice and relationship. These could be targeted to any one of a number of areas, such as impulsive actions and decisions; social isolation; mood disturbance; substance use and abuse; anxiety associated with posttraumatic stress; and antisocial traits. In addition to these, any number of other issues may have come to the forefront over the course of our working together. But for the sake of brevity, I will only focus here on those change strategies that might be categorized as matters of spirit and soul.

As previously stated, I believe that the possibility of authentic spiritual formation that can result in an increasing experience of "Christ in you" or progressive "union with God" is built on the foundation of our view of God. Jake's counselor will work to help him develop a warm, loving and healthy view of God. There are a number of resources that may be helpful to this process (see table 6.2).

The therapeutic ground already covered should provide a solid foundation for this work. Jake's God views have been explored through the memory exercise above. There will have been an element of the incarnation in the person of the counselor and the environment that has been created. Along the way we will have sought to understand how any negative views of God may be part of maladaptive patterns in Jake's life. But at this point, I would seek to work even more intentionally to provide Jake with a scripturally accurate view of God and of himself, while providing some tools for increasing awareness of divine presence—and hopefully creating a desire for spending more and more moments "with" God. Toward these ends, there are a variety of exercises Jake's counselor might use with him. The following four are among those I use most frequently.

Table 6.2. Bibliotherapeutic Resources

Books	Dallas Willard	*Renovation of the heart: Putting on the character of Christ.* (2002). Colorado Springs: NavPress.
		Hearing God: Developing a conversational relationship with God. (1999). Downers Grove, IL: InterVarsity Press.
	Richard J. Foster	*Celebration of discipline: The path to spiritual growth.* (1998). San Francisco: HarperSanFrancisco.
		Streams of living water: Celebrating the great traditions of Christian faith. (1998). San Francisco: HarperSanFrancisco.
	David G. Benner	*Surrender to love: Discovering the heart of Christian spirituality.* (2003). Downers Grove, IL: InterVarsity Press.
	Larry Crabb	*66 love letters: A conversation with God that invites you into His presence.* (2009). Nashville: Thomas Nelson.
	Adele Calhoun	*Spiritual disciplines handbook: Practices that transform us.* (2005). Downers Grove, IL: InterVarsity Press.
	Jan Johnson	*Invitation to the Jesus life: Experiments in Christlikeness.* (2008). Colorado Springs: NavPress.
	Ruth Haley Barton	*Invitation to solitude and silence: Experiencing God's transforming presence.* (2010). Downers Grove, IL: InterVarsity Press.
Periodical	Edited	*Conversations: A forum for authentic transformation.* <conversationsjournal.com/>.
DVD	Edited	DVD small group resources for *Hearing God, Renovation of the heart, Celebration of discipline* and *Streams of living water* are available through Renovaré.

First, the counselor could ask Jake to experiment with a modified version of the daily examen, which is part of the *Spiritual Exercises of Saint Ignatius* (Ganss, 1992). In this modified examen Jake would find a convenient time each day—preferably at or near the end of the day—to sit down, relax and review the previous 24 hours of his life. He would allow the most life-giving times to enter his mind. Following this, he would also allow himself to relive the most life-taking moments of the day, ideally capturing these on paper to discuss in session. The theory is that the most life-giving moments of Jake's day—those characterized by experiences of love, joy, peace and so on—would be those in which he was moving with and toward God. The opposite entries would most often involve times of moving separately and away from God. Over time the goal is for Jake to begin to pray that each new day would contain more and more moments in which he was aware of God's presence and love.

The second exercise involves *lectio divina* and Scripture memorization. In class I often have students do an exercise where they take 10 minutes to eat a raisin. The purpose is to see what can be learned about that raisin that would have been missed if it were eaten in 10 nanoseconds. I will want the counselor to show Jake, in session, how to slow down his reading of selected passages of Scripture through using a form of devotional reading known as *lectio divina*. There are many ways to approach this, but we will use a pattern of meditative reading that will provide time to approach the text through four movements: *attending*—reading as listening and silence; *pondering*—paying attention to the thoughts and images that arise; *responding* to the thoughts and images that occur; and *contemplating*—spending time in silence with God. It is possible that the counselor would ask Jake to memorize a passage of Scripture, such as Colossians 3:1-17. The purposes of both the *lectio* and the memorization are to allow for the creation of alternative, positive views of God and the invitation to transformation.

Third, the counselor may ask Jake to experiment with the spiritual discipline of solitude. This practice could range from taking advantage of the little solitudes in the day (e.g., early morning moments in bed, slowly drinking a cup of coffee with a focus of attention on God) to spending a day or two at a retreat center.

Dallas Willard (1988) says that in solitude "we purposefully abstain from interaction with other human beings, denying ourselves companionship and all that comes from our conscious interactions with others" and calls solitude "the most fundamental of the disciplines" (p. 160). Why would he say such a thing? Maybe the answer is found in reflections by Teresa of Avila, who wrote: "Settle yourself in solitude and you will come upon Him in yourself" (quoted in Moon, 2005, p. 116) and by Richard J. Foster: "God takes this 'useless' Discipline, this 'wasted time' to make us His friend" (quoted in Moon, 2005, p. 116). My hope for Jake in his practice of solitude would be that he finds within himself Jesus, as a new friend.

Fourth, we would likely use the cognitive technique of guided imagery—toward the end of imagery restructuring. Tan (1996) refers to this technique as inner healing prayer and finds it particularly relevant in "situations where the client has suffered past hurts or childhood traumas" (p. 371), and then goes on to describe the procedure (pp. 372-74). Given Jake's history with his parents—which has included rejection, abandonment and harsh criticism—and his traumatic memories from the military, he would seem to be a good candidate for this type of intervention. This particular form of prayer can be helpful in facilitating a feeling of spiritual reconciliation with God.

Blending of counseling and Christian spiritual formation. With a nuanced transformational psychology approach, there is a blending of counseling and spiritual formation from the first encounter with the client. However, even with this approach there may come a time in the process where the focus has shifted and the majority of the work would be categorized by most as spiritual direction. I have come to such a holistic view of the person—which includes *spirit* and *soul* as essential to optimal functioning—that I now believe such categorizations (e.g., this is "counseling," this is "spiritual direction") are far too reductionistic. Having said that, there have been times when I was working with clients where I have had to say, "What we are doing now no longer seems directly tied to the presenting issues we began with—or anything for which your insurance company would be willing to pay. I would be happy to continue working with you, if that is what you'd like to do. But it would be better if we redefined the relationship, our goals and how fees would be handled."

In this hypothetical case with Jake, hopefully he would want to continue meeting with the counselor for a period of time where the entire focus was on living more and more moments of his life "with" God and the continuing journey toward union with God.

Evaluation and follow-up care. How do you know when it is time to terminate? At the risk of sounding simplistic, I think counseling should terminate whenever the client believes that his or her goals—which will likely change and evolve over the course of the working relationship—have been reached. The goals in working with Jake have been myriad, and some of them were more from a case management perspective—coordinating referrals for testing, AA/NA groups and psychiatric care. In the latter phases of working with Jake I would want to monitor where he feels he is concerning each of his presenting problems and the goals established for each—mood, suicidal ideation, impulsivity, social isolation, posttraumatic stress and other patterns of maladaptive behavior. I would also want the counselor to monitor where Jake is in his journey toward viewing God in a manner more consistent with Scripture and his journey toward spending more and more moments "with" God. It is very possible that the counselor would offer to continue to meet with Jake on a less frequent basis—perhaps once per month—and with a more explicit focus on personal spiritual formation.

Conclusions and Recommendations

Eric Johnson (2010) offers a poignant quote from MacIntyre, who considers that "the person best equipped to contribute to the debate between two rival traditions [would] be trained in the discourse of both. . . . Such individuals 'are inhabitants of boundary situations, generally incurring the suspicion and misunderstanding of members of both of the contending parties'" (p. 24). A primary consideration of my presentation concerning an approach to a nuanced version of transformational psychology is that the "boundaries" both within the components of the individual and across related mental and spiritual health disciplines have more to do with training than turf. I believe that a person dually trained in a professional mental health discipline and spiritual formation is not only capable of helping a person in a holistic manner, but they may also well be in the best position to do so.

While the complexity of the case made it difficult to focus more exclusively on the spiritual formation elements of a transformational approach to psychology, I believe that the present case study, while purposefully broad and expansive, did help to demonstrate the possibility of working with a person in a manner that, at times, blurs traditional boundaries. I also believe the case showed the possibility that working in the area of soul and spirit would have implications for other aspects of that person as well.

References

American Psychiatric Association. (2000). *Diagnostic and statistical manual of mental disorders* (4th ed., text rev.). Washington, DC: American Psychiatric Association.

Beck, A. T., Steer, R. A., & Brown, G. K. (1996). *Beck Depression Inventory-II*. San Antonio: Harcourt Brace.

Benner, D. G. (1998). *Care of souls*. Grand Rapids: Baker.

———. (2010). *Opening to God: Lectio divina and life as prayer*. Downers Grove, IL: InterVarsity Press.

Brown, W. S. (2004). Resonance: A model for relating science, psychology, and faith. *Journal of Psychology and Theology, 23* (2), 110-20.

Coe, J., & Hall, T. (2010). A transformational psychology view. In E. L. Johnson (Ed.), *Psychology & Christianity: Five views* (pp. 199-244). Downers Grove, IL: InterVarsity Press.

Egan, G. (1975). *The skilled helper: A model for systematic helping and interpersonal relating.* Monterey, CA: Brooks/Cole.

———. (2009). *The skilled helper: A problem management and opportunity development approach to helping.* Belmont, CA: Brooks/Cole.

Foster, R. J. (1983). *Study guide for celebration of discipline.* San Francisco: Harper-SanFrancisco.

Ganss, G. E. (1992). *The spiritual exercises of St. Ignatius: A translation and commentary.* Chicago: Loyola Press.

Gorsuch, R. L. (1983). *Factor analysis* (2nd ed.). Hillsdale, NJ: Erlbaum.

Johnson, E. L. (Ed.). (2010). *Psychology & Christianity: Five views.* Downers Grove, IL: InterVarsity Press.

Lazarus, A. (1989). *The practice of multimodal therapy: Systematic, comprehensive and effective psychotherapy.* Baltimore: Johns Hopkins University Press.

McMinn, M. R. (1996). *Psychology, theology, and spirituality in Christian counseling.* Carol Stream, IL: Tyndale House.

McMinn, M., Moon, G. W., & McCormick, A. G. (2009). Integration in the classroom: Ten teaching strategies. *Journal of Psychology and Theology, 37*(1), 39-47.

Moon, G. W. (1993). Christian counseling: You can go home again. *The Christian Journal of Psychology and Counseling, 7*(3), 12-16.

———. (1994, Winter). Spiritual directors and Christian counselors: Where do they overlap? *Christian Counseling Today,* 29-33.

———. (1996). *Homesick for Eden: Confessions about the journey of a soul.* Franklin Springs, GA: LifeSprings.

———. (1997). Training tomorrow's integrators in today's busy intersection: Better look four ways before crossing. *Journal of Psychology and Theology, 25* (2), 284-93.

———. (2003a). Spiritual direction: Meaning, purpose, and implications for mental health professionals. *Journal of Psychology and Theology, 30* (4), 264-65.

———. (2003b). Psychotherapy and spiritual direction: Reflections and cautions on the integrative path. *Christian Counseling Today, 11*(4), 32-38.

———. (2004a). *Falling for God: Saying yes to his extravagant proposal.* Colorado Springs: Shaw/WaterBrook.

———. (2004b). *Spiritual direction and the care of souls: A guide to Christian approaches and practices.* Downers Grove, IL: InterVarsity Press.

———. (2005). *Leader's guide for celebration of discipline: The path to spiritual formation.* Franklin Springs, GA: LifeSprings.

————. (2007). Which is more important in psychotherapy, the manual or the therapist? *Christian Counseling Today, 14* (4), 51.

————. (2009). *Apprenticeship with Jesus: Learning to live like the master.* Grand Rapids: Baker.

————. (2010a). Moving out of the slums of academia. *Christian Counseling Today, 17* (1), 62-63.

————. (2010b). A tribute to Dallas Willard: My favorite psychologist. *The Journal of Spiritual Formation and Soul Care, 3* (2), 267-82.

Moon, G. W., Bailey, J., Kwasny, J., & Willis, D. (1993). Training in the use of Christian disciplines as counseling techniques within Christian graduate training programs. In E. L. Worthington Jr. (Ed.), *Psychotherapy and religious values* (pp. 191-203). Grand Rapids: Baker.

Moon, G. W., & Fantuzzo, J. W. (1982). An integration: Christian maturity and positive mental health. *Journal of Psychology and Christianity, 2*(1), 29-38.

Moon, G. W., Willis, D., Bailey, J., & Kwasny, J. (1993). Self-reported use of Christian guidance techniques by Christian psychotherapists, pastoral counselors, and spiritual directors. *Journal of Psychology and Christianity, 12* (1), 24-37.

Powlison, D. (2010). A biblical counseling view. In E. L. Johnson (Ed.), *Psychology & Christianity: Five views* (pp. 245-73). Downers Grove, IL: IVP Academic.

Smith, J. B. (1991). *A spiritual formation workbook: Small group resources for nurturing Christian growth* (p. 11). San Francisco: HarperSanFrancisco.

————. (2009). *The good and beautiful God: Falling in love with the God Jesus knows.* Downers Grove, IL: InterVarsity Press.

Tan, S. Y. (1996). Religion in clinical practice: Implicit and explicit integration. In E. P. Shafranske (Ed.), *Religion and the clinical practice of psychology* (pp. 365-87). Washington, DC: American Psychological Association.

Walker, D. F., & Moon, G. W. (2011). Prayer. In J. Aten, M. McMinn & E. L. Worthington Jr. (Eds.), *Spiritually oriented interventions for counseling and psychotherapy* (pp. 139-67). Washington, DC: American Psychological Association.

Ware, K. (1995). *The orthodox way.* Crestwood, NY: St. Vladimir's Seminary Press.

Willard, D. (1988). *The spirit of the disciplines.* San Francisco: Harper.

————. (2002). *Renovation of the heart: Putting on the character of Christ.* Colorado Springs: NavPress.

————. (2009). *Knowing Christ today: Why we can trust spiritual knowledge.* New York: HarperCollins.

7

A Biblical Counseling Approach

Stuart W. Scott

LEARNING OBJECTIVES

- *Identify how this approach seeks to rely on the resources of the Holy Spirit, the Word of God and the ministry of the church.*
- *Assess the benefits and limitations of the central premise to this approach, namely, that true help and change can only occur as the client comes to know, trust and embrace who God really is as depicted in Scripture.*
- *Formulate a personal response to the three methodological commitments of biblical counseling: gracious care, biblical truth and specific application of God's Word.*

It is both a welcomed privilege and a weighty responsibility to represent a biblical counseling approach to Jake's case. I appreciate the opportunity to offer an inside look at a widely misunderstood paradigm to counseling. I will work to represent biblical counseling as a whole while also portraying a detailed process of helping this conflicted young man. In keeping with David Powlison's (2010) important work in *Psychology & Christianity: Five Views,* my basic goal is to clarify how the triune God can work through his Word and his church to bring about change in a life fraught with difficulties.

Of course, as with any approach to counseling, there is a spectrum of emphases and practices among those within the biblical counseling camp. There is room for the individuality of the counselor, for a range of preferred resources and for variations in the application of wisdom. There can be differences in the priority of certain aspects of biblical change, as is evident as you read differing leaders in the field. Yet even with diversity, there is a great deal of consistency with respect to the presuppositions, goals, methodology and counseling content among biblical counselors. Most vital to every practitioner is that his or her counseling flow directly out of the Scriptures and into practical life application. There is an operative conviction that God's Word is relevant to all of life and can be practically applied to every heart and every circumstance of difficulty. While this does not imply that Scripture is the only source of information in the counseling process, biblical counselors are consistent in their detailed biblical analysis of information and in their overwhelming focus on special revelation—the Bible—which alone is infallible and authoritative truth. As Powlison (2010) espouses, "This care and cure for the soul systematically differs from how other psychotherapies deal with the same problems for living" (p. 245).

This chapter will reflect my fleshing out of Powlison's perspective of biblical counseling but also will reveal the influence of individuals such as Paul Tripp (2002), Wayne Mack (2005), Jay Adams (1970, 1973), Steve Viars (2011) and others. Assuming the predetermined role of "expert consultant" to Jake's primary counselor, I seek to give an overview of the case and enough specifics to display an inside look at a distinctively biblical counseling process. Given the nature of the biblical counseling model, I would advise that Jake work with someone of the same sex, so throughout this chapter his counselor will be referred to as "he" or "him."

Introductory Issues

Initial impressions of Jake. Jake is a young man in great need. He has a profound spiritual void, and he struggles with multiple past tragedies, life-dominating sins, and both emotional and interpersonal difficulties in his life, all of which need to be addressed. It is also very likely that Jake has some cognitive limitations due to brain trauma, as his status of being medically disabled indicates. All of these realities together have had a profound impact on Jake's goals, beliefs, thinking and choices. They also have a significant effect on his mental and emotional stability, as well as his functionality.

To bring this young man to a place where he can succeed in college and be free to live to the glory of God in his adult life, he will need careful and strategic care through counseling and accountability. While it is possible that

Jake may need these to an extent only available at a biblical counseling residential facility, he may be able to remain on campus under counseling carefully collaborated with school and church involvement. Examples of biblical counseling facilities are Vision of Hope (www.faithlafayette.org/voh), Twelve Stones Ministry (www.twelvestones.org) and His Steps Ministries (www.hisstepsministries.org). More facts are needed before the best venue for counseling can be determined, and we will unfold this issue as we proceed.

Initial priorities in overseeing Jake's case. Several issues will be foremost in supervising Jake's counseling.

Prayer. Prayer is a crucial element of biblical counseling both in and out of the session. We work hard to help Jake, but we do so knowing that no one's efforts—Jake's or his counselor's—will accomplish much apart from God's power and work (John 15:5; 2 Corinthians 10:3-6; 1 John 4:4).

Consultation with the school counselor. Having expressed my appreciation for the time she has invested and commended her efforts to take seriously Jake's suicidal inferences, I would explain that she will continue to be an integral part of Jake's help and accountability. With the case now under my supervision, we will assume that I have another biblical counselor in mind for Jake. In order to reveal an inside look at Jake's counseling process, I will assume I am the "Fellow" who oversaw this counselor's training and that my input would be welcomed (this refers to a certification through the National Association of Nouthetic Counselors).

Suicidality. The counselor must facilitate an immediate evaluation of Jake's suicidal threat and drug involvement (Allchin, n.d.). This evaluation will serve to abate any dangers, help determine the best venue for counseling and provide additional important data for his primary counselor. For our current purposes we will assume Jake is having the intermittent thought that death would be better than his present circumstances, but no thoughts of actually ending his own life or of any specific way to do so.

Encourage the arranging of Jake's circumstances to facilitate counseling success. His course load and other life circumstances should be optimized for his benefit. We will also assume Jake was eventually clean of drugs and alcohol after his accident, throughout his lengthy stay at the rehabilitation hospital and, for the most part, prior to arriving on campus. He admits to only minimal use since he arrived at school but agrees it is an issue. The school counselor should secure a commitment from Jake to cooperate with drug screens for as long as he remains on campus. She should ask for a renewed intent not to use while in school, a commitment to meet regularly with the new counselor and a promise to discuss his drug use with that counselor. She should advise him to move in with a roommate on campus or, at the very least, with a suite mate and share a mutual open-door policy. We will assume that Jake agrees to all of the provisions and requirements that were discussed, and thus the school administration is willing to let Jake remain on campus while lessening his course load drastically. Should Jake fail to cooperate with all of this, or evidence a regression in regard to drug use or suicidality, a temporary leave from school and a residential stay in a suitable placement will be recommended.

Instruct the biblical counselor on his preliminary responsibilities. These responsibilities would include coordinating the sharing of appropriate information gathered or observed about Jake, meeting Jake for the first time through his school counselor, and getting signed release forms for acquiring past records. The counselor should also conduct preliminary research into resources possibly needed for Jake, such as a local physician, a local brain injury rehabilitation center (or neuropsychologist for evaluation of cognitive brain functions) and a residential biblical counseling facility.

Key presuppositions going into the counseling room. It is almost axiomatic in counseling circles that the conversations that will occur in Jake's counseling are the result of presuppositions, ideas and principles that guide the counselor's thinking and assessment. All counselors enter the counseling room with certain foundational beliefs about human problems and human "rightness," and both of these are directly related to their beliefs about the nature of God and change. The following are some key guiding beliefs that are pertinent in our biblical approach with Jake.

Character of the counselor. The personal calling of a biblical counselor is to reflect Christ in the counseling room while delivering the private ministry of the Word (Matthew 22:37; John 8:36; 17:17; Ephesians 5:1; 1 John 2:6). Jake's counselor will do everything he can to have the character of Christ, the message of Christ and the methods of Christ. For these reasons Jake's counselor's help will only be as good as his own relationship with the Lord, his biblical knowledge and his integrity toward the Scriptures (Romans 15:14).

Jake's faith. Only as a believer—that is, one who has faith in Christ—can Jake experience the right kind of change and change in the fullest sense

(1 Corinthians 2:14). Jake's counselor will fully embrace that without true faith in Christ, Jake cannot have the right desires, nor the hope of God-glorifying, lasting change through God's power (Ephesians 2:12; Titus 3:3). Biblical counseling is the appropriation of God's truth and God's resources, for true change, for God's glory, from the inside out. However, as long as Jake is at least open to exploring God and the gospel in reference to his life and problems, biblical counseling can continue (John 4:1-42).

Spiritual resources. God has provided the Holy Spirit, the Word of God and the local church as the collaborative, supernatural resources needed for Jake's salvation and his sanctification or life change (John 17:17; Romans 1:16; 6:1–8:39; Galatians 6:1; Ephesians 4:16; 2 Timothy 3:15-17; Hebrews 4:12; 2 Peter 1:3-14). This means that Jake's counselor is convinced that while Jake's heart and life are fraught with issues, he is not beyond the help of God and can change if all three of these crucial, God-given resources are operative in Jake's life. It means that the counselor relies on the fact that God's Spirit works *through* the Word, thus accepting that Scripture must play a central role in Jake's counseling sessions (Psalm 1:1-3; 19:7-11; 119:11, 45, 99, 129, 130, 165). The church is the vital community in and through which Christ has chosen to facilitate this work (Matthew 28:18-20; 1 Corinthians 12:1-31; Ephesians 4:16). In the words of the Christian Counseling Education Foundation's model, floundering people like Jake can "best image the triune God as [they] live and grow in community. Therefore, we embed [Jake's] personal change within God's community—the church, with all its rich resources of corporate and interpersonal means of grace" (Lane & Powlison, 2009).

In sum, a Christian worldview (embracing the purpose of creation and the gospel) along with God's Spirit, his Word personally and specifically applied, and Christ's church are together sufficient to deal with Jake's personal issues, the impact of his circumstances, his suffering and his sins.

The influence of the past. Jake is certainly influenced by his past, yet he need not be determined by, defined by or enslaved to his past (Ezekiel 18:1-32; 1 Corinthians 6:9-11). Jake's long-standing pattern of poor responses will add an additional challenge. But according to the Scriptures, in Christ he is able and even responsible to be "set free" from the enslaving power of repeated personal sin, from the effects of others' sin against him and from living in light of tragic circumstances rather than in light of greater truth (John 8:32; Romans 12:21; Titus 2:11-14). Jake's counselor must compassionately, practically and carefully address the real and influencing factors of the past. Nonetheless, Jake's freedom does not really lie in the past, but in his present and future.

Jake as a whole person. Jake possesses both physical and spiritual components that interact and affect one another because Jake is a whole person (1 Kings 18:1–19:21; 2 Corinthians 4:16-18). Jake's counselor will place importance on understanding the interaction of both components and address them both thoroughly and practically. For example, information concerning Jake's brain damage might have a bearing on how homework is assigned and done, and may be helpful in setting proper expectations and repentance plans. But because Jake is a whole person, the counselor also should not be dissuaded from dialoguing with Jake about spiritual principles that apply to his physical situation either (Powlison, 2010; Welch, 1998).

An Assessment of Jake

The assessment process for Jake will begin with the gathering of personal information, move to organizing the data into a biblically informed framework, and end by pinpointing specific categories of issues that need to be addressed with God's truth, personal application and practical assistance. Biblical counseling relies heavily on the comprehensive gathering of information to gain an accurate understanding and to speak with relevance (Proverbs 25:11-13). Proverbs 18:13 teaches, "He who answers before listening—that is his folly and shame" (NIV). There must be careful consideration of all the facts of Jake's life, as well as his personal interaction with those facts, in order to know what is really going on with him.

Determining who Jake is. Jake will be asked to fill out a Personal Data Inventory (sample PDI; Adams, 1973) prior to the first session. This form allows Jake to give very basic information on education, job or school status, any job- or school-related problems, emotional upsets, past counseling, familial relationships, health, spirituality, and personal problems.

In Jake's case, quite a lot of information is known before his new counselor sits down with him. I would encourage the counselor to use this head start and draw from the information what Paul Tripp (2002) calls "entry gates" (p. 126). These are usually experience-based realities such as fear, discouragement, anger, bitterness and hopelessness. They may not be the primary issues, but they will help Jake's counselor to connect, communicating that he cares and that it is worth it for Jake to open up about his life. By acknowledging Jake's experience in his own world, the counselor will communicate, "I hear your concerns, I take them seriously and I want to think carefully about how to counsel you." Past disappointments, discouragements and frustrations are particularly sharp realities for Jake.

The counselor's questions will begin with easier "get to know you" types, and then move to a compassionate, progressive retelling of the information he already knows. He will invite Jake to concur or not and to add any other information. While observing "halo data" (the appearance, body language, tone of voice and attitude that surrounds what is being said), the counselor will utilize both extensive and intensive questions about each area of Jake's life. Of particular interest will be his church involvement, knowledge of God and the gospel, his relationship to God, and what he thinks about the Bible. Jake's counselor may opt to send him home with a Spiritual Convictions Questionnaire (Mack, 1986) to assess these areas further. The basic facts of past tragedies and Jake's responses to them will also be a key area of investigation. Some questions will invite specific answers, but Jake's counselor would use many open-ended ones to reveal more of Jake's thinking and desires. For the most part, more penetrating, heart-confronting, learning-based questions would be reserved for later sessions. In all of these questions, the counselor will assure Jake that it is safe to answer openly and honestly. After the first session, and having obtained past records, I would consult with Jake's counselor to assist him in formulating his follow-up questions and data interpretation.

Is Jake in the right place—a biblical counselor's office? Jake's new counselor will no doubt come to the expected conclusion that Jake does indeed need the intensive private ministry of the Word in his life. Most obviously, Jake is not living responsibly (and therefore biblically) in the simplest of terms—that is, within the law and in a way that promotes the safety of self and others. These are priority issues for the biblical counselor. Still, Jake's counselor's real rubric for determining a biblical counseling need is not so much Jake's behavior against society's norm of lawfulness or even its definition of mental or social health. It is not the presence of psychological pathology as it is described in the DSM-IV TR (American Psychiatric Association [APA], 2004). Rather, it would be whether or not Jake is able, through a relationship with Christ and dependence on the Holy Spirit, to effectively counsel *himself* with Truth toward a more Christlike manner of relating to God, others, his circumstances and himself (Psalm 16:7; 119:24, 50; Galatians 6:1-2). Obviously he is not able now.

Note that a DSM-IV TR (APA, 2004) diagnosis is not a determining factor per se because the medical (illness) model of counseling does not play a key role in the assessment or the interpretation of Jake's data. Biblical counselors do not subscribe to the clinical paradigm in its particular ideas of mental health, psychological pathology and therapeutic needs. Thus, if Jake has already received a psychological label(s), the biblical counselor will understand that the categorizations and interpretations of enslaving, abnormal and/or harmful behaviors observed and studied by those within the disciplines of psychiatry and psychology continue to be widely debated (e.g., Kupfer, First & Regier, 2002). The biblical counselor does not reject human observation but does reject related theories of personhood, problems or solutions that stray from biblical perspectives and concepts. It follows, then, that the biblical counselor will not address the validity (or not) of Jake's previous diagnoses, but rather focus attention on the obvious issues that can be addressed.

Additionally, Jake's counselor would be advised not to focus on or offer advice regarding any psychotropic drugs Jake may be prescribed. This is for his physician to evaluate, address and/or help wean him from. If he is not on psychotropic medication, the counselor may share the position that medications can have undesirable side effects and that nonorganic problems often can be improved or resolved through counseling (Fitzpatrick and Hendrickson, 2006; Welch, 1998).

Insofar as a person is unlike Christ, chaos will erupt in his or her life. Christ alone functioned according to God's optimal design in every delight, thought, desire and decision. We will never be just like Christ (even in his humanity) this side of heaven, but the farther we move from who Christ is, the more "wrong" (abnormal) we become. Only in Christ and by his truth can we begin to change this wrongness from the inside out. Jake may sometimes claim to be a believer, yet he is not evidencing saving faith, is living with multiple unresolved issues in his past, finds himself in several patterns of sin and hopelessness, and is worlds apart from Christ's desires and goals. So, yes, Jake is most definitely in the right place.

How can Jake's problem be organized and characterized? It is crucial for the counselor to pull Jake's information together in a way that facilitates seeing issues clearly, understanding them from a biblical perspective and dealing with them in manageable proportions. Considering biblical emphases in Scripture, Jake's problems can be categorized in the following way:

Critical and immediate problems. (1) Jake's despairing of life; (2) drug and alcohol abuse; (3) needed assistance with counseling homework; (4) sleep deprivation; (5) a lack of verifiable information about his medical condition, specifically his brain injury.

Basic spiritual problems. (1) No apparent relationship with the triune God as Father, Savior and Comforter; (2) confusion regarding the problem of pain and tragedy in reference to who God is; (3) often displaying anger and rejection concerning God; (4) false worship, as indicated by his life agendas and hopelessness; (5) no apparent understanding of union with, identity in or a walk with Christ that has bearing on daily living (forgiveness, eternal hope, secure adoption, power, glad obligation to follow and obey, view of self and others); (6) no understanding of sanctification (Christian growth); (7) no apparent involvement in a church—God's primary community for the ministry of the Word, growth and service.

Cognitive and emotional problems. These are placed under one category because they are so closely related. The emotions are largely driven by one's thinking, even if physically initiated. Though there can sometimes be this organic element, clearly in Jake's case there are emotional problems stemming from spiritual and cognitive ones. Concerns here are: (1) trouble focusing on the basic tasks required for school, work and daily living skills; (2) menacing memories, terrifying flashbacks and what is commonly labeled "survivor guilt"; (3) confusion regarding his past due to a lack of personal resolution about the tragedies and failures in his life; (4) thinking patterns that are void of God and Truth and tend to focus on himself inordinately; (5) habitual emotional pain, fear and anxiety; (6) depressive episodes; (7) a persistent anger at life and others; (8) memory problems.

Behavioral problems. Concerns here include: (1) retreating to false refuges with reckless abandon, particularly to drugs, alcohol and gaming; (2) habitual responses to tragedies or to provocation are characterized by rebellion, anger, hostility and other sins; (3) poor use of time and lack of clear educational or vocational goals; (4) deceit.

Relational problems. Jake exhibits: (1) general isolation; (2) poor relational skills; (3) a lack of genuine (biblical) love for others; (4) a patterned lack of confession and reconciliation with others; (5) leading his young girlfriend into sexual sin; (6) responses to his mother and to school that are characterized by rebellion; (7) uncertainty as to whether his ex-girlfriend's child is his and his being prevented from having a relationship with the child.

Medical and physical problems. Concerns in this area include: (1) the lack of clarity concerning the limitations and difficulties from Jake's brain injury; (2) possible difficulty in accepting the effects of his brain injury; (3) poor sleep habits and/or insomnia; (4) poor stewardship of his body.

Jake's personal problems and behaviors will, whenever possible, be defined, understood and communicated in biblical terms. While disease terminology for nonorganic problems implies hopelessness and a lack of responsibility, biblical terms lend hope. Jake's biblical counselor will avoid any perspective that would reduce Jake's basic problems to merely a physical, metabolic or genetic cause.

Conceptualization

As I consult with the counselor about how to help Jake, I will encourage him to step back from the details and conceptualize Jake's problems from a biblical worldview. A biblical worldview understands humankind according to the reason for which they were created in God's image (spiritual, personal, rational and moral): to know personally, rely on and glorify God in this life and for eternity (Genesis 1:26; Matthew 22:34-40; 1 Corinthians 10:31; Ephesians 1:6, 12, 14).

Jake's life is demonstrably out of tune with God's purpose for him. Because of this, his problem is not primarily something outside of him, but within. A biblical worldview insists that the fundamental corruption of the human soul (sin through the Fall of humankind) has interrupted our purpose, and the negative effects of that corruption are multifaceted and complex. Because of the presence of sin, Jake is at least prone to independence, false worship and selfishness, even if he is a believer. At worst, he is a slave to the same as an unbeliever (Romans 6:1-23). He also lives in a world with others in this same condition, where suffering is a pervasive reality. There is great hope even in light of these realities for Jake, though, because of Christ's gospel and power to change lives and work all things for good (Romans 8:28; 1 Corinthians 6:9-11).

At the center of Jake's whole person is a spiritual being in a relational context with God and others. As a result, every issue of Jake's past and present is connected to spiritual and relational ones (Matthew 22:37-40). To help Jake most, his counselor must directly relate his goals for Jake to the fundamentally spiritual and relational purposes of Jake's existence. In trying to cooperate with God's goals for Jake, his counselor will seek to facilitate an increase of personal faith and worship toward God from his inner man out, consistent with his being useful in God's kingdom and connected with others.

Granted, the goals that Jake will bring with him initially to counseling (e.g., the removal of difficulty, help with his experiential struggles and an answer from God that satisfies his demands) will be different from his counselor's. A good biblical counselor will of course compassionately address all that Jake is facing, but true help and change will only occur as Jake begins to know and trust who God really is, and as he begins to embrace a new primary goal for himself. Jake's counselor must compassionately work to reveal to Jake his distorted and destructive views of God, life and his purpose, all against God's glorious alternatives. Doing this is not easy since it requires a shift in how human beings naturally think. But the Lord delights in working his redemptive transformation of human hearts, changing their goals from inadequate to excellent, from temporary to eternal, from self-centered to Christ-centered (Psalm 119:1-2; John 15:9-11; 2 Corinthians 5:15; Ephesians 4:20-32). This transformation will also result in Jake's experience of a perfect kind of love, joy, satisfaction and purpose. Ironically, these are the true longings that Jake's felt needs point to, and yet, the only way of possessing them is to finally and truly abandon them for the ultimate goal of knowing and glorifying Christ.

The following more specific biblical realities further explain the dynamics of Jake's trouble and hope for change. They will also be useful in outlining a counseling agenda, known in other approaches as a treatment plan.

True change must flow from Jake's heart. Even though challenging circumstances have preceded Jake's obvious troubles, his personal struggles and sins are a direct result of what is going on in his own heart. Because this is true, the most loving, effective and biblical approach with Jake is to begin there, drawing out what is in his heart

(Proverbs 20:5). This spotlight on Jake's heart is necessary for at least two reasons.

First, the heart is the engine of worship for Jake and every other person. Either this worship will be the false and idolatrous worship of specific lusts, or it will be the worship of the true and living God. The human heart is always fixated on some object of worship because we were created to worship (Deuteronomy 11:16; John 4:23; Romans 1:18-25; Colossians 1:16). For Jake this means that, prior to salvation, his heart was enslaved to false worship and engaged in it constantly, having great impact on his life.

This brings us to the second reason that we must address Jake's heart: There is a natural flow from the worship of the heart into behavior (Proverbs 4:23; Mark 7:21-23). In perfect wisdom Jesus consistently addressed the critical role of the heart (Matthew 6:21; 12:34-35). Jake's counselor must follow suit for the transformation of Jake's life. Addressing the heart in counseling is not an exercise in abstraction or morbid introspection. Instead, the heart has three very concrete occupations—affection, cognition and volition—which are all critical concerns in Jake's process of change (Mark 12:29-30).

Jake's affections are those things he values, desires and pursues. This ruling occupation of Jake's heart impacts everything that flows out into his life. When his particular affections become absolute needs and reach sinful and destructive levels, they are the objects of worship mentioned above—his idolatrous substitutes for the true and living God.

The circumstances of Jake's life may have had bearing on what he ultimately chose to set his affections on or worship, but they were not the cause of any idolatry. This must be attributed to his fallen state and the lusts of his own heart. Without God, what better things to worship (or so he thought) than the "lacks" he experienced in his life and those things that were at least a measure of relief to him in this sin-sick and sometimes tragic life. A full accounting of Jake's life will reveal pursuits, choices and responses that are keeping with his desire for or loss of hope in what his affections have been set on. In the absence of Christ, this review will evidence idolatrous lusts like the approval or love of others, a life without pain, and a personal, satisfying human relationship.

The fact that salvation will inaugurate a fundamental reorientation of the worship of Jake's heart toward Christ does not mean that Jake will not have any more problems of misguided worship (1 John 5:21). Jake's counselor must eventually prevail upon him to recognize the historical objects of his affections and to seek the help of God's Spirit to forsake practically any idolatrous pursuits. Most of all, Jake needs a continued, personal conviction of the supremacy and sufficiency of Christ against the futility and emptiness of treasuring and hoping in anything else (Philippians 3:7-8; Colossians 1:13-22).

Jake has had years of disordered affections that have driven his life and that still affect him today. Also, it is possible for new idols to crop up (1 John 5:21). So it is crucial to deal with what is ruling his heart at any given time. Paul Tripp (2002) explains that too often the Christian community seems most interested in stapling great-looking fruit onto dead or poor fruit-bearing trees, as if to say that what matters is what we look like or what we do outwardly, only to find that before long the tree (or the person) is fruitless once again (Marshall, 1692/2005).

Jake's cognitions are those things about which he is thinking. His thoughts are an integral part of his heart (Luke 5:22; Hebrews 4:12). They are what comes to mind, what he dwells on and what he comes to believe. They bring about powerful emotions that also impact his responses and choices. New heart worship will precipitate new kinds of thinking, but change in old patterns (and emotional stability) will only be as far-reaching as his practical application of God's truth to his thoughts. Jake's counselor has a responsibility to help Jake recognize wrong or God-void thinking, to determine what kind of worship these thoughts are flowing from, and to learn how to take thoughts captive and renew them with truth on the spot (Romans 12:1-2; 2 Corinthians 10:5; Philippians 4:6-9; Colossians 3:10).

Jake's volitions are his personal choices that flow from his worship and his thinking. They are an act of obedience to what drives him and occupies his thoughts (Romans 6:16-17). As Christ works through his Word at the level of Jake's affections and thoughts, and Jake responds, he will experience new behavioral desires and choices more and more (Luke 6:43-45). The counselor must help Jake see the connection of his inner man (worship and thinking) to his personal choices, and teach him from God's Word what more Christlike choices would be.

The gospel keeps transforming. Even after salvation, the greatest catalyst of Jake's inward and outward transformation is still the person and work of

Jesus Christ. The appropriation of gospel truths to Jake's daily worship and thinking must be central for his practical Christian change. Jake's counselor must be relentless in helping Jake to see the multifaceted benefits and obligations of the gospel. Jake must make personal and situational application of such realities as: forgiveness through the cross, union with Christ, security in Christ, power through Christ, abiding in Christ, denying self like Christ, and loving others like Christ has loved and loves him. These truths are not mere vagaries that do not relate directly to Jake's daily experience. So the challenge for Jake's biblical counselor is to minister gospel truths throughout counseling, helping Jake see the difference Christ can and should make in his daily circumstances, affections, beliefs, thoughts and actions.

Additional biblical elements of change. A focus on gospel application and right worship and thinking do not negate the need to help Jake employ other active biblical elements of change (e.g., "putting off" and "putting on" through repentance and faith; making no provision for the flesh; accountability; practicing means of grace like prayer, Bible study and church involvement). As Jake appropriates the gospel more and has new ruling desires (Christ himself and honoring him), Jake's counselor will indeed see some attitudinal and behavioral change (Proverbs 4:23; Luke 6:43-45). Still, Jake has had many years of false worship and other refuges that have resulted in the development of strong habit patterns that may not be easily renewed. Much of Jake's thinking and responses have become second nature. God's Word teaches us that even though the flow from the disordered heart to thinking, emotions and behavior is extremely natural, the renewed heart has as its enemies the flesh, the world and Satan (Romans 12:2; Galatians 5:16-17; 1 Peter 5:8-9). But God offers hope on every level.

All this means that in addition to gospel application, proper worship and biblical thinking, the counselor will carefully lay out for Jake a proper understanding of his cooperative role in God's transforming work (Philippians 2:12; Colossians 1:29). In other words, a proper theology of sanctification as it relates to Jake's own effort will also facilitate progress. God has been very clear. Jake must be intentional at both ends of his life—heart and behavior. God has told us to "add . . . to [our] faith," "make no provision for the flesh" and "discipline . . . [ourselves] unto godliness." He has even commanded *us* to put on the fruit of the Spirit (Romans 8:12-13;

13:14; 1 Timothy 4:7-9; 2 Peter 1:5-11). Jake doing these things unto Christ and through dependence on his power is different from attempting to staple fruit onto a dead or root-damaged tree. They are different because when they are done from a heart of faith and proper worship, they are worship themselves.

So the counselor must teach Jake not only to ask, "What am I worshiping, and what truth do I need to speak to my heart?" but also, "What helpful and/or obedient action do I need to take for Christ and with his help?" He is not to presume that a right heart will easily flow into all the right actions, especially where those strong habits exist.

Not helping Jake in the discovery of practical ways to facilitate change would be cruel in that it would prolong Jake's struggles. This also would hinder Jake in his obedience of God's commands to dependently work out his own salvation (Philippians 2:13) and to go against his natural feelings (Titus 2:12).

Not all problems are a direct result of personal sin, but can lead to it. While all sin and suffering trace back to the original sin of Adam, it is also true that many problems involve trials out of the counselee's control. For Jake, these would include any clearly proven organic issues, the tragedies he witnessed firsthand that plague him and the various ways people in his life have mistreated him. Jake's counselor will be aware that often people need help and hope on how to live with or respond to these kinds of situations from faith and not from sin (1 Thessalonians 5:14; James 1:2-15). Unfortunately, sinful responses often get muddled up with genuine suffering, and it is difficult for counselees to make a distinction between the two. While compassion is an absolute must on the part of the counselor, Jake will be profoundly helped by recognizing his own responses, confessing them (if sin) and discovering the biblical principles he needs in order to change.

Strategic, well-tailored homework will be essential for change. Jake's counselor will give him weekly homework of various types to help facilitate and measure the application of truths that are being taught. On topics pertinent to Jake's past circumstances or problems, he may be given a booklet to read, media to listen to, a passage of Scripture to study in a particular way or a practical task to complete before returning. This type of application is important because God expects his children to work, with his help, to apply the truth that they are given and/or say they believe

(Luke 3:8, 10-14; John 13:17; Philippians 2:12-13; 1 Timothy 4:7; James 1:22, 25). The practice of giving homework accomplishes many other goals. It gives the counselor more information, tends to accelerate progress, and helps sustain hope and focus between sessions. It gets the counselee personally into the Word of God, which helps the counselee see that it does have relevance to his own life. It reveals the counselee's commitment level, helps to measure understanding, provides a good starting point for the next session and encourages the counselee that something good is happening. Good homework is given in accordance with the counselee's abilities, relevant to the situation or problem; it actively uses or applies the Scriptures and is solution oriented, specific, measurable and attainable (Mack, 2005). One key aspect of Jake's homework will be finding ways to involve the body of Christ in Jake's life and he in theirs, especially to help meet the many practical needs that Jake has.

As I oversee Jake's counseling I will be assisting his counselor to further flesh out these principal realities of a biblical counseling conceptualization (Romans 15:1; Galatians 6:1).

Counseling Jake: A Look at Process and Agenda

With Jake's hope conceptualized in the ways just detailed, we can reveal more specifically what will take place in the counseling sessions. Jake's counseling can be condensed into these three methodological commitments: gracious care, biblical truth and specific application.

In addition to these methodological commitments, Jake's counselor will keep in view the five stages of the counseling process. This trajectory of counsel is illustrated in figure 7.1.

Care and involvement begins the counseling process and should span all phases. While there is an initial, concentrated time of gathering information (phase two), phases two, three and four do intermingle. But once Jake is evidencing some consistent progress, phase four begins with the widening of time between sessions. Finally, when Jake is spiritually, cognitively and behaviorally holding his own, he is released to regular church-body care and involvement.

Prior to any sessions following the primary data gathering, I will consult with Jake's counselor to create a counseling agenda that will address each of Jake's needs with biblical truth and wise application.

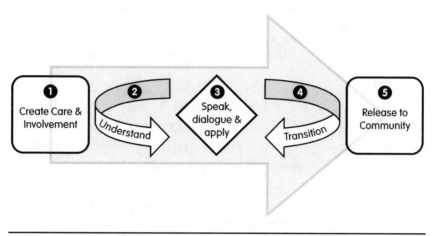

Figure 7.1. Trajectory of Counsel

This agenda will correspond to how Jake's problems were understood and prioritized in the assessment and conceptualization phases. What follows is a rough outline of how counseling can proceed. In the specifics, the order is somewhat adjustable. Actual counseling could require a different priority since all the issues are interconnected and have ripple effects into one another. I will consult with Jake's counselor on how these areas are progressing, offering any needed guidance or assistance. For each of the agenda items, helpful resources are available on biblical counseling websites, including teaching diagrams, worksheets, Bible studies, booklets, audio CDs and DVDs.[1]

Critical/immediate problems (address during the first week). As counseling begins, Jake's counselor must deal first with some issues needing stabilization. Jake's counselor should:

- Labor to instill hope and practically lessen Jake's isolation (Proverbs 13:12; 18:2).

- Insist on some assurance that Jake gets rid of all drugs and cuts off easy access to them.

- Have accountability set in place immediately. This is imperative (Romans 13:14; Galatians 6:1-2).

---

[1]These websites are a good starting point for biblical counseling resources: <www.stuartscott.org>, <www.soundword.com>, <www.CCEF.org>, <www.graceky.org>, <www.faithlafayette.org/store> and <www.biblicalcounselingcoalition.org>.

- Arrange for a person to help with counseling homework as well as some life-skills assistance as needed (possibly for managing time, good nutrition, sleep hygiene, keeping appointments, etc.; Galatians 6:2).

- Acquire past medical, counseling and army records and verify, as much as possible, the facts of his family history (Proverbs 18:13, 15, 17).

- Have Jake schedule a checkup with his general physician and possibly an appointment with a neuropsychologist (for repeat brain function testing) or a local brain rehabilitation center (depending on medical records; Proverbs 18:13, 15, 17).

- Ensure enough sleep for sufficient comprehension and interaction in counseling. Consider natural means or, if necessary, consult Jake's physician for a few nights' worth of sleep aid.

Basic spiritual problems. Jake's counselor will endeavor to help Jake understand the whole gospel and help him to know whether or not he believes in and is reconciled to the holy, powerful, gracious and faithful God of the Bible. This is in contrast to having responded to a different god or a truncated gospel that focuses on coming to Christ merely to have temporal needs met or to facilitate idolatrous lusts (Luke 14:25-35; 2 Corinthians 11:1-14). In addressing basic spiritual problems the counselor will also:

- Help Jake gain a better understanding of the problem of pain and tragedy in reference to who God is. This will probably be included in gospel dialogue and also in sessions dealing with his past (Lamentations 3:32-33; Isaiah 55:6-9; Romans 8:18-22; Revelation 21:4-5).

- Guide Jake to understand his own heart's worship, specifically highlighting the supremacy and sufficiency of Christ and identifying possible areas of idolatrous lust. As mentioned, these could be relationships, the approval of others, security, freedom from pain, control over his reality or other things. After walking through these concepts in Scripture, Jake will be graciously called to confess, repent, and begin to worship and find refuge in God alone in practical ways (Psalm 62:5-8; 73:25-28; 107:9; Isaiah 55:6-7; Jeremiah 2:13; Ezekiel 14:1-11; Romans 1:1-25; Philippians 3:8; 1 John 2:15-17; 5:21).

- Teach Jake what it means to have union with and identity in Christ in a way that affects daily living. Specific subjects that will be addressed are forgiveness, eternal hope, secure adoption, the church body, the indwelling Spirit and the power of God, the glad obligation to obey, what it means to abide in Christ, and having a proper view of self in Christ (John 15:1-11; Romans 6:1–7:25; 2 Corinthians 5:9-10, 15).

- Help Jake understand the nature of sanctification (Christian growth) as encompassing both God's work and humankind's, as being progressive in nature, and as affected by the functions of the heart (Romans 6:1–8:39; 1 Corinthians 6:9-11; Philippians 1:6; 2:12-13).

- Encourage Jake to attend and establish himself in a church that evidences a high view of God and the Scriptures, the centrality of Christ, strong evangelism outreach, a biblical counseling perspective, small groups and discipleship, and the practice of restoration-geared church discipline (Ephesians 4:11-16; Hebrews 10:24-25; 13:17).

Cognitive and emotional problems. Jake's counselor will teach Jake the spiraling dynamics of depression (including both spiritual and physical aspects) and how to reverse and avoid nonorganic causes (and even handle organic ones) by applying the biblical principles below. Jake must see the need for practical and timely faith with regard to all his emotions, suffering, desires and thoughts, and also acknowledge and deal with any sin or guilt in his life God's way. The counselor will likely have Jake track for a while his discouragement and emotional upsets on a weekly calendar that includes related events, thoughts and desires on it. In addition, the counselor will:

- Instruct Jake on not trying to work things out on his own and on how not to follow feelings, but rather choose to live dependently and responsibly at decision points (Proverbs 28:26; 3:5-6; John 15:5; 2 Corinthians 9:8; Hebrews 4:16).

- Help Jake more biblically understand his fears, anxiety, bad dreams and flashbacks that are associated with what is commonly known as posttraumatic stress disorder. Handling these in biblical ways with God's help will cause panic attacks and flashbacks to lessen and allow Jake to avoid the downward spiral of his emotions (Psalm 119:45; Isaiah 26:3; Philippians 4:6-9; 1 John 4:18).

- Work with Jake until he can understand and actively employ biblical principles of renewing the mind. He will be instructed in how to practically take captive individual thoughts by recognizing them for what they are, understanding where they are going wrong or are deficient, and prayerfully bringing in God's truth. With the aid of the Holy Spirit, turning to God and his truth when it counts, Jake will learn to develop renewed thought patterns and emotions that are more God-glorifying, profitable, hopeful, thankful and trusting (Proverbs 4:23; Romans 12:2; 2 Corinthians 10:3-5; Ephesians 4:21-24; Philippians 4:6-9; Colossians 2:8).

• Guide Jake in reinterpreting his own past with "new eyes" and in sorting it out in a way that brings spiritual clarity (Powlison, 2003, p. 256). The different events, responses and sins will be categorized in smaller portions that he and his counselor can begin to deal with God's way. This will be done with great care, being sensitive to what Jake can reasonably handle at any given time. The counselor will also address the wrong motivations, thinking and theology involved in what is commonly termed "survivor guilt," helping Jake learn how to renew these aspects of his survival perspective (Genesis 50:20; Romans 8:28-29).

• Address learning and memory problems with Jake, consulting with school, medical and rehabilitation professionals to insure that the appropriate assistance is available and that the biblical counseling model in not compromised by contradictory approaches. Also, Jake's ability to focus will likely improve some as his issues are dealt with biblically and he is more at peace (Psalm 119:165; Galatians 6:2).

Behavioral problems. It will be important for Jake to take responsibility for his actions but also discover what precedes them from his inner man (false worship, thoughts and false refuges) and outside him (specific temptation facilitators). Jake's counselor will have him track temptations and sins along with related events, desires and thoughts so he can begin to forsake old responses to his past and present and learn to respond biblically from a heart of thankfulness, worship and dependence. This will be accomplished as the counselor will:

• Exercise the Christlike character of humility, while addressing the heart worship, false refuges and thinking behind Jake's fleshly sins, wrong responses to life and wrong ways of handling guilt (Proverbs 4:23; Mark 7:21).

- Compassionately but clearly help Jake see his need to address specifically his past sins before God (e.g., anger, bitterness, sexual impurity, sins against others and self-focus) and turn to the forgiveness available through the cross (Psalm 51:1-19; Proverbs 28:13-14).

- Help Jake to learn more about his particular false refuges (e.g., drugs and alcohol, selfish pleasures, other people, computer games) against the one true and deserving refuge, God. These will need to be repented of by confession, pursuing God as refuge and learning patterns of righteous responses (Psalm 62:5-8; Jeremiah 2:13; 1 Corinthians 10:13; Ephesians 4:31-32; Colossians 3:1-17).

- Employ the biblical metaphor of *putting off* and *putting on* to explain the process of replacement (e.g., being less self-focused by thinking more about and serving others). This will also involve devising temptation and repentance plans (Ephesians 4:22-32; Colossians 3:1-17).

- Discuss with Jake the importance and ways of making no provision for the flesh and mortifying sin habits (Romans 8:13; 13:14; Galatians 5:17).

- Assist Jake in coming up with a reasonable and productive schedule for better use of time for Christ (Ephesians 5:15-16).

- Graciously point out Jake's deceit in the past and challenge him to become a man of truth for Christ, by Christ's power. He must address related desires and thoughts (Matthew 5:27-30).

- Help Jake create a plan for his future that will glorify God while realistically keeping in mind his physical disability (Proverbs 16:9; James 4:13-17).

- Repeatedly reiterate while dealing with behavior, in particular, that any element of change or cooperative work applied in his sanctification must flow from a heart that is vested with the right power, the right motivation and the right goal, all of which are Christ himself (Philippians 3:8-13; 4:13; Colossians 1:10).

Relational problems. Jake's counselor will begin in this area by instructing him in a biblical view of human relationships and how they have bearing on our relationship with God. This will lead to discussing how Jake has misunderstood or misused them in the past (Matthew 22:37-40; 1 Corinthians 12:12–13:7; Ephesians 5:1-2). Also, the counselor will:

- Challenge Jake to the Christian duty and privilege of showing Christlike love to others and forsaking a focus on self. He will address his old pattern of isolation and have him working on improving interpersonal skills (1 Corinthians 13:1-7; Ephesians 5:1-2; 1 John 3:11-18).

- Address Jake's various forms of anger toward others, leading him to see them as God sees them, face the heart issues behind them, and replace them with love, humility and returning good for evil (Romans 12:17-21; Ephesians 4:29-32; 5:1-3; Philippians 2:1-7; James 4:1-3).

- Eventually encourage Jake to address all his past sins against others with the offended party, specifically his mother, his ex-girlfriend and her parents, school authorities, and the girl in the dorm. This includes seeking to restore these relationships to their appropriate degree once he is learning how to relate to others more like Christ (Matthew 7:1-5; Romans 12:14-21; 1 John 1:9).

- Help Jake biblically process any real sins committed against him and to properly (for God's glory and others' good) address these with those individuals involved, as is necessary and possible (Matthew 5:23; 18:15-20; Luke 17:3-4).

- Depending on how details unfold, encourage Jake to have a paternity test conducted so he may begin the process of being involved if the child is indeed his. The counselor can also arrange instruction for Jake in regard to parenting principles and skills (Ephesians 6:4; 1 Timothy 5:8).

Medical/physical needs. Jake's counselor will seek to establish Jake's physical condition and address his needs in a practical and personal way. He will:

- Have any limitations as a result of brain injury clearly defined and addressed with the appropriate medical and occupational assistance (2 Corinthians 4:16-18; Galatians 6:2; 1 Timothy 5:23). The counselor will be encouraged to review findings from any brain scans or other procedures with the physicians attending Jake, and to consider the impact any findings may have on Jake's day-to-day functioning. The counselor must have Jake sign release forms in order to discuss with his doctors and any key rehabilitation professionals personal pertinent information to Jake's progress. He will then be able to encourage Jake to follow through on any recommendations.

- Encourage and challenge Jake to accept and respond to any of these limitations by renewing his thoughts concerning his God-given purposes and gifts, by being thankful for and faithful to what God has chosen to supply, by learning to depend on God's grace, and by discovering ways to help himself and to utilize needed resources and assistance (Matthew 25:14-30; 2 Corinthians 12:9-10; Hebrews 4:14-16).

- Continue to monitor Jake's sleep activity patterns and oversee sleep, exercise and work plans toward being a faithful steward of the body God has given him (1 Corinthians 6:19-20; 2 Corinthians 4:2).

The Sessions

For Jake's counselor the first session has three purposes: to begin establishing a relationship of love and trust, to understand Jake and his situation enough to offer some significant hope from the Scriptures, and to gain a commitment from Jake to continue the counseling process. This first session also offers an explanation of biblical counseling and outlines the responsibilities for both the counselor and counselee. Each subsequent session and topic will basically follow this pattern:

- *Pray:* Ask God for wisdom and for the Holy Spirit to work through his Word and assist Jake (James 1:5).

- *Connect and Review:* Refresh involvement with care, going over Jake's week and homework. Note any new data (Proverbs 18:13; Philippians 2:4-5).

- *Dialogue on Truth:* Interactively talk through appropriate Scripture and biblical principles with Jake (Psalm 119:45; Matthew 4:4; 1 Timothy 4:10-11).

- *Make Application:* Guide Jake to make application to his own heart and life through strategic questions (Psalm 119:34; Luke 3:3-14).

- *Call for a Response:* Using Scripture, address Jake's need to respond and commit in appropriate ways. Invite Jake to pray (confess and/or commit with thanksgiving) as appropriate (Psalm 119:30; Proverbs 28:13).

- *Offer Comfort and Hope:* Bring encouragement, hope and promises to bear in light of all the above (2 Corinthians 1:3-7; 2 Thessalonians 2:16-17; Hebrews 6:19-20).

- *Assign Homework:* Give Jake applicable listening, reading, Bible study and/or practical tasks to accomplish before the next session (Proverbs 9:6; James 1:22-25).

- *Pray:* Give God thanks. Ask for assistance today and until the next session and specifically with homework. Instill more hope here also (Psalm 25:4-5; 36:9).

How long it will take for Jake actually to internalize and appropriate truths cannot be known for sure. But generally speaking, it is a matter of months and not years to reach the transition stage of counseling (when the time between sessions is significantly widened). Typically, the counselee, who has responded to the gospel and continues on with counseling, becomes more and more hope-filled about Christ, the Scripture's practicality, and his or her own ability to change by God's grace.[2]

Concluding Evaluation and Follow-Up Care

As Jake's counselor continues to care for him, build trust, and minister Christ and his Word to Jake's heart—and as Jake responds—his life *will* transform. Ending regular counseling times with Jake would mean one of three things: (1) Jake now has working faith and worship and has transitioned well to regular church community involvement; (2) Jake shows a pattern of unwillingness to do the homework assigned; or (3) Jake drops out of counseling and does not respond to contact.

In the sad event of the latter two scenarios, Jake's church leaders would be notified so that they could follow up with him, care for him and implore him to continue counseling (Hebrews 13:17). (This would be consistent with an agreement of limited confidentiality signed at the outset of care, based on the premise that adequate care cannot be given without church oversight and involvement.)

Jake's flexible course could be loosely projected at 30 to 40 sessions. Due to possible responses on Jake's part and the number and severity of the issues facing this young man, this projection may yet vary in either direction. As he recognizes and turns from false worship and is able to appropriate what he is learning in an effective way, the time between sessions will widen in an incre-

---

[2]An actual in-session scenario addressing Jake's past, called *Stepping into Counseling with Jake*, is available from <www.stuartscott.org>. The website offers a helpful list of resources on biblical counseling and the training that is available.

mental manner. Even when regular counseling has ceased, there should be some checkups during the next year—some initially done by Jake's counselor and then some by his church shepherds. One of the benefits of involving the local body in Jake's life is that needed encouragement, accountability and opportunities to serve can continue indefinitely.

Wayne Mack (2005) offers insights on how to know when biblical counseling can be drawn to a close. With these in mind, here are ways to recognize when Jake's formal counseling can end:

1. His progress is seen by others as well as by himself;

2. He is able to understand his problems biblically;

3. He is experiencing a significant decrease in the frequency and intensity of certain temptations;

4. He is able to handle failures and difficulty well;

5. He is delighting in his walk with Christ;

6. He sees the importance of involvement with other believers and has established some good Christian relationships;

7. He is well established in his church, serving and ministering to others;

8. He continues to improve even when the times between sessions are lengthened;

9. He has a realistic plan for his future; and

10. His church elders are aware that counseling is ceasing, and there is a particular person in Jake's life for continued discipleship and accountability.

Conclusions and Recommendations

Hopefully, it is apparent from this chapter that Jake's case is appropriate for a biblical counseling model. Issues of the past, of suffering and hopelessness, and of destructive thinking and behavior are all issues stemming from the heart. The basic condition and perspective of the soul, the functions of the heart and God's path to change are what biblical counseling addresses so well. Of course, other resources are also important in Jake's case. Church involvement is paramount since "change is a community project" (Lane & Tripp, 2006, p. 73). Again, it is particularly important to utilize medical and brain rehabilitation resources in Jake's case. But predominantly, Jake needs a helper who will minister God's truth to his soul and his life.

As a pastor, teacher and counselor, I have seen a desperate need for Christian counselors (myself included) to know the Scriptures in depth and have it profoundly affect their counseling content and practice. Anyone interested in utilizing a biblical counseling approach should first seek training in biblical theology. Equally important is counseling training that strategically applies the Scriptures to the complexities of human life and also scripturally evaluates contemporary secular and Christian counseling presuppositions, theories, prescriptions and methodologies.

Though there are great limitations to the hypothetical case study of this book, this exercise affords a basic explanation of the goals, focus and direction of working with Jake through a biblical counseling model. My hope is that this survey reflects Tripp's (2002) description of biblical counseling: "In a nutshell: Speaking the truth in love, [so] we will in all things grow up into . . . Christ" (p. 332; Ephesians 4:15).

In actual counseling, it is a miraculous thing—a "God-thing"—to see the light dawn on a person's soul through the discovery of truth he or she has needed for so long. By the Holy Spirit's use of the Word through dependent vessels like us, Christ brings change to people like Jake every day (Scott & Lambert, 2012; 2 Corinthians 3:18).

References

Adams, J. (1970). *Competent to counsel.* Grand Rapids: Zondervan.

———. (1973). *The Christian counselor's manual.* Grand Rapids: Zondervan.

Allchin, S. (n.d.). *Why would she want to kill herself?* Retrieved September 1, 2011 from <www.biblicalcounselingcenter.org/node/5343>.

American Psychiatric Association. (2000). *Diagnostic and statistical manual of mental disorders* (4th ed., text rev.). Washington, DC: American Psychiatric Association.

Fitzpatrick, E., & Hendrickson, L. (2006). *Will medicine stop the pain?* Chicago: Moody Publishers.

Kupfer, D. J., First, M. B., & Regier, D. A. (Eds.). (2002). *A research agenda for DSM-V.* Washington, DC: American Psychiatric Association.

Lane, T., & Powlison, D. (2009, November 10). *CCEF history, theological foundations, and counseling model.* Retrieved from <www.ccef.org/ccef-history-theo logical-foundations-and-counseling-model>.

Lane, T., & Tripp, P. D. (2006). *How people change.* Winston Salem, NC: Punch Press.

MacArthur, J., & Mack, W. A. (Eds.). (2005). *Counseling: How to counsel biblically*. Nashville: Thomas Nelson.

Mack, W. A. (1986). *Preparing for marriage God's way*. Tulsa: Hensley.

———. (2005). Implementing biblical instruction. In J. MacArthur & W. A. Mack (Eds.), *Counseling: How to counsel biblically* (pp. 190-200). Nashville: Thomas Nelson.

Marshall, W. (2005). *The gospel mystery of sanctification* (B. H. McRae, Trans.). Eugene, OR: Wipf & Stock Publishers. (Original work published 1692).

Powlison, D. (2003). *Seeing with new eyes*. Phillipsburg, NJ: P&R Publishers.

———. (2010). A biblical counseling view. In E. L. Johnson (Ed.), *Psychology & Christianity: Five views* (pp. 245-73). Downers Grove, IL: InterVarsity Press.

Scott, S., & Lambert, H. (Eds.). (2012). *Counseling the hard cases: True stories illustrating the sufficiency of God's resources in Scripture*. Nashville: B&H Publishing Group.

Tripp, P. D. (2002). *Instruments in the Redeemer's hands*. Phillipsburg, NJ: P&R Publishers.

Viars, S. (2011). *Putting your past in its place*. Eugene, OR: Harvest House.

Welch, E. T. (1998). *Blame it on the brain*. Phillipsburg, NJ: P&R Publishers.

8

Distinctives and Dialogue

LEARNING OBJECTIVES

- *Illustrate the assertion that all of the five approaches are helpful groupings or categories that offer a range of options and variations.*
- *Compare your own list of similarities and differences between the approaches with the highlights identified here.*
- *Rank the five views according to your prediction of eventual counseling effectiveness with a client such as Jake.*

Jake's counselor will be in very capable hands no matter which of our authors is supervising. Each of our experts has done an outstanding job of sketching out a plan of action for Jake's multiple problems in a limited amount of space. Each author has shown a thoughtful, caring approach to serving Jake and improving his life. In any of the five directions, Jake will be well cared for.

Nevertheless, the trajectory of Jake's counseling will vary considerably depending on the approach to Christianity and counseling embraced by the supervisor, ranging from evidence-based spiritual interventions with Plante to strictly biblically based admonitions and guidance from Scott. In the predecessor to this book (Johnson, 2010), each of the five views has a representative respond to the other views to create a dialogue about their similarities and differences. That worked quite well in comparing the theoretical aspects of the differing models, yet that seems less appropriate in evaluating the five approaches in planning client care. Rather than initiate a debate, we intend to facilitate reflection as we offer dialogue about the treatment approaches.

This chapter will serve as an aid to the reader in placing the individual approaches within their conceptual models, and in assessing similarities and differences among the treatment strategies. Before reviewing our impressions, we encourage you to indulge your curiosity, ponder your reactions and reflect deeply on your observations in reading the chapters. Engage in an intentional round of thoughtful deliberation as you review the differing strategies and tactics of our five authors, and then read on and take in ours. If you are reading this for a class, the following questions might make an interesting assignment or structure a small group or class discussion.

Consistency with the Five Views

1. What surprised you about each of the approaches compared to what you expected following the *Five Views* book?

2. What was predictable about each of the approaches from what you expected?

3. Which chapter was the *least* surprising? Which was the *most?*

4. Which seems most consistent with the way you think about counseling?

5. What are some things you learned that might change how you counsel?

6. Which one approach do you see as the *most* distinctive compared to the others?

7. Which do you see as the *least* distinctive?

8. If two of the approaches could be combined into one, which would you choose?

Comparing and Contrasting Jake's Treatments

1. What does each model see as being "health" or "wholeness" for Jake? How do these differ? How do these concepts of health play out in the actual treatment plan?

2. What is the role of the counselor in the process according to each model?

3. How adaptable is each to people who are Christians and to those who are not?

4. How is assessment done? How does it impact treatment?

5. What is *wrong* with Jake? That is, what is the problem as understood by each author? What is the source for defining problems: *DSM-IV* or something else?

6. What use is made of professional sources besides the therapist? Which professions are invited into Jake's treatment?

7. How do the goals of treatment vary among the chapters?

8. What methods are employed in the counseling itself? What external sources do each draw from? Does any relevant treatment seem to be missing from any of the approaches? Are they the techniques you would expect from the model?

9. How does change occur according to each approach? How do these understandings differ? Who is seen as responsible for change?

10. How does the counselor know when to end therapy in each model? What plans are there for aftercare?

11. Specifically, how are the church and its ministry integrated into the counseling?

12. Which approach do you think will most likely be able to help Jake?

13. Maybe more importantly, which approach do you think Jake is more likely to stick with?

14. How do the differing models address Jake's relationships and relational skills?

15. What place is given in each for the role of Jake's past and its impact on the present? How do the approaches differ and/or agree on this?

16. How are Jake's physical problems considered in each approach?

17. What role does the Holy Spirit play in each?

18. Overall, which approach do you think comes closest to giving the highest quality Christian counseling to Jake? Which do you see as weakest? Why?

Five Families of Approaches

We turn now to our impressions from the five chapters depicting the five views in action with Jake. Again, it is important to be candid and acknowledge that one cannot capture in a single chapter all that would go on in any episode of counseling. This is even more apparent with a case as complex as Jake's. So wisdom dictates not focusing too much on what is omitted in any given chapter given the space constraints. It is likely fair to assume that each chapter does contain the prominent points of emphasis for each author, and we can work from there.

The five approaches are not monoliths. They are categorizations of approaches that are as varied as the persons who counsel. This is not unique to Christians, of course, as models of counseling are quite varied. It is important, though, to try to organize thoughts, as that carries important weight in discussing models. While "psychodynamic psychotherapy," for example, can refer to a very wide range of approaches, the term still carries important conceptual weight in knowing that the practitioner will focus on internal psychological dynamics. The individual therapist will identify his or her position within the broader model, be it a self psychology or ego psychology, or other "brand" of psychodynamic therapy. So it is with our five views: they are helpful groupings, but each has a range of options within the overarching family. Or, each is more of a "genus" encompassing a group of "species."

This raises a fundamental issue in evaluating the chapters just read. In choosing spokespersons for the views, we could not represent each nuance of each model. Some fit more neatly within the heart of the views than others. Moreover, like the Olympic rings, certain approaches overlap with others (and some overlap with more than others). In the following paragraphs we will try to position our authors within their broader positions.

Levels of explanation. Thomas Plante explicitly connects his approach to the levels view in noting that one should use the best available information in science (p. 61). Science is the source of knowledge and technique. Plante also neatly sets up a strategy of treatment that is more *intentionally* comprehensive than others are in that it encompasses vital "levels" that include biological, psychological, social and spiritual elements. Secular psychology today concedes that spirituality is important to many individuals, and Plante helpfully demonstrates that research has shown many spiritually based interventions can help. Plante's approach looks to science for diagnosis (using *DSM-IV*) and for assessment methods as well. Keeping with modern professional counseling approaches, it honors Jake's spirituality without imposing any spiritual ideas from outside his own system. Thus, spirituality is a resource to be utilized in pursuit of psychological health while the objectivity of God and his role in the therapy itself is not addressed. Jake will improve by application of scientifically supported, best-practice techniques that bring his spiritual values to bear on his problems in productive ways.

Plante's approach has the strength of being the only one that could be utilized in a strictly secular setting, and even by a non-Christian counselor. Its appeal to empiricism will also make it the most attractive to third-party payers. However, this also carries a potential weakness vis-à-vis the other approaches where greater emphasis is placed on the spirituality of the counselor in specifically Christian terms, and the more explicit appeal to God's actions as part of the counseling. It also does not address the Bible or Christ as resources for counseling in themselves, but only as valued by the counselee.

Integration. Mark McMinn's plan of treatment for Jake fits squarely within the integration domain that he represents and flows easily from Jones's (2010) description in the *Five Views* book; McMinn praises Jones for maintaining the "rightful authority of Christ and Scripture" (p. 85) in the model. McMinn makes clear his commitment to three primary sources of psychology, theology and spirituality, and to integrating them into a coherent model as he has done in *Integrative Theology* (McMinn & Campbell, 2007) while allowing for other models within this approach. However, his foundation of the model in the purely theological concept of "imago Dei" moves his take on integration from the center of the model's circle toward the Christian psychology and transformational views to an extent, making it more a form of what Johnson (2007) terms "strong integration." His discussion of brokenness and its role in counseling also shows a place of priority for the theological and spiritual, though he then draws freely from secular concepts such as cognitive behavior therapy (CBT). The idea of health toward which CBT and the rest of the model are directed, though, is defined from faith, not modern psychology.

McMinn is then a premier example of the integration position, with strengths in its commitment to Christian theology and spirituality while carefully drawing appropriate techniques and models from modern psychology. His approach also draws on one of the more detailed Christian integration therapy models that have been developed. Weaknesses might include its lack of empirical validation (something to be said of all the approaches except for Plante), and specifics on how and when to choose from each discipline.

Christian psychology. Langberg acknowledges the role of theory and research in the Christian psychology position as articulated by Roberts and Watson (2010), yet extends this to the work of the mental health professional. Admittedly she may have the greatest clinical challenge of the five approaches, as writers in the Christian psychology approach have had a strength in theory and intellectual models, yet to this point less attention has been given to translating these into clinical work (though see McFee and Monroe [2011] for a recent example of movement in this direction). The Christian foundation Langberg builds on is the impact of transformation by Christ on the therapist, and the therapist as representative of Christ in the session. Health is defined by Christ as its model, consistent with several other views. In the family of Christian psychology, Langberg may lean toward the integration side with her not tapping into the writings of the Christian tradition while looking to secular models for treatment techniques. Still, her focus on the presence and power of Christ as central in therapy echoes a stress of Christian psychologists who tend toward more explicit use of Christian language. She thus pioneers in this approach in thinking out practical counseling application.

Strengths for Langberg include her very clear focus on Christ (shared with the transformational view to follow) and movement into Christlikeness for counselor and counselee alike. The therapeutic process ultimately furthers kingdom-oriented character development and righteousness in daily routine. Secular techniques are placed in service of this goal. Yet this may have weaknesses in lacking a more comprehensive theory of change from within the Christian tradition and a lack of connection to historic Christian texts.

Transformational psychology. Gary Moon is forthright in his desire to avoid "silo building" and being confined to a single approach. This is more pertinent in the transformational psychology approach than the others, as it has been defined in detail by Coe and Hall (2010a) as the most precise and specific of all the approaches. A focus of their model, and the transformational approach in general, is the importance of spiritual formation and spiritual disciplines in transforming persons in counseling. It overlaps more with spiritual direction (as traditionally understood) than the other views. Here is the core of commonality that Moon shares with Coe and Hall, putting his approach more within this camp than any of the others. Yet he is also careful to distance himself from their approach, as he sees it as "too ambitious, optimistic and somewhat exclusive of the other four positions" (p. 135).

Moon is correct in seeing his position overlapping with others. His focus on Christ is explicitly shared with all the views except levels of explanation, and his focus on spiritual formation through the disciplines clearly overlaps with the levels view (where several of the disciplines are shown to have empirical evidence as helpful) and the biblical counseling view, though the other two would likely give place to these as well. But the transformational approach stresses these more than any of the others, and movement beyond counseling to spiritual formation and transformation is more explicit here than in other models. Therefore, Moon's model does fit within the transformational mold, despite numerous divergences from many of the specifics of Coe and Hall (2010b).

Strengths of Moon's approach are his focus on Christ and the centrality of living in fellowship with him, and his clarification of psychotherapy versus spiritual direction on the road to optimal health. A point of interest is that Moon endorses the application of numerous standard procedures and techniques for the early phase of treatment and reserves the most overt formative efforts for the later stages. He freely draws from psychology to organize his approach to therapy yet cites spirituality authors more than psychologists or theologians in incorporating faith into Jake's counseling. Weaknesses for this approach might include a need for more specific rules on incorporating empirical and other modern psychological material into the model and a need for more specifics in the treatment approach.

Biblical counseling. Our colleagues in the biblical counseling approach are evolving and changing, and the term now encompasses a variety of styles while maintaining the distinctive of a focus on the sufficiency of Scripture for counseling needs. Scott may draw more from the tradition of Jay Adams than directly from Powlison's (2010) description in the *Five Views* book. The consultant in his chapter is defined as a fellow in the National Association of Nouthetic Counselors (NANC), and he uses materials developed by Jay Adams. This would place Scott in what Johnson

(2007) calls the traditional (rather than progressive) camp of biblical counselors. While many biblical counselors might reject Johnson's categories, there would likely be consensus on the assertion that Scott's approach is more strictly nouthetic (using the term coined by Adams [1986/1970] drawn from Romans 15:14 and used to summarize his approach to biblical counseling) and more strongly authoritative than that of other biblical counselors. This is seen, for example, in his stating that "Jake's counselor must eventually prevail upon him to recognize the historical objects of his affections and to seek the help of God's Spirit to forsake practically any idolatrous pursuits" (p. 169). Powlison and others in this tradition might dedicate more attention to deep listening and to the relational engagement with the counselee. Thus, Scott is certainly representative of a mainline strand of biblical counseling, but he may be further away from the other four approaches than some of his contemporary colleagues in this area.

A definite strength for Scott's presentation is his thorough use of the Bible and appeal to its authority, an obvious bookend to Plante, who uses no Scripture. Yet this strength may also relate to a weakness in that the approach is more directive and sermonic than the other approaches. It also leaves little or no room for input from secular psychology in either understanding or treating Jake, though Scott makes place for the cognitive impacts of Jake's head injury.

It is apparent, then, that the five approaches overlap and interweave to quite an extent, yet there are distinct emphases in each that carry through. Many counselors generally would label their approach to counseling as eclectic in some sense; Christian counselors may glean from each of the approaches to form their own. The explicit strategy for how the reader might do that will depend on the nature of training (psychology/counseling versus pastoral ministry/theology) and the context where he or she counsels (private practice versus church versus public or parachurch agency). Individuals vary in their training to use the different models, and the models vary in how well they can adapt to different settings. For example, the majority of biblical counselors would not seek the governmental endorsement of a professional license, would not bill insurance companies and could not work in secular counseling agencies as a rule. Practitioners within the other approaches may be limited in how they involve faith in counseling because of licenses that subject them to limits in their practice.

We will offer a few thoughts comparing and contrasting the views on some of the vital aspects of the counseling process to assist the reader in thinking through these and other implications of the five approaches.

Distinctives and Commonalities

Certain aspects of the counseling process are endemic to it and thus transcend individual models. We will walk through some major dimensions of the counseling process to consider ways in which the five approaches presented above are similar and dissimilar.

Assessment. Each of the five approaches involves some assessment as one must identify what is wrong before one knows how to go about fixing it. Unique to the five is Scott's taking care to consider whether Jake is indeed a Christian in the first place, as biblical counseling is suited only to Christians. If it were clear Jake is not a Christian, then exhorting him to the faith would be in order. Scott uses a formal assessment form from his tradition, and he is the only one of the five to give explicit consideration to residential treatment.

All five at some point see need for further clarification of neurological issues, though this is most systematically approached as the "bio" of Plante's biopsychosocialspiritual strategy. Plante also details the assessment most formally and is the only author to make reference to a validated measure related to the use of faith in coping. Most address suicidality as a critical issue to evaluate. McMinn is the only author to explicitly explore diversity issues, also being alert to self-awareness and brokenness, which are central concepts in his model. Likely the least specific in the assessment area is Langberg, though she might have appealed within the Christian psychology approach to Johnson's (2007) overview of an assessment model. She is most specific in stressing the need of a treatment team to work alongside the counselor. Moon recommended a thorough evaluation according to the standards of best practice, although he only mentions a few specifics, such as use of a depression inventory and investigation of suicidality. The practice of conducting a careful spiritual evaluation is detailed and endorsed to address the core spiritual problems.

All except Scott work with *DSM-IV* to one degree or another, though *DSM-IV* itself comes from secular psychiatry (American Psychiatric Association, 2000). Though all the approaches save biblical counseling see some value to it, none appears to limit treatment to specific diagnoses that might stem exclusively from *DSM-IV*. The trend is for each approach to leave generous space to address spiritual concerns that are only peripherally mentioned in *DSM-IV*.

What is health? Much training for counselors leans heavily on the side of pathology and disorder, leaving less room to address healthy functioning. One must, however, know what health is to recognize disorder. Our five authors share differing visions of what health and disorder look like.

One way to sort the views is by category of health. Plante and Scott essentially collapse spiritual and mental health together, albeit in opposite ways. Plante quickly moves to the *DSM-IV* to place Jake into categories of psychological disorder, implying health to be freedom from diagnosis (at least to some basic extent). While spiritual aspects are addressed, these are not necessarily loci for "unhealth" but are coping resources to promote health and may or may not be used effectively in the service of mental health. In contrast, Scott eschews the *DSM* and conflates psychological disorder into the spiritual problem of sin. For Scott, Jake's health is to be freed from enslavement to sin in his past and present and to the impact of the sin of others.

The other three authors intertwine psychological and spiritual definitions of health in various ways. For example, McMinn and Moon both consider sanctification as ultimate health, though both also draw lines between counseling and pursuit of this. McMinn says that sanctification cannot be a goal for licensed therapists, rightly noting that it goes beyond their training and commitments to the counseling professions. Moon might transition to spiritual direction (and more overtly in the direction of sanctification) when psychological disorder is resolved, having a background in spiritual direction as well as counseling. McMinn adds that sanctification takes place in the context of relationship, so the process of sanctification will still often move forward in the therapeutic relationship, though not as an explicit goal. Moon sees health more basically as abiding in Christ, which will end in sanctification ultimately, but to abide in Christ, submitting to his will each moment, is to walk on the road toward ultimate health.

Langberg sees Christ as the model of health and wholeness, though she gives little detail as to how to pursue that outcome. She does stress that the growth of the counselor into the health of Christlikeness is a vital part of effective therapy. Interestingly, she sees the end of Jake's therapy (which is not to be confused with health) as determined by less lofty goals, such as his being more productive in his life, managing his affect and being in a supportive network of people. In this regard psychological and spiritual health appear to intertwine, but the mechanism is not described.

What is pathology? Knowing how our authors see health, we look at the lack of mental and/or spiritual health: pathology. What is wrong that needs to be treated?

As we noted above, four of the five views work at least to some degree within the *DSM-IV*. As expected, Plante stays most consistently with these definitions of disorder, though he acknowledges that Jake's ambivalent faith may negatively impact his decision making. Plante's use of standard psychological assessment tools also argues for a focus on traditional psychopathology. As we now see as common, Scott lies at the other end of the continuum. While he describes several things as "problems" that might overlap with *DSM-IV* categories (e.g., alcohol and drug problems, sleep problems), spiritual problems are the real pathology, revealing a faith that is unhealthy. Why? Because Jake's life is out of tune with God's purpose for him.

It would not be anticipated, however, that Langberg, representing the Christian psychology position, works more from secular diagnostic labels than either McMinn or Moon. She places much weight on Jake's having posttraumatic stress disorder. Then again, her astute noting of Jake's fatherlessness as an issue leaves room to point to the pathology of lacking a model of God as Father.

Mark McMinn sees psychological disorder in the traditional sense, but also finds pathology in a need for brokenness, a better sense of self and improved relationships. For Moon, pathology is "living apart from the Tree of Life" (p. 143), though he concedes such language may not be helpful to Jake in early sessions. This does, however, point to treatment addressing Jake's relationship with God, though Moon does see some of Jake's pathology in terms of *DSM-IV*'s concepts of maladaptive functioning.

Treatment goals. How one defines pathology leads directly into determining the goals of treatment. Plante utilizes evidence-based treatments that have been demonstrated as effective with the diagnoses Jake receives, with the implicit goal of eliminating symptoms of the diagnoses, though goals are delineated at each level of the biopsychosocialspiritual model. Moreover, he sees better physical health as a "side effect" of the improvements that enhanced spiritual coping will bring. Langberg, too, establishes goals based on diagnosis, but goes beyond this more explicitly. Her three phases of safety and stabilization, grieving and recognizing trauma, and newness of life follow from a treatment focus on trauma, but with both psychological and spiritual goals in mind.

Three stages make up the structure of goals for McMinn as well, as he moves through the functional, structural and relational issues facing Jake, noting interim goals along with longer-term ones. Gary Moon's explicit goal for Jake is to reconnect to God in a profound way, harking back to Adam and Eve's pre-Fall walk with God. Improved psychological and emotional functioning may be addressed to clear the way to spiritual formation, a focus that is at the crux of transformational psychology.

Scott's goals, too, are spiritual, though they are such from top to bottom without psychological subcategories. Jake will move to a working faith and worship that is also marked by active involvement in the Christian community. He shares such a relational goal with McMinn, though Scott is more explicit in the relationships being a church community that utilizes church discipline. In keeping with his more authoritative approach, Jake will remain under a spiritual authority even after his counseling is over. This is a goal unique to the biblical counseling perspective, but a point that other approaches might need to consider more.

The person of the therapist. Several of the approaches extensively highlight the spiritual life and formation of the therapist as an essential aspect of treatment. While this is clearly outside the realm of the levels-of-explanation view (not that the counselor's spiritual life is not important; it is just not a major issue in the effectiveness of counseling), it is noted in the other four. Prayerfulness is a focal point for all (and even Plante alludes to the counselor's saying a prayer as work with Jake begins). Langberg specifically sees the growth of the counselor into Christlikeness as integral to the Christian psychology approach, while Moon stresses the importance of training and spiritual formation for the counselor. Scott here finds common ground with these models as he emphasizes the character of the counselor being such that it reflects Christ in the counseling room. McMinn would likely agree with this, though it is not made explicit in his chapter.

Counseling methods and the process of change. Methods serve counseling goals as the means to achieve them. Therefore, they should fit consistently with goals and with the model's theory of how people change.

Gary Moon's chapter may spell this out as well as any of them. Change is rooted in pain and love, to which Jesus himself appealed in Matthew 11:28-30. Beyond these, Jake will need to show motivation, though part of that will be an outworking of the therapeutic relationship. The Willard model (pp. 136-37) shows that in this context, the Word and Spirit of Christ work in the person from the spirit out through the other levels of the person, producing faith and restoration. Techniques, then, will be primarily those spiritually rooted activities that facilitate the work of God's Spirit in Jake's spirit, though Moon leans toward those that have empirical support (which are those listed by Plante). He says less about the psychological aspects of change and how they tie into the three stages he borrows from secular psychology. Overall, the spiritual change process is readily apparent, and his references offer a helpful gateway into the resources of Christian spirituality for counselors less aware of these.

Scott's model may be closest to this, as he too maintains that change flows from the heart (which is used in a way similar to Willard's use of "spirit"). A caring relationship also is helpful and complements the motivation for spiritual change endemic in the true believer, but change for Scott is more educational and instructional, with Jake being encouraged to act on knowledge rather than to seek more spiritual experience. In keeping with this more didactic approach, each session is clearly planned and draws from other biblical counselors for resources and homework (a central tenet for Scott, who stresses this more than any of the other authors, though Moon gives it an important role as well). Change is the gospel transformation effected by Jesus, yet Jake is required to act as well—it is not a passive process in Scott's view.

For McMinn, change is in a sense opposite from the Willard model presented by Moon, as he begins by addressing the functional problems that are more superficial and symptomatic. True to the model, the methods are an integration of psychological and theological/spiritual strategies and techniques. Change deepens as therapy moves into the deeper, structural needs; McMinn stresses not always changing underlying psychological schemas but accepting them to a degree. This draws from psychological research yet serves spiritual purposes for McMinn. Relational change is the final area and develops a context to maintain progress made. So McMinn is clearly an integrationist in drawing freely from both spiritual and secular sources to promote change.

Though many Christian psychologists might start from a more specifically Christian point of view, Langberg organizes her interventions around a well-documented trauma model from which she gets much of her strategy. Using scientific approaches is certainly within the realm of the model, though she utilizes it in a manner almost more in keeping with an integration approach. In other words, she seeks to blend seamlessly techniques for trauma recovery with interventions aimed at spiritual maturation. This may not be typical for her, however, as she avoids being too overtly Christian early in therapy given Jake's distorted faith. Once stabilization has occurred, she gently moves into addressing and using his faith as a resource, as being exposed to God's truth is a source of change. Langberg is the only author other than Scott to specifically address Jake's sin as such (though from other writings [McMinn, 2008] it is clear that McMinn is also comfortable discussing sin). An important emphasis for Langberg, appropriate to a Christian psychology approach, is that God is seen at work on *both* sides of the counseling relationship to promote change. In doing so she may give the therapist's faith a larger role than any of the other authors, or at least she is more explicit in doing so. Langberg's third stage matches McMinn's in its focus on Jake's relationships and that they can be strengthened. They thereby join Scott in stressing a healthy relational context as needed at the end of Jake's counseling.

Plante's model of change is more purely psychological, seeing change occurring when using techniques that research has proven to help. Yet research does not dictate, but merely informs, professional practice, giving leeway to customize treatments to individual clients. This is consistent with the ethical value of autonomy of the client and giving Jake input into the counseling (again, on the opposite side of the one-directional approach of Scott). The levels view supports a systems approach to counseling, with the differing levels impacting each other. For example, we just mentioned how a better spiritual life improves health, but also with Jake, a head injury could cause cognitive deficits making praying and maintaining relationships harder. Still, the overarching theme is to use only things that have been proven to work, making his model the most appealing to insurers while still allowing Jake's spiritual needs to be addressed. Recall that Moon also prefers spiritual disciplines that have empirical support and thus displays his respect for the insight that research can shed even on matters where the Holy Spirit is operative.

Termination of counseling. Each of the five authors offers insights into how to know when it is time to terminate. Consistent with a more empirically rooted strategy, Plante looks for measures of treatment outcome, or data to support progress. This would include possibly the readministration of some of the tests given at the outset of treatment. He encourages Jake's involvement with outside resources such as the Veteran's Administration or Alcoholics Anonymous for ongoing support outside of the counseling office. He also suggests follow-up or booster sessions after formal treatment ends.

McMinn shares three "exit points" in the counseling process, noting that some clients choose to leave after the shorter-term functional concerns are addressed, just as Jesus addressed only the physical needs of individuals at times. Other clients will stay through the structural phase and address schemas, while even others may stay to engage in long-term relational work. He recommends a maintenance phase before termination.

Langberg had clear goals that signal the optimal time for termination, including more focus and productivity in Jake's life, satisfactory management of affect in his life and a supportive network of people around him. Termination is incremental, including a titration of session frequency as the end nears. This sets it apart from the first two models. Also, relationships within the body of Christ are a vital part of aftercare for Jake.

Moon gives more of a role to Jake in deciding when he is ready for termination, allowing him to assess when treatment goals are met. Yet the counselor would also monitor Jake's progress toward goals on the various presenting problems. Moon, too, suggests a slowing down of treatment and potentially a shift to spiritual formation rather than counseling per se.

Scott wisely mentions that two ways treatment might end would be due to Jake's dropping out (a possibility for any approach given Jake's history), or Jake's refusing to do homework and thus lacking investment in counseling. Biblical counseling is unique among the five approaches as seeing itself not being practiced most often by licensed counselors. Rather, it is firmly resolved to be an extension of pastoral care (though both Christian psychology and transformational psychology might be readily conducive to church-based counsel in some of their iterations). Jake has completed counseling when he "has working faith and worship and has transitioned well to regular church community involvement" (p. 180), though Scott suggests additional criteria as well. Scott would ensure that Jake's church leaders are aware of this and follow up with his care.

All of the approaches see varying forms of aftercare as important, with the church community's being part of it more explicitly in the Christian psychology and biblical counseling chapters. The integration and transformational chapters are more overt in empowering Jake to participate in a mutual agreement to end counseling.

Role of the local church community. Finally, most of the chapters overtly discuss the role of the church in Jake's counseling and ongoing maintenance of treatment gains. Two of the empirically supported spiritual interventions listed by Plante include participation in religious rituals and community support. These easily translate in the Christian community to participation in the sacraments and involvement in the local church. The Christian psychology and biblical counseling chapters are most direct in incorporating Jake's involvement in a local church as part of his growth and spiritual care, though for Scott this is about accountability and not just social support.

McMinn does not speak directly about the role of the local church, but approaches this in seeing a church-based support group as an ancillary to counseling, though he sees this as one option along with mentoring or involvement in a campus ministry. Moon is the only author to not mention the church directly, and it is true that much current spiritual direction is done outside of the bounds of the formal church community. However, Moon would likely concur that much spiritual direction has been done within a church context (as is true of many of the orders of monks, for example).

As we have noted before, in such short chapters omissions cannot be interpreted as negations of aspects of counseling. There are numerous other areas where we could compare the treatment approaches taken by these five counselors representing different approaches, but the discussion above serves to cover major points. In many ways, the overlap of the approaches is more than one might expect after reading Johnson's (2010) book, for different theories sometimes lead to surprisingly similar practices. Yet many aspects are quite consistent with reasonable expectations based on the models presented in the *Five Views* book. And in some ways, there are surprising differences, such as the ability of Plante to appeal to research to incorporate spiritual interventions, or the comfort Langberg has as a Christian psychologist to draw from secular models of treatment. Moon's transformational approach allows for continuity with standard therapeutic practices in ways that one could not predict given the tone of the corresponding theoretical articulation of that model in its inaugural presentation.

To reiterate an important theme of the current book, these models are families, and like your family and mine, some individuals bear more of a familial resemblance than others, despite the ties that bind. Moreover, each family is not orthogonal from the others, as there is extensive overlap in understanding and approaches—even though they come to those from different theoretical orientations. This is exemplified in the happy convergence of Moon's devotion to the spiritual disciplines and Plante's scientific justification for the same practices.

Models and specific approaches are important, and likely will only increase in importance as current trends push counseling to be more specific. Yet as Plante noted, science (and theory) inform but do not dictate counseling. By its very personal nature, counseling will always be different for every combination of counselor and counselee. God gives a variety of gifts and works in a variety of ways. It is the wise counselor who knows the models, abides in Christ, and applies the wisdom of training and experience to the unique needs of each client.

References

Adams, J. E. (1986/1970). *Competent to counsel: Introduction to nouthetic counseling.* Grand Rapids: Zondervan.

American Psychiatric Association. (2000). *Diagnostic and statistical manual of mental disorders* (4th ed., text rev.). Washington, DC: American Psychiatric Association.

Coe, J. H., & Hall, T. W. (2010a). *Psychology in the Spirit: Contours of a transformational psychology.* Downers Grove, IL: IVP Academic.

———. (2010b). A transformational psychology view. In E. L. Johnson (Ed.), *Psychology & Christianity: Five views* (pp. 199-226). Downers Grove, IL: IVP Academic.

Johnson, E. L. (2007). *Foundations for soul care: A Christian psychology proposal.* Downers Grove, IL: IVP Academic.

———. (Ed.). (2010). *Psychology & Christianity: Five views.* Downers Grove, IL: IVP Academic.

Jones, S. L. (2010). An integration view. In E. L. Johnson (Ed.), *Psychology & Christianity: Five views* (pp. 101-28). Downers Grove, IL: IVP Academic.

McFee, M. R., & Monroe, P. G. (2011). A Christian psychology translation of emotion-focused therapy: Clinical implications. *Journal of Psychology and Christianity, 30,* 317-328.

McMinn, M. R. (2008). *Sin and grace in Christian counseling: An integrative paradigm.* Downers Grove, IL: IVP Academic.

McMinn, M. R., & Campbell, C. D. (2007). *Integrative psychotherapy: Toward a comprehensive Christian approach.* Downers Grove, IL: IVP Academic.

Powlison, D. (2010). A biblical counseling view. In E. L. Johnson (Ed.), *Psychology & Christianity: Five views* (pp. 245-73). Downers Grove, IL: IVP Academic.

Roberts, R. C., & Watson, P. J. (2010). A Christian psychology view. In E. L. Johnson (Ed.), *Psychology & Christianity: Five views* (pp. 149-78). Downers Grove, IL: IVP Academic.

9

Conceptualization and Contextualization

LEARNING OBJECTIVES

- *Critique the idea that counseling in Christian wisdom means building a comprehensive case conceptualization and humble application of expertise.*
- *Debate the notion of location and the value of contextualization in the application of the specific approaches to psychology and theology.*
- *Review with counseling peers your responses to the ten orientation questions designed to clarify convictions and promote wisdom in counseling practice that is decidedly Christian.*

Counseling and Christian Worldview

The transparent display of the five Christian counseling approaches presented will encourage readers to freely compare and contrast. It may be a surprise to learn that an improved grasp of viewpoint distinctions or even a more fervent articulation of a favored position is not the ideal criterion to evaluate progression in counselor development. The best gauge of helper proficiency for bridging theological perspectives and ethical Christian service is the active application of a cognitive framework that facilitates counseling connections and conversations. An essential learning outcome from this case-based exploration of perspectives is internalization and expansion of a Christian worldview. This inner, faith-attuned framework needs to be versatile enough to facilitate well-delivered, client-sensitive and thoroughly Christian applications in a wide range of service delivery settings and cultures. The intention of these pages is to guide counselors to initiate a lifelong helping journey with confidence and conviction.

In chapter 2, a representative set of mental health professionals (MHPs) were introduced. Andy, Sonia, Ray and Anita, like numerous novice people helpers, will seek out an effective conceptual model to join their deeply held spiritual passions with their counselor training. Beyond the necessity to merge information and techniques to function adequately as a people helper, those who follow Christ often have an inner curiosity to explore how spiritual formation, personal growth and counselor development actually coincide.

- Andy, a social worker, came through the early life experience of being a child of an alcoholic by a firm reliance on his Christian faith. Currently he invests his therapeutic efforts into supporting struggling families who face economic hardship in addition to mental health concerns.

- Sonia has training in pastoral care. She is the first member of her immigrant family to achieve an advanced degree. A Bible school degree focused her career aspirations on a counseling role closely aligned with a church. After all, career missionaries and a local congregation made all the difference in the physical and spiritual destiny of her family.

- Ray selected counseling as a second career. As he stepped away from a successful identity as an accountant, he prepared himself to pursue generativity in midlife out of his enthusiasm for discipleship (Erickson, 1982). As a therapist, he thrives as a mentor to those who wish to grow in a walk of faith.

- Anita, in addition to being a mother of teenagers, is a psychologist whose professional identity is bound to a core conviction: her personal well-being and counseling skills are the result of a multitude of miraculous blessings.

These representative MHPs will gravitate toward a distinct method of establishing the parameters to manage the relationship between Christian theology, Scripture, the movement of the Holy Spirit and principles derived from social science. Their choice of a uniform method will also influence how each merges client information to formulate a conceptual template to understand the whole person. The client's life narrative and issue-relevant material gathered via assessment and empathetic listening move through an internal assembly framework to shape a coherent story of the whole. In other words, these approaches tie worldview to counseling activity by ordering perceptions and establishing priorities.

This chapter seeks to stimulate learning and assist MHPs to build explicit connections between their own Christian worldview and a particular area of practice. Our intent is not to favor any single approach. Our tactic will be to introduce central operational concepts and priorities to guide counselor development. We will move stepwise through a progressive series of questions. Counselors will identify their theological beliefs. Finally, Christian counselors will consider how these inform the plan and procedures applied to the art of helping others.

Defining Key Terms

Case conceptualization is the deliberate combination of data related to presenting concerns, background information, personal attributes and interpersonal tendencies into a clinical profile ample enough to elucidate client issues and options. Our expert consultants demonstrate that core beliefs about faith and practice impact their conceptualization of Jake's case. For example, Langberg observes that in Jake's initial presentation, he exploits faith for his own purposes. His distorted view of God and Christianity ties to a wider misuse of others. He will resist change in this core area until there is a coherent sense of stabilization. Once there is progress in basic functioning, more focused work to nurture a healthy and authentic relationship with God can proceed. This insight and structure to connect the dots in Jake's chaotic story displays the benefit of a theologically and therapeutically grounded worldview.

Case conceptualizations contain hypothetical links regarding cause and effect, informing the plan to secure change. Theoretical grids establish working assumptions to predict connections and pilot treatment. What is distinctive about each of these five approaches is that theological, biblical and spiritual principles are brought to bear in different ways on the client scenario. Thus, the case conceptualization forms in a manner consistent with a Christian worldview. This is the benefit derived from the appropriation of an explicit interface model. Case information is organized within an overarching anthropology reflecting Christian tradition and spiritual resources. Thinking as a follower of Jesus Christ permeates conceptualization and allows counselors to remain attentive to the leading of the Holy Spirit.

Building accurate and useful conceptualizations is a common activity in advanced counseling courses. Considerable education and supervision is invested in cultivating a counselor's skills in this arena. Clients themselves typically actually collaborate and contribute to a thorough conceptualization of the forces contributing to their presenting issues. The five Christian views take this a step further as they aid in sorting out broad matters of epistemology—how we know what we know—and are utilized when assembling case information into a comprehensive life story—why we do what we do. A therapist's overall understanding will structure the route offered to clients to realize restoration and growth.

The following term, a pivotal one in global Christianity, is admittedly not a common one within the mental health literature. Yet it may be productive in extending the practice applications that flow from this extensive case exploration. *Contextualization* is the process of communicating the gospel in word and deed into a specific sociocultural setting (Chang, Morgan, Nyasulu & Priest, 2009). This expression has been extremely important in the area of Christian mission and theology for decades. Experts in mission began to realize that spreading the good news of Jesus Christ meant sharing the essence of the message using words, metaphors, stories and practices that communicated as crosscultural equivalents. This was not merely a matter for translation of Scripture but a consideration for the essentials of Christian living as Western culture recognized the value of indigenous communities. Missionaries became aware that sharing the wonder of the gospel did not necessitate furthering the cause of economic colonization or enforcing Western customs. Becoming a member of God's family for eternity requires recognition that the Creator God became a human person, willingly consented to death on a cross as an atoning sacrifice to destroy the stronghold of sin, and not only rose from the dead, but ascended into heaven (Romans 1:16-17; 1 Corinthians 15:1-8). Living as a disciple of Christ does not require conformity to a peculiar style of clothing or singing hymns to melodies imported from other eras, cultures and customs. Careful reflection on how to contextualize core factors of the gospel, along with ministry formats, allows the advancement of the spread of Christianity without the repudiation of local culture (Moreau, 2006).

Contextualization is an intentional activity conducted by Christians committed to evangelism across cultures. It requires adaptation of the forms, content and routines of the Christian faith to communicate the gospel core in the best possible way to the minds and hearts of people with diverse cultural backgrounds. Here is the rationale for adopting this term in relation to counseling. Christians who engage in conversations to heal must evaluate not only how the gospel themes of creation, fall and redemption inform the client's story and circumstances; it is also essential to ponder ways that service delivery will respect, cohere or conflict with cultural, institutional and client values. This applies to the export of these approaches to other geographic locations or as they are implemented nearby with sojourners displaced from their homeland. Further and of the utmost importance in a pluralistic age, select principles associated with contextualization are applicable when engaging clients within a dominant secular culture where Christianity is no longer welcomed or tolerated as a religious tradition. Christian counselors, who serve as sheep among wolves, need to heed well the words of our Lord to be as shrewd as snakes while as innocent as doves (Matthew 10:16).

What MHPs such as Andy, Sonia, Anita and Ray may discover across their careers is that while a certain approach may be personally preferable and useful for case conceptualization, it may not be the ideal fit for a particular setting or client. Having the flexibility to apply another view may be prudent and display discretion. Wisdom may reveal that adjusting one's approach results in a superior means to contextualize a faith-based hope. After all, counseling is not a matter of what one thinks personally but what one delivers in service to a client with distinct characteristics. Beyond client considerations, services flow through a specific organizational structure and into an established community. Let's set the stage for Christian counseling across a full spectrum of settings, clients, issues and goals by way of an old anecdote with a novel twist.

Blind-Sided by an Elephant

An ancient Asian fable featuring an elephant timelessly illustrates the foolishness of making broad assumptions about a whole based on limited information gained through a narrow slice of data. What is especially interesting about this often-cited folklore gem is that it is most widely recognized in the Western world through its telling by a nineteenth-century American satirist, attorney and Vermont poet, John Godfrey Saxe (1816-1887; Linton, 1878).

Saxe begins his poetic telling of the tale by introducing six blind men of "Indostan" who were much "inclined" toward learning. The fascination of their day was to discover the nature of an elephant through personal, hands-on observation. Each of the six sight-deprived examiners latches onto a different part of the grand beast, then proceeds to describe the whole mammal through the characteristic discovered in the lone factor encountered. The first blind man touches its broad side and declares the elephant to be like a wall. The second grabs a tusk and determines that an elephant is certainly like a spear. The third locates the trunk and decides that the elephant is most comparable to a snake, whereas the fourth takes hold of a leg, concluding that its structure is more like a tree. The fifth happens upon an ear and deduces that its likeness is to a fan. And the last man reaches the tail and accordingly classifies the elephant as a rope. Hopeless argument erupts. Each blind "seer" clings tenaciously to his personal conclusion based upon empirical data that are, unfortunately, too restricted in scope. The poet ends with the resounding lament. Each was partly right, yet all were exceedingly wrong!

This poem, with its pleasant rhyme, enduring message and childlike simplicity has found countless applications about perspective drawn from its main eight stanzas. In its slightly longer version, Saxe explicitly adds his own salient moral to the story in a ninth stanza. In this he points his satirical finger at theologians who rail on tirelessly about an elephant that none, according to this poet, have experienced through the use of their fundamental senses. Saxe settles the disagreement among these finite investigators decisively. He asserts that the limits of empirical experience restrict our human ability to achieve a comprehensive understanding. Moreover, the implication is that it is sheer foolishness to be adamant in an assertion when one cannot possibly perceive the whole. There are those who display an attentive interest in learning; nonetheless, when a mind closes prematurely, capacity is limited. In the end, Saxe closes his little ditty with these six unfortunate blind men looking virtually as foolish as their ridiculous assertions.

Certain adaptations of this tale may go back as far as 2000 years before Saxe ever picked up and Americanized the yarn. The story is generally attributed to Indian, Chinese or Muslim tradition, and the claim for origin resides in folklore or in religious writings. Curiously, when non-Westerners release the antiquated story, the blind men are not depicted as quite so silly, stubborn or empty-headed. The intense manner of the arrogant disagreement displayed within the sarcasm of Saxe's poem is blunted or removed (Blubaugh, 2011). Non-Western versions do not have these five characters left in unceasing noxious competition. Instead, the urge among these curious elephant investigators is to *collaborate*. The blind men may initially draw improper conclusions based on what their hands actually touched, but they do not remain long in ignorance. There is honor in joining observations through genuine communication and cooperation. Pooled perspectives achieve a fuller picture of the physical form of the elephant.

Before leaping to suspect a proposed link between our expert consultants and the blind elephant researchers, rest assured there will be no such association! The insights of these consultants with their extensive counseling room experiences amply demonstrate that each is far from blind. The direction ahead involves stimulation of the imagination. The intension is to promote a nuanced schema to govern the approach to conceptualization, so it is necessary to awaken creative tendencies. This is an occasion to recall that genuine people helping is a hybrid venture requiring the use of strategic interventions with artistic application. Counselors bring helping techniques validated through extended practice and replicated success. In addition, interpersonal skills build relationship with intentionality. The maintenance of a Christian faith dimension throughout the helping process requires merging acquired methods and creative abilities with attentive receptivity to the Holy Spirit.

Consider counselors as investigators who enter helping encounters in much the same way as the famous blind men become acquainted with an elephant. The experience is direct, and all sensory inputs are operating. Still, Christian counselors seek understanding beyond the client's dilemma manifest through the unfolding story. They strive to gain a transcendent vantage point in order to address the condition of the soul. Although this statement may be controversial, the proposal at the outset of this text was that counseling is a contemporary adaptation of soul care. "Soul" in this sense is the whole human person including the unique quality to reflect and relate to the Creator. Thus the view of the person and scenario most desired would be that of Jehovah. Such comprehension is indeed an undertaking of elephant-sized magnitude and proportion.

For the sake of exercising imagination, picture an elephant rescued from a traveling circus by representatives of a radical animal-rights group. The lost creature has been set "free" but cannot thrive because it is virtually trapped in the status quo of captivity. It is unable to adjust to its new routine, unstructured lifestyle and free-range living in spacious surroundings. Helpers would not be seriously interested in the size, shape or physical likeness of the elephant. Unfortunately, the whole functioning and dilemma of the elephant cannot be seen with the naked eye. Compassionate keepers would have limited capacity to tap into its inner well-being, social patterns, symptomatic behavior and inner life. It is not feasible to take in the mammal's full characteristics, areas of vulnerability and the developing scenario purely by visual inspection. Each counselor must individually encounter the beast by listening, watching and intimately following its ongoing story.

The first therapist might readily center on the elephant's trauma experience throughout years of captivity, constant travel, unnatural performance expectations and enslavement to fulfilling the insatiable entertainment lusts of human beings. The cumulative impact of this trauma may be severe. Memories may not fade with time alone, as allegedly, elephants never forget. A second counselor may hear of the elephant's escalating, desperate attempts to show off, demand attention and draw a crowd. Although admittedly this creature was conditioned through training to perform, such narcissistic tendencies on a continuing basis would not go unnoticed or unaddressed. Perhaps a third helper would empathize exclusively with the breakup of the established herd following the rescue. The tragic loss of familiar social supports, along with intense experiences of isolation, could be cause for much discomfort. A fourth counselor may conjecture about the new surroundings as a poor environmental match for the elephant's genetic constitution. This may appear to be an African elephant, but its derivation could either be from the savanna or the forest. Besides the possible dispositional irregularities, rumors of a splendid pink elephant may undermine its dignity and self-esteem. Finally, a fifth counselor may postulate that the elephant is disoriented and without a sense of purpose. It has no existential core. Its days are dulled by a lack of purposeful activity. The circus may have been enforced barbaric slavery, but the daily hoisting of the big top and prancing for peanuts positioned the elephant in surroundings where it enjoyed a highly regarded, pre-scribed role and function.

There is a vital lesson to this far-fetched stretch of the ancient tale: counselors meet clients in need at a single point in time. From the present, they strive to unravel the past and fathom a hopeful future. A client is not static but is a whole being, constantly developing and experiencing unique transitions. Counselors make inferences about the total based upon direct experience with only select parts: story samples, affective displays, behav-ioral reports and immediate relational encounter. In addition, clients do not have their lives on pause. New experiences, events and relationships occur as they are in treatment. Even if a well-fashioned description is rea-sonable following an intake appointment, new data is constantly available.

Reflect back on Jake's scenario. Each of those initial counseling ses-sions not only gained novel information about his past, but fresh chal-lenges surfaced. The visual picture of becoming acquainted with a moving elephant may not be such a metaphorical leap. Entering the life experience of a client with the purpose of delivering soul care involves attending to the organizational layers of biological, psychological, interpersonal, be-havioral and spiritual dimensions (Johnson, 2007). Forming a compre-hensive conceptualization requires a humble application of therapeutic expertise. Impressions form, but the counselor must remain open to re-vision over the course of treatment.

Furthermore, change is contemplated, strategized and pursued in an appointed relationship. This is precisely the point where the theme of con-textualization becomes useful. Case conceptualization is the process of gaining understanding for the purpose of healing and nurturing the soul. Contextualization is the considered implementation of scriptural truth, Christ-exemplifying relationship and the practical delivery of refreshment to a unique client immersed in community and culture. With clarity re-garding worldview and faith convictions, counselors are protected from being blind-sided and missing the whole. The intent is to counsel toward change in a manner reflecting Christian wisdom regarding an individual in unique circumstances without falling into the pits of relativism or to the whim of random preferences.

These ideas extend the recommendations found within the concluding chapter of the predecessor volume, *Psychology & Christianity: Five Views* (Johnson, 2010a). The reader is encouraged to revisit that summary directly to deliberate on the outcome evaluation criteria for shaping an internal mental grid allowing for the utilization of a multiperspective system and a customized view of persons in transition. For the sake of a smooth flow into the clinical considerations that follow, here are two key assertions from Johnson's concluding chapter.

The necessity of humility. Johnson (2010b) makes the case that each view on the relationship between psychology and Christianity must be appraised from within the virtue of humility to produce mature understanding. A diligent search for wisdom commences with an open admission of the need for greater understanding. Wisdom is sought because a gap is recognized between acquired knowledge and the insight deemed essential to proclaim mastery. Surprisingly, as greater awareness is gained, this acknowledged gap does not readily remit. Instead, an ironic realization tends to surface. A steady increase in learning promotes a balanced appreciation for what one has yet to grasp. Epistemic humility and modesty about what one has come to know will maintain the requisite eagerness to earnestly refine and expand knowledge.

Moving through multiple perspectives is indeed an iron-sharpening-iron endeavor (Proverbs 27:17). Thus a reasonable outcome of this process is increased depth in epistemic humility. On the other hand, this is not an educational venture calculated to wear seekers down until there is resigned abandonment of the search. Being unassuming about what one knows produces a quiet and resolved confidence. This is quite distinct from sensations of being overwhelmed, confused or discouraged. There is no justification to cease a vigorous exploration for a faith-enhancing, organizational framework by settling for an anemic relativism. A superficial or passive relativism may have a core belief that echoes the following statement: "It is evident that conflicting but credible positions exist; thus personal beliefs in this area do not really matter." On the contrary, this bland, uncritical acceptance will not forge guiding principles useful to increase case conceptualization skills. Rather, this represents an avoidance of the furnace where deep values are forged and pressed firmly into one's consciousness. Instead of giving in to a nondiscerning position, one must seek to pursue a more comprehensive resolve.

The most advantageous result to an investigation of approaches is progress in obtaining the best possible grasp of God's outlook on the subject. Well-articulated models may seem rational, reasonable and biblically grounded. Yet not all may be uniformly valid when the ultimate criterion is conformity to God's perspective. Despite the pervasive and contrary contention of this postmodern age, there are viable, correct, Creator-oriented perspectives. The beginning of genuine wisdom is founded on the conviction that submitting one's mind and heart to the Lord is the basic starting point in any learning quest; what must follow is a worship offering of any astuteness gained.

The scrutiny and anointing of the Holy Spirit is available by submitting to the Lord in worship. Johnson (2010b) contends that genuine dialogue modifies understanding and that distinctly Christian dialogue helps participants anticipate God's transcendent perspective. Such conversation would best begin with prayer as the seeker addresses and listens to God. The next step is to consider Christian tradition, especially as expressed by the inspired authors of Scripture. The discourse continues, becoming an active interaction with material offered by credible professional leaders who have thought deeply about Scripture, theology, psychology and helping approaches. Counselors absorb what these specialists have to say about critical interdisciplinary relationships by turning our ears toward wisdom and our hearts toward understanding (Proverbs 2:2).

God is a triune communicative agent who engages in action to reveal his nature, purpose and wisdom. Scripture is the written masterpiece of his various communication strategies. Human agents assist us, by grace and the activity of the Holy Spirit, to grasp this imperative communication (Vanhoozer, 2002). The optimal perspective on a subject is the one that readily conforms to the reality that God created and sustains. Human finiteness accompanied by sin's vision-dimming effects on cognition and relational priorities make our egocentric assertions prone to error and distortion. In order to ascertain how our models for clinical work may reflect a robust Christian theological worldview, it is essential to faithfully band together in community. Members of the body of Jesus Christ who investigate Christian tradition and the Scriptures gain perspective on the reality God creates, speaks and reveals.

The contention in these pages is that such high-minded and lofty ideals can not only be pursued but practically achieved. This is demonstrated through the survey of treatment approaches targeted to assist a wandering and confused college student such as Jake. This grand scheme to move from model to counseling praxis is intricate yet simple. The cognitive components and considerations are certainly complex, but the hope for the results of this effort is a matter of childlike faith. The initial step forward is to return the conversation back to the Lord and to bring key questions before him. This furthers discernment on how an approach might contribute to client change efforts while honoring and pleasing the Lord.

The recognition of location. The second premise to evaluate in conjunction with a multiple-perspective review involves the recognition of location and how this is incorporated into the functional advantages of a *metasystem* (Johnson, 2010b). The term *location* is appropriated from the economic realm of property valuation. Real-estate experts are fond of citing a repetitive phrase to explain why homes with comparable features can command a wide range of price expectations. The answer is "location, location, location." The phrase is a haunting reminder that value is not solely determined by a discrete set of notable characteristics; worth is influenced by features *and* placement. For example, a weather-worn, clapboard shack with an airy porch and occasionally leaky roof may not command much investment interest based upon a series of close-up photos. Display that identical crude dwelling perched royally on a cliff overlooking the ocean, and its potential will be immediately apparent. The asking price will leap from affordable to astronomical. The question shifts from, "How much for that rundown shack?" to, "What is the asking price for that quaint, rustic seaside getaway with the stunning vistas?" Features *and* location combine to establish value.

Borrowing that popular phrase, Johnson (2010b) points out that each interface of psychology and Christian faith does have a prime location. That is, each approach is associated with a unique practice domain where its central principles particularly thrive. There may be a best fit within the academy, psychological laboratory, local congregational ministry, counseling clinic or discipleship forum. For example, a social science researcher may realize the great value of the levels-of-explanation perspective when employed at a major university hospital. The capability to logically, realistically and effectively compartmentalize faith while vigorously pursuing scientific research would be viewed as an asset. Transfer that identical researcher into a leading role on a grant project for a private, faith-based college. In this location, Christian psychology might be the interface position of choice due to its extraordinary resources to formulate foundational assumptions and faith-affirming hypotheses. In discussion regarding personal counseling, this notion of location will take on particular clinical significance.

Perhaps the assumption is that the most productive analysis of psychology and theology views would be to conduct an evaluation to ascertain which perspective successfully serves Christians in helping roles across the most counseling locations. The goal would be to select the approach with the most extensive application power. This process of elimination would be most comforting. Since only a single model would be found worthy, only one would have to be mastered. However, a one-size-fits-all decision grid has an unfortunate downside: the models ruled out have distinct worth in other locations. Further, fitness for the most locations cannot be the sole value for approach selection.

Consider this illustration. The predominant trend across the contemporary mental health setting is to promote evidence-based treatment, and in many locations (particularly served by third-party or government funds), it is a requirement of any counseling (Norcross, Hogan & Koocher, 2008). Levels of explanation as a system respects to a high degree the credible contribution of modern science and grants allegiance to its chief method for determining the best techniques—empirical research. This explains its diligence in the application of evidence-based treatments. This indeed grants it favor for most secular and medical agencies. Does its widespread applicability and compatibility make it the optimal or exclusive ethical approach? Despite the credibility of the approach, the answer is an obvious and emphatic "no!" For example, the integrationist view also gleans insight from empirical research, so it too can blend into settings with a preference for interventions informed by research. Christian psychology invites research to demonstrate the empirical value of Christian concepts and approaches.

Furthermore, the elevation of empirical investigation by social scientists as the arbitrator of best practice displays an ideological bias favoring empiricism, scientific methods and a nontheistic worldview. These priorities can distract attention from biblical revelation. The trend in professional mental health care toward an evidence-based model thus might pull Christians who counsel away from practices embedded in our faith and theological convictions. This trend may foster discrimination against techniques that flow logically from the storyline of Scripture and may deprive clients who respect the authority of revelation the benefit of this perspective. Finally, though location may make a particular view more suitable, it may not provide the most fitting care for each client scenario. The point is that while location is important in model selection, it cannot become the sole criteria for establishing optimal interventions or, more pointedly, in determining what constitutes genuine soul care.

The establishment of a broadly based evaluation grid, a scheme to guide the implementation of systems, may allow for commitment to a select combination of models. Such an overarching structure to manage systems would allow a counselor to hold two approaches as viable even when these contain vastly different assumptions. The internal logical procedure to guide the choice of a complete set of preferred principles and practices is labeled a "metasystem." Such a strategic, thought-shifting mechanism allows for fluid application according to location expectations in ways that are sensible and feasible to achieve a Creator-honoring perspective.

Having an effective, flexible cognitive application grid might be compared to the stability of an operating system on an electronic device, such as a computer or mobile phone, to navigate between programs. These programs run in the background while opening the possibility for applications to perform seamlessly in the foreground. It is realistic to have multiple programs open simultaneously. The operating system permits smooth transitions between effective tools that have applicability in unique circumstances. This is no appeal to haphazard, random or wobbly whims; on the contrary, the development of a metasystem is a concerted effort to validate a disciplined and sophisticated style of cognitive processing capable of utilizing diverse approaches in a complimentary design.

In the complex realm of direct counseling care, there are more factors in play than location. To put it another way, if counseling were a song, it would not only have a single melody but would resonate with full, enriching harmonies (Brown, 2004). For practitioners, the faith-psychology approach in use must adapt not only to service site requirements but also to clients whose needs and expectations may be in flux. There may be conflicting motivations, fluctuating circumstances and variable outcome goals. Most importantly, there are immediate and intermediate spiritual concerns as well as lifelong and eternal issues at stake. Counseling is an interpersonal helping procedure to aid clients as they contend with change. Thus by necessity, there are forces to ponder such as unique life trajectories, cultural heritage and relational interactions. Counselors need to navigate multiple perspectives as well as an assortment of dimensions. Despite the science-fiction motif to such an undertaking, it is plausible to bring these concerns to the practice level.

Orientation

Moving forward, the remainder of this chapter offers ten "orientation" questions to provoke reflection. Orientation is an identification procedure to launch a lasting direction of thought and inclination. The design is to stimulate introspection as well as prayerful meditation on theological and kingdom concepts that add substance to case-level understanding. Counselors will formulate an inner framework for aligning service delivery that is client and context sensitive as well as thoroughly Christian. Envision counselors such as Anita, Ray, Sonia and Andy gathering to make applications from the previous chapters. These orientation questions can initiate discussion and bring critical themes to the surface. Let's begin.

Clarifying faith experience and beliefs. Helpers who aspire to counsel in a robustly Christian manner would do well to begin with an appreciation for their personal faith journey and core doctrinal commitments. One's walk with God and theological underpinnings will be integral to the selection of an interfaith approach.

CONVERSION

Describe how you came to love and commit the passion of your life to Jesus Christ. Consider the people, persuasive concepts, personal circumstances and Spirit-enabled awareness that brought about repentance, conversion and the realization that you are a new creation in Jesus Christ.

There is a connection between the development of a functional meta-system for case conceptualization and one's personal confession of the gospel. The realization that God's grace alone transforms our life by the movement of the Holy Spirit, along with the recognition of servant qualities of our Savior, does much to maintain a gospel-centered, epistemic humility. Our unique spiritual narrative along with its prominent forces, people and layers is worth considerable contemplation before coming alongside another to offer comfort or facilitate change. The second orientation question builds on the first.

CONVICTIONS

What doctrinal statement, creed or concise theological treatise best reflects your central beliefs? Consider the faith statements of your denomination, local fellowship, cherished ministry, academic institution, and the Nicene or Apostles' Creed. Explain the reason and hope beneath your convictions on the core beliefs of Christianity.

The trend to position counseling as Christian reflects a common ground in the unity of faith. When it comes to making informed choices between approaches, one's doctrinal footings reveal much and are perhaps the largest contributing factor in adapting a preferred approach. For example, one's convictions regarding revelation, the Trinity, salvation or sanctification become the criteria to evaluate the credibility of each proposed view. Beliefs operate as the footings for worldview, approach preferences and practice priorities. Finally, since theological core values inform one's inner sense of calling, these greatly influence career ideals and trajectory.

Transcending dimensions to perceive the whole. Christian counselors will not find in this text or in their entire Christian education that elusive formula to guide once and for all their clinical role, function, focus or treatment recommendations. Such "cookbooks" simply do not exist, nor should they. However, there are guidelines to manage the forces that converge in the counseling encounters. The counselor seeks to blend a selected faith-based approach with artistic creativity and respect for the person receiving services within a specific location. Four factors combine to promote healing relationships and to realize wisdom. These will be described using the following terms: *context, contact, contract* and *content* (Greggo, 1998; 2001; 2002). These are not discrete dimensions that make sense in isolation; rather, they overlap and interact. Each must be examined in conjunction with the other three. Taken together, these assist MHPs to examine not only what is instantly obvious as they interact with a client but also the unseen elements.

Context. Counseling takes place in an explicit organization location such as an educationally affiliated guidance clinic, private office, medical facility, church ministry or social service agency. The factor of context alerts the counselor to the dimension of purpose, both in terms of the primary setting and from a broader theological standpoint. The privilege to offer care derives from the goals of a social and institutional framework. Still, it may well represent a divine appointment. A temporal concern instigates a client to consult a helper. Should Anita, as a psychologist, offer therapy within a setting where medical insurance will reduce the cost of the service, then diagnosis as well as treatment using evidence-based methods would probably be required. It is thus compulsory to consider the mission of the clinic along with the intentions of a third-party payer. Mental health concerns that place overall health or the ability to function at risk activate the health care system to offer care that alleviates the illness. In a culture that considers health care to be a basic entitlement of employment or citizenship, there are multiple service-delivery implications. When Anita, functioning within this medical/mental health system, seeks a model to merge convictions with practice, the chapter by Plante, with its firm empirical grounding, would be a prime resource.

On the other hand, if Sonia were to join a client in a pastoral care ministry, the personal difficulty or life challenge under consideration may not be observed through a health care lens. Instead the setting encourages the crisis to be perceived as means to promote spiritual formation or earnest discipleship. Any physical or psychological symptoms would not be ignored, but the essential purpose in coming alongside as caregiver would tie to the intentions of the ministry hosting the encounter. The context surrounding the client's request would cast the role of the helper as pastoral over professional. Further, ministry values would influence the expectations for service and boundaries regarding the type, length and methods emerging from the counseling conversation. Sonia may find the direction offered by Scott regarding the primacy of Scripture as healing balm to be particularly salient.

No matter what the setting or presenting issue, a Christian counselor will still deliberate over how the client is being called into a dependent relationship with the Creator and into a closer walk with Jesus Christ. Two theological premises guide discernment of purpose within the helping framework. Human beings are unique, created in the image of God to be stewards of the natural creation and to expand human civilization. In this dominion role, human beings impact their surroundings in ways that reflect our holy, divine Creator and his will or in a manner that displays sinful, selfish and shortsighted disobedience. The entire biblical narrative provides details and commentary on how human persons struggle with the autonomy-dependence paradox (Hoekema, 1986). This tension is referenced as the person-creature mystery. Human persons have freedom to will and to act. Still, human beings must accept the reality that created creatures need to submit to and be reconciled with their Creator (2 Corinthians 5:20). Human ingenuity and the desire to be free of our ultimate dependence may bring about action that ignores the Creator God and attempts to carry out our stewardship role in self-serving ways (Genesis 3:6-7). In response to humanity's fallen state and the subsequent need for order in social relations, God allowed human institutions to assist human beings in efforts to be fruitful and multiply.

Therefore, each Christian counselor reviews personal mission and calling in light of divine expectations as well as in light of the cultural definitions that establish the parameters for the direct setting. The orientation question to prayerfully consider is what faithful stewardship will look like within a defined helping role.

AMBASSADORSHIP

How do I serve as an ambassador of Christ and glorify God within the cultural and temporal context in which I am placed? Furthermore, how might this counseling relationship at this juncture address God's purpose in this counselee?

God may be doing an active work in the counselee at this time in his or her life journey. The counselor may not presume to fully recognize the transcendent view, but there is comfort in knowing that there is a divine purpose.

The counselor who humbly and submissively weaves this essential theological perspective purposefully into the practice context is in a wonderful position to be moved by the Holy Spirit as a faithful steward in the counselor's vocational calling. This application acknowledges that the counseling process is a potential way in which God may reach, redeem and re-create human beings through the means of these counseling conversations.

EXPECTATIONS

What is this counselee requesting, presenting, needing and anticipating? What does the setting host—the employer, payer, provider panel, church board, mission organization or medical team—expect of these services, and what are the rules, limits or ethical guidelines that I agree to follow in this appointed position?

The counselor does well to evaluate the vocational role to grasp the expectations embedded in the work setting. Professional status, ethical codes, provider agreements and employment arrangements have important implications. For example, Sonia's life experience makes her an ideal candidate to accept employment with a social service agency executing a government grant to support the relocation of international refugees seeking political asylum. Under this structure and in this role, Sonia would not abandon her faith or her earnest ministry orientation. Still, its expression would be tailored to respect the principles of religious freedom that stem not only from the stipulations of the grant but are central to her clients' hopes of life in a new country. Thus the MHP comes to grips with the ideal way to honor Christian convictions as the client is assisted through a particular institution and cultural context. The setting itself establishes certain entitlements, ethics and boundaries that need to be respected. This moves our consideration into a parallel dimension.

Contact. God promised a Redeemer from the moment sin was confronted (Genesis 3:15). By sending his own Son as the Word incarnate, God took the lead in addressing the broken relationship with the very creatures designed to represent him in creation. In a helping relationship, the counselor takes the initiative in assuming the functional role that will facilitate the necessary restoration as a healing application of grace and redemption through Christ. Clients may enter counseling hurting or hiding. No matter what level of interpersonal openness or characteristic personality style, the counselor makes use of advanced interpersonal skills to make the desired connection to address the current agenda. The human connection or therapeutic alliance is activated to facilitate the internal or external changes necessary to accomplish the purpose of the counseling arrangement (Bordin, 1994).

Counselors are trained to increase sensitivity to personal patterns of distorting or misusing relationships. The point of this is to obtain genuine contact with clients. Supervision and personal therapy create alertness to common relational breeches. Unfortunately, blindness to our own sinful tendencies cannot be fully eliminated. Counselors intentionally establish "good enough" bonds with counselees who may not have identical levels of insight or motivation to make a genuine connection. Fortunately, not every helping scenario requires an identical type of bond. The intimacy level or optimal style of relating finds a balance by considering conditions in the other three dimensions.

ROLES

How well prepared am I as a counselor to meet counselees as unique persons with wide-ranging levels of readiness to engage, relate and bond in such a relationship? Are there roles that I readily gravitate to fulfill and others that I might do well to enter yet tend to avoid? In what ways must I effectively represent an agency, health care system, governing authority, pastoral leadership team, hospital or professional guild in this customized interpersonal conversation?

Andy may be required to relate to an alcoholic in recovery as a rigid authority figure when he functions in an oversight role to enforce a court order mandating substance abuse treatment. The decision to withhold permission for unsupervised visits with vulnerable children could appear to clash on the surface with images of Jesus Christ offering grace and forgiveness. Still, a protector for little ones is also a critical relational responsibility (Matthew 18:1-6). With another client, Andy may move into the position of reliable advocate for an insecure soul who has never enjoyed such a safe and secure union. In either scenario, for Andy the treatment context remains the same; the dimension of how to make the helping role therapeutic is vastly distinct. Heeding the dimension of contact is not only good therapeutic counseling but wisely demonstrates the love of Christ.

RELATIONSHIPS

How might I represent my Lord to persons whom he loves within the therapeutic alliance? In what ways might certain counseling experiences be a means of grace to alter the quality or nature of a client's relationship with the Triune God: Comforter, Savior and Heavenly Father?

The Christian counselor recognizes forming alliances with counselees is crucial to facilitating change in a client's other relationships. Thus, a counselor often assumes a mediator role and may exemplify Jesus Christ in this dyad (Greggo, 2007). Mystery of mysteries, the counselor can also experience Jesus Christ in the dyad *through the client* as one who is thirsty, broken or imprisoned (Matthew 25:31-46).

Ray may discover that opportunities ripen to engage with Christian clients who desire to deepen their faith. His expertise as a spiritual mentor may rise to greater prominence in clinical relationships once immediate concerns are not paramount. Moon presented a convincing argument that spiritual direction can be both ethical and appropriate in the later phases of care. Moon went on to describe specific formative activities where grace may flow. Whether counselors represent the Holy Spirit as Comforter by compassionate listening or through direct speech in the midst of spiritually enhancing conversation, we can convey the presence of our Lord through helping relationships.

Contract. Contemporary counseling proceeds according to agreed-upon arrangements. Early on, counselors and clients discuss concerns, wishes and potential outcomes with the aim of reaching a common understanding. Goals may be hammered out that are S.M.A.R.T.: specific, measureable, attainable, realistic and time-framed. These features are reflected in a customary treatment plan. In addition, there is discussion and documentation of other administrative facets of the procedure, such as informed consent, financial policies, confidentiality limits, etc. Overall, the verbal and written components of the structure and rules that operate to keep the counseling relationship productive fall under the heading of the contract.

The term *contract* in reference to counseling conveys the business, legal, ethical, operational and temporal aspect of the relationship. The theological principle most applicable to the contract dimension is the golden rule. Counselors who are Christ followers do for others what they would desire others to do for them (Leviticus 19:18; Luke 6:31; Romans 13:9). In addition, counselors keep God's covenant in mind when entering explicit agreements.

Christian counseling does have a business component when services have fees and where accountability to outside parties impacts payment. While counseling typically becomes much more than a cool business transaction, it cannot be less. Finances and time frames are one aspect of the contract. Also included are the risks, methods, clarification of treatment options, adoption of a reasonable and realistic plan, and pre-planning for how to evaluate effectiveness. There are settings where the contracts are brief, broad and simple. Other mental health organizations, such as an inpatient hospital or residential facility, will have extensive written treatment and informed consent documentation.

The initial counseling dialogue may also establish a number of underlying implicit agreements beyond the explicit contracts. Frequently these need to be addressed forthrightly as the relationship progresses. For example, Ray becomes a sought-after career counselor for the county under a federal grant to assist those in employment transitions impacted by downsizing and a shifting economy. He is thrilled to let his faith become transparent with clients who openly declare Christian values. Nevertheless, sessions by design will maintain an employment-over-discipleship priority, even when Ray and the client candidly are in full agreement that God's will is the most critical aspect of search success and career satisfaction.

INTENTIONS

How will I ensure that explicit and implicit agreements are genuinely consistent with the charter, outlook, limitations and freedoms understood in the counseling setting? In what ways can I ensure that each contract will address the client's current circumstances and conditions in order to reach desired goals?

Counseling encounters involve client growth and change. In Christian counseling such contracts are formed in cooperation with the Holy Spirit. Life transitions are outward expressions of the Spirit's movement to produce holiness and Christlikeness, the process of sanctification. Thus Christian counselors contemplate agreements in light of God's eternal covenant through prayerful reflection. As believers, the plans that occupy our clinical efforts, energies, words and heartfelt compassion need to be consistent with our values, beliefs and commitments as informed by the Word of God.

SANCTIFICATION

What types of client-change goals could signal that the counseling contracts may facilitate the ministry of the Holy Spirit by furthering his calling or sanctifying work?

Sonia offers guidance to folks transitioning into a new culture much as her own family once did. In the early phases of care, practical matters take center stage. Survival is the priority. Eventually, when clients settle, counseling conversations may focus on the morals and commitments that these refugees will maintain within the surrounding culture. Should her clients seek to be salt and light to lift up the Lord, counseling could explore matters of holiness, character and obedience. Cultural identity takes on new meaning when there is recognition of our dual citizenship, one on earth and the other in the kingdom of God (1 Peter 2:9).

Content. The essence of the Garden temptation, when Adam and Eve considered eating the forbidden fruit, was the accuracy and authority of the Word of God (Genesis 3:1-6). The manipulation of the tempter and the awakened desires of the humans turned God's straightforward statement— "You will surely die" (Genesis 2:17 NLT)—into an ambiguous phrase left open for dispute. Thus from the beginning, the special revelation of God's Word and its accurate recalling is portrayed as a matter of life and death. The power of Scripture to govern and guide has persistently been crucial in Christian counseling (2 Timothy 3:16). Each "psychology and Christianity" viewpoint has a defined platform on epistemology to address this issue. When moving from a position into specific helping conversations, the approach will also set parameters for the prominence of reason and revelation.

The content factor customarily draws the most fire in any dispute regarding the intersection of Christianity and counseling. The subject matter being addressed is the dimension of primary focus in the talking cure. This is the material that occupies the dialogue. Content encompasses the conversation topics and themes shared in the session. Thus content is the obvious element for each approach to influence. Content displays the authoritative explanation for distress, problems, behaviors and relationships. How much emphasis will be placed on empirical psychology, evidence-based interventions, personal value clarification, heavy introspection or the implication of biblical teaching? Scripture may directly or distantly speak to the matters at hand. Consider the orientation question related to this factor.

AUTHORITY

What authority oversees the content material that I bring into counseling conversations, and how well will it represent best-practice strategies from the professional discipline from which I speak? How will the subject matter of sessions directly reference or align with special revelation as understood through responsible biblical theology? What place will be granted to matters of general revelation, reason and science, including the social science of psychology?

Anita, functioning in her professional role as a psychologist, encounters a client on probation who perpetrated sexual abuse on a young victim. Anita can sense a palpable rise in her internal rage during the session as her outspoken client exemplifies a classic maneuver lifted right from the personality disorder depictions within the *DSM* (American Psychiatric Association, 2000). The words spoken rationalize gross mistreatment and neglect of the dignity of another human being. Projection, denial, blame and entitlement are running rampant. Biblical passages with clear prohibitions permeate her thoughts while she seeks to soothe the impulses of her heart. Attempting to concentrate, she internally but intensely prays that this client would sit under the teaching of a local pastor so that Scripture carried by the Holy Spirit would soften his heart. A reflective question passes through her lips. Her intent is to raise a semblance of empathy for the victim. Chapter and verse will remain outside of this conversation. Instead, variations of the golden rule guide her gradual excavation of the client's defensive layers. This decision regarding the content of this session reflects her best clinical judgment and leading of the Holy Spirit. Yet she recalls her mission adopted in response to this final orientation question.

GOSPEL STORY

How can the Word of God and the gospel story of creation, fall, redemption and consummation have a substantial influence on the conversational directives introduced in response to the suffering, stubbornness, questions, beliefs and enduring personal narratives shared by my counselees?

The food pantry at the urban ministry was only one of several on the list Andy had given to the single mother who was now seated in his office with her two rambunctious children. How was he to know that the pantry's service volunteer, who greeted this overwhelmed mom, had herself once stared at an empty refrigerator while her own children whimpered with hunger? While several grocery bags of essentials were packed with generosity, the volunteer kindly shared an invitation to get to know the Bread of Life. A local Bible study fellowship was custom-designed for women like them. Andy listened in awe and amazement as he heard from his client what she was learning from this new supportive community and from an ancient Book she had never before opened or understood.

Christian Approaches: Seeing and Sensing

Again, the four dimensions of context, contact, contract and content do not compose a formula nor delineate a particular Christian counseling approach. These dimensions help organize one's internal meta-model. These orientation questions can assist counselors like Andy, Sonia, Ray and Anita to move through a thoughtful progression from conversion to conviction to a missional-professional commitment to further the gospel. Becoming acquainted with clients may be a challenge of the magnitude of blind men getting to know a moving elephant. The helping process requires seeing and sensing how to weave together a case conceptualization with supernatural discernment and human sensitivity. Then, prayerfully, the overall clinical portrait can be lifted before the Lord in humility as one listens for the whisper of the Holy Spirit. How will personal Christian faith be communicated to the unique, complex and culture-bound person before me? This is a matter of contextualization. There are untold numbers of clients such as Jake who are struggling to make sense of the past, present and future. Whether a counselor meets a client such as Jake in the office down the hall from a physician, pastor or probation officer, our approach can still reflect the Savior. No matter what ethnic background, geographic location or personal customs, a counselor brings training, interpersonal skills and Christian calling to come alongside a counselee and extend greetings from the great Comforter.

Intentional Christian counseling is about faithful ministry. Christian counseling therefore requires loyal dependence of submissive creatures on the Creator. These expert consultants have displayed with openness how they would bring their expertise to bear on a soul needing rest and restoration. It is the responsibility of each counselor to hone the conceptual understanding necessary to follow the examples displayed. There is a season to reflect on the best way to administer soul care, and a season to offer that care for healing in service to our Lord. We hope the latter does not supplant the former.

References

American Psychiatric Association. (2000). *Diagnostic and statistical manual of mental disorders* (4th ed., text rev.). Washington, DC: American Psychiatric Association.

Blubaugh, D. (2011). *The blind men and the elephant.* Retrieved February 24, 2011 from Peace Corp Stories, <www.peacecorps.gov/wws/stories/stories.cfm?psid =110>.

Bordin, E. S. (1994). Theory and research on the therapeutic working alliance: New directions. In A. Horvath and L. Greenberg (Eds.), *The working alliance: Theory, research, and practice* (pp. 13-37). New York: John Wiley.

Brown, W. S. (2004). Resonance: A model for relating science, psychology, and faith. *Journal of Psychology and Theology, 23*(2), 110-20.

Chang, E., Morgan, J. R., Nyasulu, T., & Priest, R. J. (2009). Paul G. Heibert and critical contextualization. *Trinity Journal, 30,* 199-207.

Erikson, E. H. (1982). *The life cycle completed: A review.* New York: Norton.

Greggo, S. P. (1998). Therapeutic relationship in managed mental health care.

In J. F. Kilner, R. O. Orr & J. A. Shelly (Eds.), *The changing face of health care* (pp. 177-91). Grand Rapids: Eerdmans.

———. (2001). Integration art in a postmodern age. *Christian Counseling Today, 9*(3), 32-41.

———. (2002). Artistic integration: Theological foundations for case-level integration in contemporary Christian counseling. *Trinity Journal, 23,* 145-60.

———. (2007). Biblical metaphors for corrective emotional relationships in group work. *Journal of Psychology and Theology, 35,* 153-62.

Hoekema, A. A. (1986). *Created in God's image.* Grand Rapids: Eerdmans.

Johnson, E. L. (2007). *Foundations for soul care: A Christian psychology proposal.* Downers Grove, IL: Intervarsity Press.

———. (Ed.). (2010a). *Psychology & Christianity: Five views* (2nd ed). Downers Grove, IL: Intervarsity Press.

———. (2010b). Gaining understanding through five views. In E. L. Johnson (Ed.), *Psychology & Christianity: Five views* (2nd ed., pp. 292-313). Downers Grove, IL: InterVarsity Press.

Linton, W. J. (1878). *Poetry of America: Selections from one hundred American poets from 1776 to 1876, with an introductory review of colonial poetry, and some specimens of negro melody.* London: George Bell. Retrieved February 23, 2011 from <books.google.com/books?vid=LCCN28016886&id=hdrGIl0rnhgC&pg=PA150&lpg=PA150&dq=Poetry+of+America++Saxe#v=onepage&q&f=false>.

Moreau, S. (2006). Contextualization that is comprehensive. *Missiology: An International Review, 34*(3), 325-35.

Norcross, J. C., Hogan, T. P., & Koocher, G. P. (2008). *Clinician's guide to evidence-based practices: Mental health and the addictions.* Oxford: Oxford University Press.

Vanhoozer, K. J. (2002). *First theology: Scripture, God and hermeneutics.* Downers Grove, IL: InterVarsity Press.

10

Case Scenarios
for Further Exploration

LEARNING OBJECTIVES

- *Summarize the training advantage of exploring complex cases where developmental issues, relational binds and faith dilemmas are evident.*
- *Compose a list of potential research questions for the case of Miguel, Audrey and Jason, or Grace to investigate ideas gleaned from psychology, biblical studies, Christian theology and spiritual formation.*
- *Project your own Christian approach to at least one of these cases following the example provided by one of the five consultants.*

Complexity in Clinical Scenarios

Each consultant to this project is an outstanding representative of a specialized approach, and we honor the gracious willingness each shows in sharing his or her invaluable competence with us. Despite the exemplary skills of our consultants, we need to be candid about their early reactions to Jake's case scenario. This intentionally intense story was the framework for these accomplished clinicians to demonstrate the benefits of their particular models. Despite their skills and experience, Jake was daunting even to them, given the depth, severity and complexity of his problems. Comments we received suggested that these fine counselors were humbled to deal with such a challenging case, and doubtful that they could do it justice in the short space allotted. How could Jake's convoluted cry for help be thoughtfully engaged in a single chapter? Further, the matters at stake in Jake's life are significant in terms of disruptive relationships and serious suffering. The case may begin as a straightforward mental health check at a small college counseling center but unfolds into an intriguing narrative with a compelling combination of behavioral, neurological, interpersonal and spiritual elements.

The justification for posing a case embedded with challenges of this magnitude was never a calculated attempt to stump the panel or to pose an unsolvable mystery. Rather, the reality is this: clients such as Jake are *not* unique. There are numerous military veterans, children of alcoholics and struggling college students in our country today with comparable mental health, interpersonal and career difficulties. Details may vary, but numerous risk factors and formidable variables remain constant. Counselors, from novices to senior practitioners, frequently find themselves making empathetic eye contact with clients whose stories are equally packed with double binds, unresolved losses, developmental stressors, physical disabilities, substance abuse and multifaceted interpersonal resistance. Despite what may play well in the entertainment industry, mental health professionals (MHPs) do not spend the majority of fifty-minute hours with the worried well. Those who engage the helping services of a pastoral counselor or MHP present relational ruptures, family chaos and interior conflicts that echo the strain of a client such as Jake. If counselors are going to cultivate a distinctively Christian case approach, it must be robust enough to address the intricate life stories and sin-infested state of affairs that clients actually unburden during in-vivo counseling sessions. In counseling, MHPs and clients together are often required to make hard choices regarding priorities, resources, ethical dilemmas, relational ties and bringing honor to Jesus Christ.

In the journey of professional counselor development, there are occasions when it is best to address case examples that spotlight limited concerns and include succinct social histories. Brief case vignettes allow for pointed illustration of particular presenting features or diagnostic aspects. A tightly framed clinical example is ideal to illuminate a line of intervention strategies or tactics to address resistance. For example, Jake's case details could be restricted to solely address his military trauma, the care of the child he apparently fathered, the compounded grief he carries, his identity as an adult child of an alcoholic or his spiritual hunger that waxes and wanes. For instructional purposes, a case profile can be tailored to tackle a single clinical feature. Consider the focal point in this example as Sandra approaches her pastor for ministry responsibility relief.

Sandra (31) makes an appointment to speak with her pastor. She and her husband of six years have been active leaders in a thriving church ministry. Her story begins with her decision to step back from all ministry responsibilities due to "personal issues." Life is crowded with too many demands, and the timing is ripe to reassess even worthwhile commitments. Initially she is hesitant to reveal more.

The pastor responds by thoughtfully emphasizing how she and her husband have contributed to the discipleship of so many as the home Bible study they direct is a source of solid Christian teaching and revitalizing fellowship. He agrees to pray with her about being sensible and strategic about family priorities. After Sandra hears his perspective on her valuable contribution, her disclosure goes further.

One month ago to the day, Sandra miscarried for the second time, something few people know. She admits that this is impacting her entire life as she is keeping distant from all of her former friends, all of whom have children. She is beginning to envision what her life might be if she never has a child of her own. Sandra does not imagine that people in the church have any idea of her inner anguish, and if they did, she believes that each would cease to respect her as a follower of Jesus Christ.

Sandra's presentation flows steadily with restrained emotion until the pastor inquires gently about the impact on her marriage. She becomes tearful, sobs intermittently and has difficulty putting full sentences together. The ragged explanation reveals that the marriage tension is high and conflicts intense. The most distressing alarm is the escalating rage in the arguments between Sandra and her husband.

This abbreviated case scenario provides an excellent opportunity to sharpen powers of observation and case conceptualization. Discussants can practice assessment strategies related to diagnostic categories and interpersonal patterns. The ministry scenario allows for exploration, not only from a mental health perspective, but from theology, biblical stories and contemporary community life. The benefits of empathetic listening and relational support are evident.

As presented, this counseling scenario does not provide extensive social, developmental or faith journey details. Leaving aside these particulars allows the resulting professional training conversation to remain focused on a central issue along with its impact on Sandra and her marriage. A brief case such as this does suggest the significant nature of important clinical concerns. On the other hand, it does not offer ample specifics to display circumstances and interpersonal tensions that would inhibit the effectiveness of therapeutic efforts. Consider how the dynamics of this case intensify with the addition of the following highlights from a developmental and family history.

> Sandra was the sole adopted child among three biological siblings. Her adoptive mother was a respected leader in her church. At home, she was a stern disciplinarian who routinely withheld affection and affirmation to exert control or execute punishment. Sandra's husband is from a large family with no strong church ties or faith customs. Family gatherings on special occasions with numerous siblings, spouses, nieces and nephews are common.

These points may appear as minor tidbits of background trivia. Yet depending on how Sandra offers this information, there are abundant implications that such details would stir in a clinician's disciplined, clinical imagination. Such description would add dimension to a counselor's view of Sandra's treatment plan. The reason is because relevant historical perspective tends to enrich the depth of understanding in one or more of the following areas: the context (treatment setting), contact (therapeutic relationship), content (conversation topics and themes) and contract (treatment agreement). As evidence for this assertion, ponder how the added case detail could reveal aspects of Sandra's spiritual life or how the effort to join with a compassionate pastor or therapist might stir transference.

The purpose in this text is to arouse advanced contemplation of how pivotal Christian worldview convictions have implications for the discourse between medical, social science and theological disciplines. When moving the focus of discussion from epistemology, theology and philosophy to case planning, there is benefit in pondering genuinely realistic case presentations. The messiness of a complex case requires that clinicians set priorities after evaluating risks and contemplating resources. There is also room for plausible alternative case conceptualizations. In such clinical stories, the whole cannot be seen immediately or completely. Pieces may not fit neatly. There are often signs of ambivalence, mixed motivation and hidden emotional baggage. This allows developing mental health professionals a realistic occasion to explore how each of the various Christian discourse models may contribute to clinical care procedures by informing case conceptualization and contextualization strategies.

This chapter offers three additional case scenarios for group conversation and/or individual practice in case analysis. Review these options for focusing the direction of case analysis for professional development. Using either adds structure to the discussion.

Case exploration method A: Approach analysis. This style of exploration for clinician development is on display in this case study. Replicate the approach analysis used by the consultants here. Look at any or all of these cases through the lens of one particular model. Place yourself in the functional role of a clinician doing direct service or as consultant advising the counselor on how to therapeutically engage these clients in a manner consistent with one's Christian convictions. When one viewpoint has been thoroughly applied, mull over a different perspective that offers a complementary or perhaps an alternative means of proceeding with treatment. To replicate the approach used in this volume, follow these instructions.

1. Select one of the five Christian approaches—levels of explanation, integration, Christian psychology, transformational, biblical counseling. Use this grid as the overarching perspective to analyze the client's dilemma, the interpersonal dynamics and presenting problem.

2. Move methodically through the assessment, conceptualization, intervention and evaluation sequence. Take into account the clinical context, session content, counselor contact and treatment contract.

3. Refer back to the chapter in this text that amplifies the rubric in use as well as the corresponding chapter in *Psychology & Christianity: Five Views* (Johnson, 2010).

4. Pause to deliberate and discuss the ten evaluation questions offered in chapter 2 (pp. 40-41).

5. When the process has generated a reasonable understanding of the client's concerns, present your perspective to others who have scrutinized the same scenario from a different Christian perspective.

6. Compare and contrast contributions from each approach.

Case method B: Critical issue investigation. A second style of counselor training and preparation offers a worthy variation to the portrayed approach analysis. This method of case review does not adopt a favored Christian perspective in advance. Rather, it identifies and researches the worldview clashes within the case itself. Once personal, mental health, moral and ethical issues are identified, the MHP selects a framework that offers the most guidance on addressing the significant tension points within the clinical scenario. Conducting a case review that places emphasis on critical concerns offers noticeable advantages. Such an investigation will identify specific points of friction surrounding worldview convictions apparent within the case scenario. These issues are abstracted from the case to pursue research. Then these serve to press further into in-depth discourse between evidence-based treatments derived from social science methods and Christian wisdom as located in Scripture, theology and Christian tradition. Critical concern investigations require prudent case review to discern embedded ethical, lifestyle or spiritual facets.

There are turning points in every case where Christian convictions may be at odds with a largely secular approach. The research question initially is to identify aspects of the case where worldview influences tend to inform clinical decisions. In such instances, it would be important to explore at length the theological and biblical material that speaks to the values inherent in explanation or solution to the issue. In addition, a review of social science, psychological and/or psychiatric research related to the identified matter may be conducted. What evidence-based treatment protocols are located in the literature? Perhaps the client is facing a moral dilemma. It will become apparent that Christian identity greatly influences goal setting or may limit potential outcomes. Or a case may display a controversy related to diagnosis or raise disputes over an intervention that might clash with a conscientious Christian understanding of the Word. For training purposes, it would be worthwhile to comb the Scriptures to locate passages and biblical principles that require detailed exploration. Further, a review of how other Christian writers have addressed this or a similar issue would be an invaluable exercise. The wise teacher in ancient Jerusalem declared that there is nothing new under the sun (Ecclesiastes 1:9), and yet much has happened since then! Believers struggle with matters common to people of faith across the ages, so gleaning soul care insights from within our Christian heritage deepens identification with the universal church. Once the theoretical, empirical, theological, biblical and/or ethical matter has been studied from these vantage points, it is possible to return to the case scenario to apply the newly discovered material.

Clinically oriented research should track not only contemporary trends and common solutions but establish a profound faith perspective derived from reliable and authoritative Christian sources. In the hurried day-to-day routine of people helping, this is not always feasible. Counselors in training or MHPs undertaking professional development will discover the educational value of such a pursuit. The Scriptures tell us that in the making of many books there is no end, and much study wearies the body (Ecclesiastes 12:12). Yet quality clinical care is not purely a subjective or internal process. Good information and understanding is necessary, and accessing the best knowledge available does require academic prowess. A counselor does prepare homework outside of sessions. This often entails theological, biblical and psychological investigation. Reviewing realistic cases in this fashion provides an ideal opportunity to hone skills of biblical exegesis and theological research, as well as how to glean lessons from Christian history. It is useful to make inquiries into how the Christian community has spoken into such matters in the distant and recent past. What is most productive in this type of investigation is the press to determine how far to direct research into each area and how to merge the results. This process takes clinicians back to the foundational premises beneath each Christian helping approach. Each view has a method to manage the discourse between Christianity, social science literature and the practice parameters of mental health disciplines. Cases that stir up worldview clashes tend to display the distinctions between Christian approaches. Here are the basic steps to proceed with a critical issue investigation.

1. Read thoroughly the case scenario to highlight each instance where there is evidence of a potential worldview concern or turning point. Identify these issues in language that fits with psychological and/or theological terminology.

2. Working with this derived list of critical issues, make an effort to categorize and prioritize. Select the key issue(s) of interest for further investigation.

3. Develop a research question. These queries guide a targeted exploration of themes, questions, assumptions or treatment options. For Jake, these questions might generate productive investigations: (1) Given the emergent understanding of psychological trauma in veterans, is faith and spirituality a protective or healing factor? (2) How have biblical experts defined the responsibilities and roles associated with fatherhood? and (3) What insight and instruction does Scripture offer regarding behavior change in regard to alcohol and substance abuse? Once a subtopic is selected, step back from the case itself to pursue related research from sources that address with authority the issue in the abstract (e.g., peer-reviewed journals, professional books, theological texts, biblical commentaries).

4. Identify the optimal strategy from the assortment of Christian options—the one that aids in the organization, distillation and formulation of conclusions from these relevant sources. Maintain the ultimate goal of arriving at the optimal Christian approach to guide clinical care.

5. Move back to the case itself and apply the information gathered. Notice sources that shed light on the conceptualization and treatment plan. Consider the implications on context, content, contact and contract.

Similar to the scenario of Jake, there are no easy answers or simple solutions to the following three clinical vignettes. These are not brainteasers to attack like a puzzle until the pieces are neatly joined. Rather, each story represents a life in crisis. The worldview of the helper matters, as does the perspective of the client. Pray through the following biblical command as each case is considered in unpretentious anticipation of sitting directly with clients such as Miguel, Grace, Audrey and Jason: "Therefore, prepare your minds for action; be self-controlled; set your hope fully on the grace to be given you when Jesus Christ is revealed" (1 Peter 1:13 NIV).

Miguel

Miguel is only days past his fifteenth birthday. His big brown eyes and impish smile suggest that he is just another fun-loving kid, but his behavior and manipulative style with adults indicates a more devious pattern. The intake social worker assigned Miguel to a counselor at a community service agency to begin his court-ordered, mandated therapy. The family and Miguel have had contact with mental health professionals in the past, and success has been limited and temporary. This is the first court-mandated treatment that has specified a family emphasis for this active, trouble-prone adolescent.

The issue that pushed the juvenile justice system to demand clinical treatment is that Miguel was arrested for breaking and entering. Once, when working with his father, he had been to this house. Later, Miguel entered the residence by himself after breaking a basement window. He consumed alcohol, played video games, ate a quart of ice cream and pocketed a small amount of cash. After spending an hour or so in the home, he called up a few friends to invite them over and they readily consented. Unfortunately for Miguel, when his friends arrived in a noisy car with music blaring, the police soon followed.

When arrested, he protested loudly stating that he had permission to be there. The broken window left the police unimpressed by this explanation. Miguel threatened to jump out of the police car and hurt himself if they did not immediately take him home. Due to the persistent verbal assault on the officers and his threats of self-harm, he was taken directly to the emergency room. Following a psychiatric evaluation, he was admitted to the inpatient unit. The diagnosis was bipolar disorder, and a medication regime was begun during his five-day hospital stay. He was discharged to the care of his parents with the legal charges pending regarding the break-in. A prevention program that provides services in conjunction with the juvenile justice system picked up Miguel's case. This arm of the court reported to the judge that individual and family therapy was warranted. The hospital psychiatrist directed ongoing medication for bipolar disorder. The court order included in the conditions for eventual dismissal that Miguel follow treatment guidelines of medical and mental health professionals.

Miguel is the middle of five children, with two older siblings and two younger. His older brother (18) lives in the household whenever he is at "home" but is known to the police for being involved in gang activity. Miguel does associate with his brother and gang friends but is not yet a "member." His older sister (20) also resides in the home and attends a local community college. She is the only family member thus far not to drop out of school, and even pursue schooling beyond the basic legal requirements. This sister has often taken Miguel under her wing and is deeply frustrated with her brother's poor choices. Over the years, her investment in her dear "kid" brother has been significant. She loves him and has openly committed to remain involved in family treatment as her schedule permits. Additionally, there is a large extended family network throughout the surrounding area.

Court documents note that there is a family history of gang involvement and drug and alcohol abuse on both sides of Miguel's family. One uncle is in jail for a murder charge related to gang activity. Miguel's father, Juan, was issued a DUI summons five years ago when he hit a stop sign with the company truck that he was driving. Fortunately, no one was injured and his employer was well connected. The charges eventually disappeared, and the incident now only lives on in his wife's memory. After that legal skirmish, he "quit" drinking. In actuality, this meant that he ceased to drink as intensely during and immediately after work. He now drinks primarily in the home. Juan consumes beer and hard liquor heavily in the evening and on weekends. His family states that Juan never appears drunk or disorderly. He does maintain steady employment. His wife, Eva, reports that all of Juan's coworkers, many of whom are friends or relatives, drink alcohol in a similar manner. Thus this practice is both custom and completely socially acceptable. Juan has never had an accident other than the isolated stop-sign incident. He is never mean or abusive and has never harmed anyone. Juan does fall asleep in a chair in the evening after a late dinner, but not before drinking a considerable amount of alcohol. The only reported hardship this brings into the family is that they do not have much money. Eva wishes she had more funds to buy items for the household. Juan's pay is in cash, and alcohol purchases are made before he turns his earnings over to his wife. Since this is his only undesirable practice and he does not physically hurt anyone, she does not view Juan's drinking as a family problem, only as a spiritual concern.

Eva was raised in a religious home. She fully embraced Christianity for herself following her father's death 10 years ago. She now describes herself as a devout follower of Christ who attends a Latino charismatic fellowship faithfully. She speaks Spanish primarily but does have command of conversational English. Her own father died from a heart attack after a difficult life employed in construction. In his history of alcohol abuse, he would leave the family for days on drinking binges. On some occasions her father would hit her, her five siblings or her mother. Eva is adamant and outspoken with pride that the family handled these matters quietly. The police were never involved. Eva's mother told the children that this was what fathers do. Good children would be wise to stay clear when a man is doing his drinking. Eva portrays her husband as a hard-working man much like her father. He maintains a firm commitment to his native tongue and has always provided steadily for the needs of his family. Eva describes herself as blessed because Juan remains with his family and is nonviolent.

Miguel does not profess to be religious or a Christian; however, he occasionally attends church with his folks and siblings. Juan attends church every week except for the rare exception when he is asked to work on a special project. Juan will nod "yes" when asked if he is a follower of Christ. He never openly expresses any faith commitment. In fact, Juan hardly speaks at all. He seems to comprehend English but speaks very little. He is cooperative with his wife in attending church as Eva is enthusiastically committed to her church ministry and personal faith. It is by her insistence that the court allows Miguel and the family assignment to a Christian counselor. For this reason, her pastor comes with the family to the intake appointment. He offers to interpret and translate and remain involved. Miguel's older sister also assumes this role. The current court involvement stirs an intense sense of family shame.

Miguel began drinking and smoking cigarettes at age nine. His older brother snuck hard liquor and cigarettes from their father. Miguel continued occasional use through age 11. He laughs when reporting that he used liquor at family get-togethers with cousins or in his own house with his brother. Miguel admits that he began to enjoy drinking, and his use increased at age 12 and peaked at 14. Miguel sounds boastful when he reports drinking twice per week with intake of 5-10 drinks per episode.

He began smoking marijuana at age 12, also with his older brother. Miguel smoked pot on the weekends with friends, and in the last year increased his use to three times a week. He reports that he currently has fewer drinks and gets into less trouble when he uses pot. In the last six months, Miguel's marijuana use has apparently escalated. Before his arrest, he was using daily, often by himself after school. In the past year Miguel began dealing small amounts of marijuana to close friends and is often approached by peers looking for marijuana or other drugs. Miguel breaks into homes or sells pot in order to pay for his daily use. He states without hesitation that he can steal the liquor from the grocery near his home but needs cash for marijuana.

During elementary school, Miguel demonstrated average academic skills. Teachers have described him as demonstrating attention difficulties and as being restless. Medication was initiated on and off, but the family never followed through on a regular basis. Miguel currently attends an alternative school. Most of the adolescents in this setting have not succeeded in mainstream schools and are identified as having learning or behavioral disorders. Miguel was taken out of his mainstream school after getting into a fight with another kid between classes. This was the last straw, as Miguel had already been in several fights that academic year and attendance was irregular. Miguel has been in trouble with the school for petty theft in the past. Once he was disciplined for stealing an iPod from the locker room at school. It was further suspected, but never proved, that Miguel stole $20 from a teacher's wallet when the teacher left the room. While these are the only two known incidents, there have been multiple occasions when this client has stolen from the school locker room, perhaps taking as much as $100 in one day. This information was reported by his older sister, who heard it while her brother was bragging to peers.

Even now within the alternative school setting, Miguel gets poor grades, mostly Ds with an occasional C or F. He can speak English well but has difficulty with reading and written expression. He receives English as Second Language support with other Latinos in his school. Recently, Miguel stopped attending this particular support because there are opposing gang members in the room. He wants to avoid interaction with these other boys, especially after all the trouble he's already been in. He boldly claims that he is not afraid. Instead, he is acting smart to stay away from trouble. These boys do intentionally provoke him to watch him melt down or get into authority disputes. Miguel's intent is to be quiet and go unnoticed. When he turns 16 in another year, the court and the school will have less control over what he does. Much to Miguel's annoyance, the school social worker is active and encourages academic progress.

Upon Miguel's return to school from the arrest and hospitalization, he was confronted by one teacher for not doing homework. This assignment was specially provided for him at the request of the social worker. It was brought to him at the hospital. Miguel ignored it. When the teacher challenged him, Miguel became angry and impulsively yelled at her, claiming that he would bring back his brother's friends who could blow her away. The school is considering expulsion because the teacher is afraid to have him return to her classroom. Such threats certainly must be taken seriously. However, the psychiatric involvement in Miguel's life is new. The local pastor is speaking up for the "rights" of his people. The school does not attempt to pursue this matter. Instead, Miguel is placed on home tutoring with the proposed plan that he will be able to return to school once the medication routine has been established for four weeks and there are no further personal threats or community incidents.

The recent court attention has everyone paying close attention to Miguel. It is evident that Eva and Juan have not been able to control their son for years. Their ability to impress or enforce discipline at this point is doubtful. Eva prays with church leadership for a miracle in Miguel.

Audrey and Jason

Audrey (32) has been married to Jason (33) for six years. They met during a student teaching assignment in their final year of college. Both were involved in a Christian campus fellowship group at the state university where they obtained their degrees. Audrey is now an elementary school art teacher, and Jason is an elementary school physical education instructor working in different school systems. They do have the benefit of a common work schedule in terms of days off and routine hours. Thus far, during the summers they have enlisted as staff members together at a YMCA youth camp.

Audrey is now entering outpatient counseling with a Christian mental health professional due to an episode of discouragement and depression. Such experiences are unfortunately not new to her—she has had two hospitalizations during their marriage for major depression with suicidal ideation. Her psychiatrist is supportive of counseling, for while he manages her medication, he does not provide talk therapy. Audrey does not appreciate his broken English or his gruff style. She doubts that he fully understands or actually listens to her. Yet since this psychiatrist accepts her insurance, she continues to see him twice a year. Audrey has been in and out of counseling for years. Extremely selective in her choice of therapists, Audrey does not tolerate what she considers to be incompetence. She has "fired" several counselors, and she now drives an hour to see an experienced counselor with a longstanding, favorable reputation within the Christian community. This counselor is on her insurance panel, which requires that her mental health care be monitored through a national managed care organization. Prospective treatment plans are required.

The reason for entering counseling at this juncture is that Audrey has become increasingly eager to start a family. Jason confided in their pastor that Audrey is obsessed with having children. While the desire for a family has never been a question between Jason and Audrey, the discussion of the particulars has become the topic of intense and bitter arguments. This is not the only matter where they have conflict, but it does capture the hot button of marital tension at the moment. The relationship has been fraught with intermittent turmoil since when they were dating. Jason tends to be laid back and easygoing and enjoys activities such as watching sports with his friends, playing league softball and participating in outdoor activities in general. Audrey states that she does not mind these recreational outlets, but she relentlessly presses him to do chores around the house, frequently pointing out things that need to be done that he simply overlooks. Honestly, Jason does not enjoy home improvement or maintenance, and he was perfectly content in their apartment. According to Jason, Audrey was restless from the day they moved in, always wanting the home of her dreams. Jason gave in to her demands, and they purchased a starter home that Audrey berates as needing lots of TLC. Jason admires the artistic flair that Audrey brings to their house, but he is not interested in learning how to implement the projects that Audrey is desperately intent to get underway. Jason admits that he is not detail-oriented in terms of planning and organization. Thus there is heated friction, in the form of four to five arguments per week, about the allotment of time spent together, finances, family visits, how and how much to be involved at church, and of course, home improvements.

Audrey admits that pastoral marriage counseling has been helpful. The pattern to the marital conflict is reasonably predictable, and goes something like this. Audrey notices something that needs to be done or a promise that Jason has forgotten to fulfill. She gets quiet, tearful, sulky and angry. This brooding may build for days. Jason may notice, but if he does, he will ignore it for as long as he possibly can. Eventually he will be forced to ask what's wrong. According to Jason, Audrey then unloads a laundry list of issues that may run back to when they were dating. The exchange escalates until Jason is overwhelmed and has to leave to "cool off." He admits that he would prefer spending time with his friends to being at home when Audrey is in one of her dark moods. These cycles are far from uncommon, and Audrey acknowledges that she does get emotional and irritable at times. Yet she vehemently supports her complaints regarding the lack of care that Jason gives to her, their marriage and their house.

Last year when Audrey was planning to remodel a bedroom during spring break, she learned that Jason had planned a trip with his friends to Arizona to watch exhibition baseball. The persistent conflict during that period became so severe that Audrey entered the hospital for nine days due to threats of self-harm, missing nearly two weeks of teaching. After medication adjustments, she felt strong enough to resume her routine. Jason canceled his trip and committed in marriage counseling to devote one weekend day to do household chores. He may "hire" or borrow a friend from church to hang out with him and tackle the never-ending "honey-do list."

Jason has a large extended family. The clan has remained loyal to one another, but gatherings are spontaneous and communication is limited. Holiday parties and special occasion surprises tend to be quite lively events. The lack of planning irritates Audrey, who would prefer not to be with Jason's family at all. The children running around everywhere upset her, stirring internal awareness of her biological clock and discontentment with her marriage.

Audrey does not have any extended family within reach. Her younger brother lives on the opposite side of the country and does not maintain contact. Her father was an alcoholic who died when she was a teenager. Her mother was diagnosed with bipolar disorder decades ago and has been in and out of the hospital for most of Audrey's life. It is Audrey's contention that she raised herself and her younger brother. Her father was quiet, withdrawn and not all that active in her life. When he was alive, he did manage his wife's outbursts and hospitalizations. He would coordinate with medical personnel, get her into intensive care as necessary, keep prescriptions current and intervene whenever an incident caught the attention of police. Since his death, Audrey is yanked into her mother's crazy episodes. Not only does her mother need help with everyday living and routine psychiatric care, she has been a lifetime heavy smoker. Numerous bouts of serious breathing and heart-related concerns are reported. Her mother lives by herself in a subsidized-rent apartment for seniors even though she is only 59. Audrey is legally responsible for her mother's financial and health decisions. This is an increasingly difficult burden.

The marital and family issues are only part of the current challenges facing this couple. Audrey wants to have children and begin a family. Her desire is to have a biological child, yet given her mental health history, she is afraid of the genetic risks in passing along mental illness to her child. Audrey is adamant that she will come off her antidepressant medications when they attempt to get pregnant. Jason becomes speechless in these conversations, yet he is hesitant to break these off given his wife's propensity to become seriously depressed. He has muttered that they should have six months of peace in their marriage before they even think about having a child. This does not appear likely.

The first two counseling appointments with Audrey are extremely tense. During the initial session she pressed the counselor with inquiry after inquiry. The counselor senses that he is on trial and must tread lightly with this fragile but obviously strong-willed client. Audrey is already under psychiatric care, so the counselor is aware that medication may not bring immediate improvement. The pastor is willing to continue marital support if necessary, but he admits that this couple is above his ability to counsel with only occasional contacts. The counselor considers how to best proceed.

Grace

Grace is a 24-year-old graduate student working toward a business degree. Grace is the name that she has always used at school, with friends and throughout her American life. In her household, with her extended family and at her ethnic church, she uses her Asian name given at birth. These two names reflect the rather significant cultural divide in her life. Her family has lived in this country for 16 years. In most settings and in her entire social life, Grace lives, thinks and speaks as an American. As if living a divided existence, however, her family maintains strict values and traditions from their ethnic culture.

Grace enters counseling due to complaints of a lack of energy, difficulty sleeping, plus feelings of stress and dread about most activities. She describes her eating habits as poor because she has no motivation to shop, prepare healthy food or eat well. She is petite and thin by American standards. There are no known health concerns, and her medical history is unremarkable. According to Grace's description during the initial consultation, "nothing is certain or makes sense; my life is like an empty seashell, without purpose, and I'm thrown around in any direction the waves decide to move me." When asked about her Christian faith, she glumly declares that since she has committed the unpardonable sin, God will never want anything to do with her ever again.

Despite this, Grace opts for a Christian mental health professional, though her parents are opposed to counseling. After consulting with their pastor, they conceded their support to Grace seeing a Christian therapist. Grace is glad to be able to speak with this counselor who shares her family's faith background, but she has doubts that counseling, even with a Christian approach, is going to help all that much. Grace has been fighting off the persistent thought that she would like to go to sleep and never wake up. She denies any active plan to harm herself, though she admits thoughts about disappearing, fading away or falling off a cliff. When pressed by her counselor, she indicates that she has had these thoughts at least five out of the past seven evenings before going to bed.

Her family has been attempting to discuss marriage plans for her. On each occasion, she becomes increasingly discouraged and confused. After a difficult conversation between Grace and her father, her long-time pastor was consulted. The pastor agreed fully with her father that this was the proper juncture in Grace's life to consider marriage. He accused Grace of harboring disrespect and exhibiting an ungrateful attitude toward her father, for which she should repent. Despite this direct challenge, he recognized the intensity of her inner distress and recommended a Christian counselor of whom he approves.

Grace graduated from an expensive private college associated with a mainline Christian denomination. Her education was essentially secular. Grace reports friendships with a variety of students who were mostly from affluent family backgrounds similar to her own. She says that she once had more friendships than she does now. In order to start graduate school, she moved back home with her parents. She knows few people as her parents moved to a larger home in this city while she was away at college. Many of her former college acquaintances were not close with their own parents. Most were from families with at least one divorce. She was one of the few among her peers who would identify herself as a Christian. During college, Grace occasionally attended the campus church and sang in the choir for special services. There was no Christian fellowship group like she had once experienced and enjoyed in high school. During a meaningful youth group retreat, she prayed the sinner's prayer to invite Jesus Christ into her heart to be her Lord and Savior. After the dismissal of the youth pastor following a moral failure, the high school fellowship group dissolved. Grace has had no Christian discipleship since her junior year of high school. During college, she spent limited breaks with her family, preferring to frequently pursue trips with friends. The family "home" has long felt boring, stressful, cold and without emotional ties. Formalities no longer are appealing, and keeping up the pretense of a Christian family appears empty to Grace.

Grace discloses to her counselor a statement that neither her parents nor pastor know. She dated on occasion in college but has never been in any serious romantic relationship. Her parents told her that they would make marriage plans when the season was right. There was apparently freedom to practice dating at college like an American as long as nothing became serious. What she has not told her parents is that during her senior year of college, one of her housemates, Samantha, came out as gay. This housemate persistently expressed strong feelings of attraction toward Grace and did make physical advances. Samantha once told Grace that she was not only beautiful, but stunning. Grace had never heard such complimentary words. Grace admits that she felt close to this friend, and there were sexual feelings that she never fully understood. Other than a couple experimental kisses and touching, there was no sexual relationship. Her friend moved on when Grace cautiously resisted taking the relationship further. Her friend has since had several lesbian relationships. Grace and this friend continue to have casual contact, and Grace follows her friend closely on Facebook. She daydreams about what might have been. She struggles to answer this question for herself: "Could I be gay like Samantha?" When she says this out loud to her counselor, her neck and face have dark red blotches, her voice becomes shaky, her hands tremble, and her eyes well up with tears. She cannot seem to get past intrusive thoughts of this gay friend who has an active life, a fascinating lineup of friendships and a clear identity. "Samantha knows who she is and where she fits in, but I . . ." Grace does not finish this sentence even when prompted to do so by her counselor.

Her family has been a consistent, active pillar in a Christian church. Her parents remain married after 26 years. She is the oldest daughter, and she has three younger siblings who are even more overtly American than she is in identity and lifestyle. She is the only one who can remember the family's former life back in their home country. Her father returns to their country of origin on the other side of the world for weeks and months at a time. The rest of the family has never been back since he established their new home in America. When he speaks to his children, he instructs them to fit in with their American peers. He invites them to enjoy the good life comprising the fine material things this country and his resources have to offer. On the other hand, he demands that they follow cultural traditions under his roof when it comes to his authority. Within the home, only their native language is spoken. Grace's mother does not have any education or employment outside of the home. Her mother speaks little English and has few social connections beyond the women at church.

Grace does not provide much family background information during the early interview. The counselor does probe to get a sense of her Christian training and upbringing. Her father is a wealthy and highly successful businessman who is involved in importing and manufacturing. His business has done extremely well, allowing the family to dwell in an elaborate, upscale neighborhood, lacking nothing in terms of material possessions. When in the States, he spends much of his time with other men in conversations about international business. Dialogue with his children is short, serious and stern. Grace describes her mother as private, withdrawn, hardworking and perhaps "unhappy" for most of her entire life. They came to this country because her mother was distressed with the filth and decline in their native land. Grace cannot recall ever seeing her mother smile, laugh or speak anything to her children except to issue threats or repeat stories of social shame. Her mother can go through an entire day without uttering a word. Grace does not report any meaningful signs of a Christian life at home. In fact, she would describe herself as the one in the family who was once most interested in church and spiritual things. She has never heard her father pray. The household Bibles are more for show than reading.

Grace struggles to describe her parents' marriage as the counselor seeks to obtain a depiction of it. She does share in a somber mood that once when she was in high school, a girl from church announced with confidence and details that Grace's father had another family back in their homeland. According to this peer, who taunted Grace relentlessly, everyone at church knew this to be true. No one would dare say anything about this, as his giving was a significant portion of the church budget. Grace became distraught and angry, so she spoke to her mother. Her mother forbade her to talk so disrespectfully of her father, to advance the accusation further or ever to speak about such a thing in her house. Grace mused over the realization that her mother never denied the rumor. Instead she alluded to saying that there are matters related to how men are that she was too young to understand. Grace could never ask her aloof and absent father about these allegations. Instead, she avoided him, resented his frequent travel and vowed silently to hate him forever. Given that he continued to pay for all of her wants and wishes, she pushed aside the incident and attempted not to think of it further. As Grace is not close to her father, there was no immediate sense of loss. Still, Grace will admit that from that point onward, she also began to distance herself from leaders at church. It was during this period that she rejected her parents' wish that she attend a denominational college. Instead, she pressed for one with a strong program in international business. Hinting that she may want to enter the family company, her parents agreed to this plan. Her father has consistently paid for her entire education. Grace has never secured any employment and carries no educational debt.

The counselor was given advanced warning from the pastor who made the referral that Grace was moving through a rebellious period. Therefore, she might tend to question her loyalty to her cultural heritage. The pastor wanted reassurance from the counselor that the traditions and values of her culture would be respected. The father is paying the session fees. The counselor has many questions for Grace regarding her ethnic and sexual identity. The most pressing matter on the counselor's mind is exploring the extent of the recent period of depression and increasing self-doubt.

Beyond Case Scenarios and on to Christian Counseling

It matters little if such hypothetical scenarios are explored using a case approach analysis or a critical issue investigation. These are likely to offer ample occasions to plunge into discourse between expectations surrounding the role of being a mental health professional and the implementation of Christian counseling. Counselors who desire to honor a personal Christian faith need to develop a way to move models of faith and theology into practice parameters.

In one Gospel account, Jesus Christ commissions his close band of disciples to proclaim the good news of the kingdom of heaven and to heal in his name (Matthew 10:1-42). In the midst of offering leadership and instruction, he introduces a theme that provides a fitting close to this endeavor. Jesus informs his disciples that while ministry to the needs of others is miraculous and full of grace, fulfilling this charge would bear a daily resemblance to living as a sheep among wolves. Included in his carefully chosen words, he illustrates the tension of living and caring in the age between his first and second coming. He instructs his followers to be "as shrewd as snakes and as innocent as doves" (Matthew 10:16 NIV). A worthy prayer would be that this directive, under the resources of his grace and presence of the Holy Spirit, would be our guide. For people helpers serving his kingdom, it is both critical to operate within the ethical parameters of our respective mental health discipline and yet provide thoroughly competent, wholeheartedly Christian counsel.

Five expert consultants openly displayed how to combine wide-ranging theological convictions and clinical skills into counseling care. Their efforts are a transparent portrayal of clinicians who desire to remain true to both their profession and a life of Christian discipleship. Having the benefit to experience these approaches, along with opportunities to improve our capacity to follow suit, we face a new challenge. The moment will come when exchanging words over clients like Jake is no longer relevant. What will be most urgent is how the presence of Jesus Christ is made manifest in refreshing dialogue within the divine appointments the Lord has on your schedule. In those encounters it is no longer a matter of smoothly articulating ideals, but how intentionality translates conviction into compassion. When a counselee expressing need becomes a neighbor in the seat before you, this becomes your moment to pause, pray and offer restorative soul care (Luke 10:29-37).

Reference

Johnson, E. L. (Ed.). (2010). *Psychology & Christianity: Five views.* Downers Grove, IL: IVP Academic.

Author and Subject Index

Scripture Index